Jil Oslo

Palestinian Hip Hop, Youth Culture, and the Youth Movement

Jil Oslo
Palestinian Hip Hop, Youth Culture, and the Youth Movement

Sunaina Maira

TADWEEN PUBLISHING
Washington, DC

This publication is produced in part with the support of the Middle East Program at George Mason University, with which the Arab Studies Institute is affiliated.

All photos in the book were taken by the author.

Table of Contents

Acknowledgements   6

Introduction   7

Jil Oslo: The Search for an Alternative Politics   31

Palestinian Hip Hop: A Different Kind of Map   70

The Youth Movement   111

Surveillance, Counter-Surveillance, and Feminist Questions   155

Conclusion   181

Acknowledgements

I want to thank Muwatin, The Palestinian Institute for the Study of Democracy, in Ramallah, Palestine for a research grant that supported this study. Muwatin's generosity was expressed not just in funding, but also with intellectual support and opportunities for me to share my work. For that I am grateful to the institute, and in particular to May Jayyusi for her encouragement and interest. I also want to thank Mada Al-Carmel, the Arab Center for Applied Social Research in Haifa, and especially Nadera Shalhoub-Kevorkian and Suhad Daher-Nashif, of the Gender Studies Program with which I was affiliated as a visiting scholar, for their support. Nadera's work has been a source of intellectual and political inspiration during this project.

I am deeply grateful to all the artists, activists, students, and young people who shared their time and thoughtful insights with me, as well as the other people I interviewed for this research. Especially in a place like the West Bank, which is inundated with researchers, these individuals readily offered their reflections and were willing to help. These were some of the most astute, refreshing, and critical discussions that I had during my time in Palestine, and the cultural production and political work of these young artists and activists inspired and sustained me in so many ways. Many friends and colleagues helped me in doing this research and while I cannot mention them all, I would like to extend my heartfelt thanks to Lisa Taraki, Rana Barakat, Sahar Qawasami, Falastine Dwikat, Riad Bahhur, Linda Tabar, Ala'a Azaa, Rania Jawwad, Nathalie Khankan, Inas Margieh, Morgan Cooper, and Rita Giacaman. I also want to thank my able research assistant, Trisha Barua.

Last but not least, I gratefully appreciate Tadween Publishing's interest in this project, Bassam Haddad's support, and my editor Nehad Khader's feedback and gracious assistance. Thanks also go to Nader Atassi for his help with the production of the book and to Nidal El-Khairy for his investment of time and effort in producing a cover image especially for the book, which I truly appreciate. Without Magid Shihade's strong support, help with translation, thoughtful feedback, and constant encouragement, I do not think this book would have seen the light of day. It is to him and all the young people I spoke to that I would like to dedicate this book.

Introduction

On 11 January 2013, over 200 Palestinians erected a village that they called Bab Al-Shams (Gate of the Sun), on Palestinian land that had been confiscated (i.e., stolen) by Israel to build illegal Jewish-only settlements in the West Bank. The proposed 4,000 new settlement homes would be built in Area E1, a corridor between Jerusalem and the Jewish settlement of Ma'ale Adumim that would dissect the West Bank, extending Israel's strangulation of Jerusalem and preventing the formation of a contiguous Palestinian state. The Israeli settlement plan was a retaliation, in part, for Palestinian President Mahmoud Abbas' successful bid for recognition of Palestine as a non-member observer state in the United Nations in 2012, and it was also a continuation of Israel's policies of land theft, home demolition, Judaization of Jerusalem, blockage of movement, siege, and repression. Bab Al-Shams was, in fact, named after a novel about Palestine by the Lebanese author Elias Khoury which is about the displacement of Palestinians in the war (the "Nakba," or catastrophe) of 1948 that displaced at least 700,000 Palestinians. In a statement about the camp, the protesters declared their right to create communities on their land:

> We, the sons and daughters of Palestine from all
> throughout the land, announce the establishment of
> Bab Al-Shams Village (Gate of the Sun). We the
> people, without permits from the occupation, without
> permission from anyone, sit here today because this is
> our land and it is our right to inhabit it. . . . Therefore
> we hereby establish the village of Bab Al-Shams to
> proclaim our faith in direct action and popular
> resistance. We declare that the village will stand
> steadfast until the owners of this land will get their
> right to build on their land. . . . Bab Al-Shams is the
> gate to our freedom and steadfastness. Bab Al-Shams
> is our gate to Jerusalem. Bab Al-Shams is the gate to
> our return.[1]

The protesters from "the north to the south" of Palestine who had gathered that cold winter day in this act of popular, non-violent resistance announced plans to hold discussion groups, film screenings, and artistic activities.[2] But the Israelis issued an "eviction" notice to Palestinians ordering them, ironically, to remove the tents from their own, occupied land. The Palestinians refused to leave, and thousands of Israeli forces attacked them and tore down the tents, forcing the activists onto buses. In the following weeks, four more resistance villages sprang up across the West Bank, also erected by Palestinians of various ages, including many youth, who made similar proclamations asserting their opposition to settler colonial policies of displacement, control, and annihilation. The camps created their own village councils, creating facilities such as a media center and clinic at Bab Al-Shams village, and provided a context for Palestinians from various locations a rare chance to meet in person and organize with one another.[3] The sites of the camps were kept secret even from participants in the protests. In one incident, Israeli soldiers stopped activists who were trying to return to Bab Al-Shams after they had been evicted, traveling in cars festooned with ribbons as if for a wedding, complete with a young woman who had come wearing a bridal dress (and who was later chased by soldiers up the hill in her white gown).

A Palestinian hip hop artist from Israel, Tamer Nafar, of the well-known rap group DAM, wrote a moving song about Bab Al-Shams. The song draws on lines from Khoury's novel which tells the story of a Palestinian fighter, Yunes, and his wife, Nahilah, who meet secretly in a cave called Bab Al-Shams after the creation of Israel and the exodus and dispossession of Palestinians in 1948:

> Oum Hassan passed away, and years after
> We gathered, men and women from all around Palestine,
> To congratulate the groom and bride.
> Younis al Asaid and Nahila al Shawah. . . .
> On January 11, 2013,
> We rode the bus to celebrate their wedding . . .
> For tonight's wedding, we set up fifty tents.
> Everyone is invited to Bab Al-Shams.
> Carrying a gift card in one hand and a present in the other
> We are walking to the sunrise of Bab Al-Shams. . .
>
> Some of us playing the oud, some are playing percussion
> And some are playing on the rifles in Bab Al-Shams.
> Nahila has candles on her ten fingers, stepping on grapes

Her hair is long like a horse's tail
And her perfume is a mixture of coffee beans and
thyme
And from a distance, a soldier is screaming at us,
"This is Area E!"
We told him, "Area what?" He said, "Area E."
No, we said, "It's Area A!!!" He said again, "No, E."
Keep dancing Oum Hassan . . .

The video for the song shows images of Palestinians traveling in pick-up trucks and waving Palestinian flags, setting up tents on the hill, sitting together around a fire, and drinking coffee, as well as footage of Israeli police and military jeeps with flashing sirens, as the song concludes, "Yes, we all return to Bab Al-Shams."[4]

Bab Al-Shams and the other "resistance villages" were as much a theatrical enactment of a Palestinian future as a courageous attempt to resist displacement and dispossession in the present. Performance was key to this movement, as it has been to many creative stagings of political protest in Palestine over the years that have created new theaters for resistance and new narratives for articulating the nature of this protracted struggle. The resistance villages were all quickly destroyed by the Israeli forces, who assaulted and arrested the protesters, but Bab Al-Shams was followed by Bab Al Karamah (Gate to Dignity), Al Asra—in solidarity with Palestinian prisoners, Al Manatir, and Canaan. On 20 March 2013, protesters erected a new Bab Al-Shams camp on a hillside in Eizariya, opposite the spot where the original camp had been torn down two months earlier.[5] The protesters included many young activists engaged in grassroots efforts to stage alternative forms of resistance in a moment of political fatigue, hopelessness, and cynicism among Palestinians, imagining what collective political struggle and autonomous life in Palestine might actually look like.

The eruption of resistance villages can be seen as an extension of independent political movements that young Palestinians have been actively involved in since the 15 March 2011 protests in the West Bank and Gaza and also inside Israel. During the so-called Arab Spring, a series of protests organized by youth erupted in Ramallah and in other sites across the West Bank, as well as in Gaza and among Palestinian youth in Israel. The protesters set up camps in the center of Ramallah and in other cities, demanding an end to the division between Fateh and Hamas and calling for a change in the political status quo. This new "youth movement," inspired partly by the Arab revolutions and in solidarity with

Palestinian prisoners in Israeli jails, is just one phase of ongoing resistance against Israeli occupation, colonialism, and apartheid. But this movement largely remained in the shadow of the much more dramatic revolts in North Africa, and the much more difficult struggle, in a sense, that Palestinian activists were trying to wage for democracy as well as national liberation.

Graffiti art, Ramallah.

At the same time as Palestinian youth were engaging in this political mobilization, using new strategies and languages of protest against colonial dispossession and displacement, young Palestinian artists were also using various media to resist Israeli occupation and apartheid policies. All of these youth have been engaging with important questions of national identity and nationhood, at a critical time for Palestine and the region at large. From music and visual art to dance and theater, Palestinian youth in the West Bank, Gaza, and Israel have been continuing a tradition of using the arts to oppose the erasure of their collective identities and to (re)imagine what collective struggle might look, or sound, like. One of the striking new expressions of this cultural politics is that produced by Palestinian rappers and graffiti artists who are drawing on hip hop culture and combining it with Palestinian and Arab musical and visual idioms to express political critiques and express solidarity with political struggles, within and beyond Palestine. Young hip hop artists are experimenting with aesthetic idioms and with new cultural practices, and they are also often deeply engaged with political movements as well as social critiques that involve a reshaping of the public sphere and national politics. This book links these two fronts of resistance and experimentation—the political and the cultural—in order to offer a preliminary discussion of the ways in which new youth cultures and new political movements in Palestine are responding to and challenging the dominant political paradigms of the era after the Oslo Accords.

In particular, this book focuses on Palestinian hip hop as an expression of the social and political identities of a new generation of Palestinian youth in the West Bank and also in Israel. Based on ethnographic research, it explores how hip hop produced and consumed by Palestinians is rethinking "politics" itself in this generation. In the last decade or so, it is apparent that there has been a proliferation of political hip hop produced and consumed by Palestinian youth in Israel, the West Bank, Gaza, Jerusalem, as well as in the diaspora. Palestinian hip hop draws on Arab musical and lyrical traditions as well as American/Western genres of rap, deejaying, breakdancing, and graffiti, and is a fundamentally hybrid cultural production. Music is a particularly important medium for political critique because it relies on discourse (words) as well as sounds and can travel across spatial and social boundaries, producing new political imaginaries in music and building social collectivities affiliated with musical genres. Graffiti art is also a potent medium for political communication, particularly of subversive or dangerous messages, as it can be produced anonymously on walls and in public spaces, and so it is not surprising that it is increasingly visible in places such as Ramallah, Bethlehem, or Jaffa. Both rap and graffiti or stenciling do not require expensive equipment or elaborate training, which also explains their allure for youth who cannot afford to buy instruments other than a laptop for producing beats or recording music and a paintbrush or spray can for producing street art.

I was interested in exploring, through ethnographic research, if Palestinian hip hop has lent itself to the politicization of a new generation of youth and the formation of an alternative public sphere and what it represents to young Palestinians, both within and outside of the hip hop subculture. What can Palestinian hip hop tell us about young people's views of politics and nationhood, particularly in the wake of the Arab uprisings and the youth movement in

Palestine that emerged in 2011? While I was in the West Bank in the fall of 2011 and when I returned at the end of the summer in 2012 to live for a year in Ramallah, there was a wave of intense protests, involving or initiated by youth, in solidarity with the Palestinian prisoners on hunger strike and against the Palestinian Authority's (PA's) economic policies and the Oslo accords, that evolved out of the protests in solidarity with the Arab revolutions in early 2011 and against the splitting of the West Bank and Gaza. I became interested in what the Palestinian youth movement represented through its public protests and political discourse. Was this offering an alternative political framework? If so, how and to what extent was it recreating, reviving, or rethinking earlier political frameworks and national narratives?

Youth at protest in the Manara, Ramallah, September 2012.

But it quickly became apparent to me that these two sites, hip hop and youth activism, were interconnected and spoke to each other through shared political critiques, primarily, but also through cultural idioms and imaginaries that resonated with many in the generation that has come of age in the Oslo era, or what I call here "jil (generation) Oslo." This book is an attempt to think about Palestinian youth politics and culture in the post-Oslo moment through the reverberations across these two sites. It is by no means an exhaustive study, nor does it claim to answer all the questions it raises, but it is rather a small sketch of Palestinian youth in specific geographic sites, in a particular historical moment in 2011-2013. It examines the emergence of Palestinian hip hop artists and young activists on the public stage, the ways they transformed that arena, and the sentiments of inspiration, consternation, excitement, disapproval, and solidarity they have evoked.

Thinking Hip Hop and Protest Together

Youth culture is a key site where young people express their social identities, political perspectives, and imaginings of the future. My research considers hip hop not just as a musical form but as a youth subculture, that is, a group of young people defined by consumption or production of specific cultural forms, in this case hip hop, in relation to the social contradictions faced by these youth in particular political and historical contexts. Furthermore, young Palestinian activists, or those engaged in various ways with "politics," are also in some sense part of a youth subculture—or multiple subcultures—based on political protest and organizing, and in some cases overlapping with and drawing on subcultural expressions such as hip hop, but also on many other cultural forms. In thinking youth culture and youth activism together, this book explores the ways in which both these sites are grappling with the meaning of what it means to be "political," and what "politics" means, in a moment in Palestine in which it seems that political vocabularies and strategies have been exhausted or eviscerated, and when political skepticism and fatigue is pervasive. In this sense, it speaks to the question of what it means for youth, especially, to "do" politics not just in Palestine or in the region, but also to some extent globally. Clearly, the Palestinian context, as also the local contexts of Palestinians in the West Bank, Gaza, refugee camps, and the diaspora, are very specific and so the Palestinian youth movement is addressing questions very different from those facing the Occupy movement in the United States or the revolutionary movements in Egypt, Tunisia, or Bahrain.

One of the major political interventions of the youth movement, highlighted in the chapters that follow, is the call for a unified national identity linking the West Bank, Gaza, Jerusalem, and Palestinians within the 1948 borders of Palestine—whom Palestinians call "1948 (or '48) Palestinians." I want to note that I use the term "'48 Palestine" throughout the book because it is the category that Palestinians, including youth and hip hop artists, themselves use and generally prefer for referring to Palestinians in Israel. This appellation is not a denial of the existence of Israel, as some are quick to assume, but it is a complex geographic as well as temporal label that encodes a critical analysis of the colonial nature of the condition of Palestinians in Israel that is rarely acknowledged, and is, in fact, often denied.[6] The insistence on a unified Palestine is significant because it challenges the Oslo paradigm that fragmented and divided the nation by situating what could be Palestine only in the West Bank and Gaza, and deferring the status of Jerusalem, within the degraded terms of sovereignty supplied by Israel. Similarly, Palestinian hip hop has helped (re)connect geographically dispersed groups of Palestinian youth and offered a medium for reimagining the political itself, often in tandem with the youth movement and in solidarity with the Arab revolutions. This is not a new national narrative in Palestine, and these are not the only sites in which the call to resist the partitioning of Palestine is being revived or recreated. However, it became apparent in this research that this cultural production and political movement, in their different strands, are an expression of this desire for national unity in a new generation but one that does not erase the specificities of place and history and has, in fact, connected different groups of youth who are involved in political organizing and cultural movements across Palestine.

I argue here that Palestinian rap is a poetics of displacement and protest, which simultaneously unsettles and recreates national cultural imaginaries. Palestinian rappers in the West Bank, Gaza, Jerusalem, "1948 Palestine," and in refugee and diasporic communities around the world have used hip hop to address the Palestine question, and become part of a globalized Arab youth culture that is inflected by local traditions and is often mixed with other subcultures. As Nouri Gana observes, Arab rap is an "emergent form of cultural and communal intelligibility and solidarity" and a youth movement that has become an "increasingly transnational collaborative project," one embedded in the "rich cultures of resistance to colonial, neocolonial, and late capitalist entrenchments in the Arab world."[7] Palestinian hip hop artists, particularly '48 Palestinian rappers, are some of the most well known Arab rappers in the world and have helped push the boundaries of progressive political hip hop, not just for

Arab but also for global rap. They have created a youth subculture that draws on American rap but is also distinctly Palestinian and Arab, rapping in Arabic and sampling Arabic music and poetry while narrating their daily realities and articulating political and social critiques. The production and consumption of popular culture by youth demonstrates their agency, but it is also a commodified form that lends itself to the containment of threats to the status quo or subversions of the social order. It is important not to romanticize the potential of resistance through youth culture or popular culture—indeed much work in cultural studies for the past three decades has thoroughly addressed this question —but it is clearly a site in which the contradictions and tensions in political and social struggle are expressed, negotiated, challenged, and rewritten.

I found in my conversations with young Palestinians that there are deep tensions and complex debates about national identity and cultural authenticity that surface in discussions of Palestinian hip hop. One of the key arguments that emerged from this ethnographic study is that these tensions are indicative of deeper concerns about the social and political that Palestinian youth grapple with in the context of cultural and political shifts. The youth movement in Palestine that erupted in spring 2011 also provoked debates about its political authenticity, framed by the familiar dialectic of resistance and co-optation. This signals what I think is the always ambivalent response to the specter of youth as political, not just generational, subjects. As Linda Herrera and Asef Bayat suggest, "The 'question of youth' often gets articulated as a paradox, as a problem and an opportunity."[8] Youth politics is always suspect, because youth are seen as either too "radical," and thus naïve or utopian, or too conformist, and thus available for co-optation and manipulation. These binaries and contradictions, as I have argued elsewhere, are what make it so difficult in many cases, including in the case of Palestinian youth culture and youth politics, to think the category of "youth" outside of these overdetermined polarities.[9] But this is what I will attempt to do here, using this small case study to link two seemingly disconnected sites where the notion of "youth" itself is produced and negotiated.

(Re)Thinking Palestinian Youth Culture

In this book, I view hip hop as a youth subculture and as a form of cultural production that is inextricably intertwined with the political and the social. That is, like all genres of popular culture, hip hop is an expression of social and political identities and is embedded in particular relations of power and historical contexts. However, Palestinian youth culture has generally been

Introduction

neglected in scholarly research in favor of psychological studies focused on issues of trauma, self-esteem, and coping skills for Palestinian youth, and quantitative studies assessing young people's political views within a largely pre-determined framework of existing political movements and what counts as "politics" itself.[10] Khaled Furani and Dan Rabinowitz point out that, in general, ethnographic research in and about Palestine was not considered "admissible" in mainstream anthropology until the 1980s. They argue that while ethnographic engagement with Palestine is growing, there is a need for more work that would go beyond a narrow definition of national political struggle to include explorations of other cultural and political sites.[11] I suggest that Palestinian youth culture is one of these sites that deserves greater ethnographic attention and that could illuminate the "critical potential of ethnography" in colonial and postcolonial studies, as well as in youth/cultural studies.[12]

More recent research on Palestinian youth has highlighted the agency of young people in conflict situations or refugee youth in the context of intergenerational shifts in national identity, and there is a small body of qualitative research exploring how religion, gender, class, and generation shape the political perspectives of Palestinian youth.[13] Some of this work is focused on Palestinian refugee youth in Lebanon or Jordan, and much of this literature is situated in the context of the first or second intifadas, that is, spanning the late 1980s to the early 2000s. Other studies have highlighted the gendered dimensions of adolescent identity and political commitment for Palestinian youth, exploring issues of education, social life, and also the experiences of Palestinian male and female youth in the diaspora who return to live in the West Bank.[14] However, there is a need for more research that investigates how this generation of Palestinians that has come of age in a globalized youth culture is producing political and national identities through new cultural expressions. I should note that there are, of course, many youth subcultures in the West Bank, Gaza, Jerusalem, and among 1948 Palestinians, and there is much work that could be done on Palestinian youth cultures that may or may not be directly engaged with questions of national politics—from car racing that involves young men and women (or drag racing) and fandom among youth who support Real Madrid and Barcelona soccer teams, to parkour (an acrobatic sport popular among young men in Gaza) and Islamic fashion styles—all of which raise a range of interesting political and social questions.[15]

The gap in existing research on youth culture in Palestine studies is addressed by Rebecca Stein and Ted Swedenburg, who argue that "most radical scholarship on Palestine and Israel has ignored questions of popular culture—or, at best, consigned popular culture forms and processes to the margins of scholarly debate and investigation."[16] In their view, "this act of marginalization has seemed a necessary response to the severity of the national conflict, the harsh violence of the Israeli occupation, and/or the enduring struggle for Palestinian national liberation."[17] While there is an ongoing political imperative that has marginalized the study of popular culture in the field of Palestine studies at large, at least until recently, Stein and Swedenburg go further to suggest that there is a conceptual limitation in the dominant approaches that leads to the notion that popular culture is "epiphemenonal to questions of politics and power." They trace this gap in the literature on Palestine (and Israel) to the dominance of "the national paradigm" and the "Marxist historiographical and/or political economic paradigm."[18] They argue that the national paradigm tended to conceive of the (Palestinian) nation as both "politically determinative" and "largely enclosed and discrete," evading cultural imaginaries not wedded to dominant nationalist logics and the complexities of identities that tend to bubble up in popular culture.[19] While the nation-state was the determinant logic for this approach, class politics and class struggle was the dominant logic for Marxist scholarship that viewed popular culture as inherently based on commodification and hence de-politicized. This dismissiveness of popular culture is, in part, the legacy of critiques of mass culture waged by the Frankfurt School theorists who were concerned that the commercialization of culture inevitably led to conformity and containment. So both approaches view popular culture, and mass culture in particular, as having a "troubled, even treasonous, relation to national interests and struggle agendas."[20] As Gana points out, Arab rap has in many cases been dismissed by Arab cultural critics and commentators as "a commodity detritus of consumer culture—or, worse, as a vehicle of Euro-American cultural imperialism."[21]

Stein and Swedenburg point out that there has been a shift since the late 1990s and more work on popular culture in Palestine has emerged that considers cultural production seriously and also critically (their own edited volume being a case in point).[22] Yet this conceptualization of cultural production as "troubled, even treasonous," especially if it is imbricated with commercialization and globalization, continues to haunt popular culture and youth culture in sites where political struggle is intense and ongoing—in particular, in locations where the production of national imaginaries is crucial, a matter of survival in zones of colonialism and occupation. In other words, the management of life and death in sites such as Palestine, that is, the biopolitics of colonial rule, means that popular culture and youth culture continue to be contested expressions of what is truly "popular" and what is authentically "national." Furthermore, it is also generally apparent that "the popular" is a notion deeply invested with imaginaries of what "the people" think—or what they should think or can think—in relation to hierarchies of "high" and "low," elite and mass, authentic and inauthentic, resistant or accomodationist cultures. While it is indeed the case that the national and Marxist paradigms speak to important tensions that cannot be taken lightly, inserting the question of popular culture, and especially youth culture, provides a missing piece in the puzzle that deepens, rather than diverts from, analysis of Palestinian politics and national struggles.

In this, my approach—like that of Stein and Swedenburg, to a large degree— is informed by the work of cultural studies theorists, and particularly of the Birmingham School. Cultural studies scholars at the University of Birmingham drew on Marxist analyses of culture by the Frankfurt School and sociological work on youth and delinquency by the Chicago School, as well as notions of hegemony developed by Antonio Gramsci, to theorize youth subcultures in relation to questions of class, nation, race, and gender. Seminal texts such as Stuart Hall and Tony Jefferson's *Resistance through Rituals: Youth Subcultures in Post-War Britain*, based on ethnographic research about largely white, working-class, male youth in Britain, signaled the ambivalent assessment of the politics of youth culture at a time of economic and social transition.[23] The neo-Marxist analyses of the Birmingham School suggested that the youth subcultures of the 1960s and 70s, such as mod or punk culture, provided "symbolic resolutions" to the dilemmas facing urban, working-class youth, but that they were not structural solutions to the crisis of class. "Youth" had to be situated within the larger economic and social contradictions that these subcultural rituals were invented to address but which they were unable, ultimately, to transform. Thus, the Birmingham School did not romanticize the possibilities of resistance waged on the cultural terrain, but was invested in the heuristic of "resistance" (primarily in relation to class) and in the everyday struggles and dilemmas of young people that were being expressed, they argued, through cultural consumption. This subculture theory has laid the foundation for much work on youth cultures that analyzes the cultural consumption and production of youth in political and historical contexts, and has been extended to study diverse groups in a range of locations.

It is important to note that youth subculture theory offers a critique of the production of "youth" itself, as a concept that articulates the category of generation with class, nation, race, gender, and sexuality. That is, youth is not a category that can be taken for granted but is a social and cultural construction—

a deeply ideological construct. The core definition of youth in Western psychology, in particular, and social sciences more generally, that shapes much work today across various national sites, is a transitional period or stage of development between childhood and adulthood. In many cultural contexts, prolonged education for and the delayed entry into the labor market of those who are anywhere between thirteen and twenty-five years has led to the association of this period with a condition of liminality, that is, an uneasy location between one social space or political status and another. Youth are not yet adults and not quite citizens so they presumably must be shepherded into proper adulthood and, as they acquire that status, into the social order. As such, youth is a signifier that can be empty but also invested with fraught meanings. The persistent conceptualization of youth as a moment of socialization into or rejection of social norms, as subjects in the making, is why youth culture is so often a political battleground.[24] I want to note that while some scholars point out that youth movements are not adequately addressed in social movement theory and tend to be discussed as youth subcultures or student movements,[25] I think it is productive here to critically use the lens of youth subcultures, and cultural politics more generally, to think about youth movements because it helps to interrogate the meaning of "youth" as a generational category rather than taking this as naturalized location. Furthermore, it is important to clarify that the Palestinian youth movement was not a protest movement focused solely or even largely on the concerns of young people per se. It was a movement by youth, not necessarily about youth, if expressing a particular critique emerging from a specific generational location and intertwined with youth culture idioms, including hip hop.

The notion of youth as a site associated with liminality and instability often permeates discussions of Arab and Palestinian youth as well. Scholars suggest that youth in the Arab world and Middle East, as elsewhere, are generally viewed as a site of crisis due to their association with the project of "national and social reproduction," and thus with the possibility of both a threat to or continuity of the status quo, for their own societies and also, in particular, for Western states invested in the region.[26] Discussions of the "youth bulge," or youthfulness of the Arab population, as well as youth unemployment and underemployment in the region, position youth as a demographic problem and an always present threat to social and political stability—a threat that was realized in ways that many did not anticipate with the Arab revolutions in which youth were deeply involved. On the one hand, mainstream discourses generally "position Middle Eastern youth as lacking in agency, needing protection and requiring the tutelage of state institutions, experts and the national intelligentsia."[27] Herrera and Bayat observe that in dominant frameworks and policy-related research, "youth are treated as a group that needs to be understood and trained for purposes of political containment, ideological monitoring, and economic reform" and youth from Muslim societies, in particular, are framed through the discourse of securitization and the war on terror.[28] Youth are seen as especially vulnerable to what Western counterterrorism experts call "radicalization" or indoctrination into militant or Islamist movements, and to the potential for too much agency. But on the other hand, national as well as (mainstream) Western state and media discourses often frame Middle Eastern and Arab, including Palestinian, youth as a threat to the "integrity of the nation" and to Western strategic interests and neoliberal capitalism in the region, respectively.

Youth are associated with modernity, with progress and with the telos of the nation, but for some observers the fear is that they may be too modern. John Collins argues these tensions are acute in the case of Palestine—a nation without an actual state—because the notion of generation has always been used to inscribe the struggle for nationhood, and the "processes through which social identities and political projects are symbolically produced, reproduced, and transformed."[29] The use of the word jil (generation), as in jil al-Nakba (the generation that endured the Nakba of 1948), jil al-Thawra (the generation of the Palestinian revolution of the late 1950s and 1960s), or jil al-Intifada (the generation that experienced the first intifada that began in 1987), underscores the national significance of the concept of generation in Palestine and also the historical experiences of different generations in resisting colonialism and warfare, including before 1948.[30] Given that the question of resistance, across different national contexts, is generally pinned onto youth, this often becomes an overdetermined site for thinking about the question of political dissent or social movements. Yet the actual social, political, and historical experiences of Palestinian youth continue to be evaded in much of the dominant (Western as well as, to some extent, Palestinian) discourse, which tends to reproduce the image of the younger generation as either alienated and apolitical or as agents of radicalism and hyper-politicization.

In the case of Palestine, there is also a prevailing awareness that the conventional conception of childhood as a period of innocence and the dominant (Western) stage models of the transition to adulthood via adolescence have been broken down by the conditions produced by settler colonialism, occupation, and warfare. While these models of childhood and youth have already been critiqued as universalizing frameworks that are not relevant across time and space, there is a prevailing narrative that childhood and adolescence in Palestine are out of sync with dominant conceptualizations, including of what youth should look like. So while youth are generally seen as exceptional, and occupying a unique or liminal position, Palestinian youth are doubly exceptionalized—they cannot be "normal" young people, and the assumption of youth as being in a state of crisis is magnified for this category. There is a pathologizing of Palestinian youth in dominant discourse, and especially in humanitarian frameworks, as exceptionally troubled, traumatic, and perhaps even non-existent, due to violence, suffering, loss, and deprivation of freedoms. But there is also a desire, including by Palestinians themselves, for young people to experience something other than violence, suffering, and loss, and to enjoy freedom, not to mention basic human rights or the right to life itself. This tension is powerfully captured in a song by a Palestinian hip hop group from Jerusalem, Egtya7 Underground, in collaboration with the Lebanese rapper Edd Abbas, titled "*Ta3 Ta Gollak*" ("Let me Tell You"):

> I opened my eyes to bulldozers destroying our house,
> I was not aware then, I had no idea what was
> happening,
> I was five years old, and we will build again even in
> the dark.
> In Palestine, the child is born naturally a mature man.
> I went over the rubble to see how many good stones
> remained,
> I put them on the top of one another, and so the
> house is built anew.[31]

The notion that Palestinian children, who have been subjected to exceptional circumstances of violence and instability such as the experience of home demolitions and displacement, quickly become adults and are politicized very early in life is a very common refrain in any discussion of Palestinian youth.

If adolescence has been conceptualized, in Western psychological theory, as the period for exploring political commitments, Palestinian children are, in a sense, always already born into adolescence—if not into adulthood—and so these categories are necessarily in flux in Palestine. Egtya7 Underground's song evokes the painfulness of this disappearance of childhood, in the context of the destruction of not just a home but also an entire society and its way of life. It also invokes the will to resist and rebuild, the concept of steadfast resilience or *sumood*, which is so central to Palestinian political discourse and identity. The rapper Rajeh Dana, from al-Khalil (Hebron), said, "We are sick from this situation, but we will continue to resist by living in our homes," adding that for him, hip hop "makes everyone outside know that we're still alive, we are not dead yet." Studies such as that by Viet Nguyen-Gillham et al. point out that unlike traditional Western models of coping, sumood is a collective and not individual construct; the authors go further to critique the ways in which international agencies have transplanted Western, generally individualist, models of psychosocial development, trauma, and coping to the Palestinian context.[32] Thus, it is important to question in any research on Palestinian youth what the ontological framework is for thinking "youth" in this specific context, without either overly pathologizing or romanticizing the tropes of victimhood/passivity and resistance/agency that generally trouble notions of youth.

Grappling with the epistemology of youth helps us understand what is at stake in thinking about hip hop in Palestine—and why it seems that there is always so much at stake in discussions of this musical genre and youth culture. Thinking "youth" with "popular culture" conjoins two sites that are often viewed with some unease in the context of political debates about national liberation, and adding hip hop into the mix inserts the equally, if not more, fraught questions of globalization, Westernization, and cultural authenticity. Palestinian youth culture and youth activism overlap but they are also distinct sites and I do not want to collapse them into a seamless narrative nor do I want to suggest these are the only arenas in which new cultural identities and political frameworks have been forged. I do, however, think that they offer a lens into the politics of the Oslo period that highlights some key tensions and important questions about youth culture and youth politics for jil Oslo.

Research Methodology

The book is based on ethnographic research that I conducted in the West Bank and Jerusalem and with '48 Palestinian youth between September and December 2011 and from September 2012 through May 2013. It also draws on earlier research I did on hip hop produced by Palestinian youth in Israel and issues of political and national identity between 2007-10. The research in 2011-13 included fieldwork and interviews in the West Bank (Ramallah, Dheisheh camp in Bethlehem, and Balata camp in Nablus), East Jerusalem, and Haifa. During this time, I interviewed thirteen rappers and artists (including one vocalist in a hip hop-reggae band and one visual artist involved in a hip hop/arts collective); nine young activists; two young artists who have worked with youth creating graffiti, break dancing, and hip hop; and four youth NGO or youth program workers.[33]

I also did focus group discussions with college students in the West Bank in fall 2011 in order to learn what young people, who were not themselves hip hop artists or even hip hop fans, thought about this youth culture and the youth movement. I conducted three focus group interviews with forty students enrolled in social science classes at Birzeit University which allowed me to speak with youth coming from different cities, towns, villages, and camps beyond Ramallah.[34] Since these youth were not pre-selected, I was able to hear a wide range of views about hip hop and youth activism, and at the end of the focus group discussion, I asked students if they would be interested in meeting individually or in pairs for a follow-up interview to talk in greater depth.[35] I also had discussions about Palestinian hip hop with a group of undergraduate students at Al Quds-Bard College in East Jerusalem in the spring of 2013, after screenings of the film *Slingshot Hip Hop* and videos of DAM's music. The field work in the West Bank included attending several music performances, cultural festivals, political demonstrations and talks involving or organized by youth, and events related to Palestinian youth, some of which included youth from Jerusalem as well as '48 Palestine (less so youth coming directly from Gaza given the difficulties of travel for Gazans living under siege).

I did a total of thirty-one individual interviews in the West Bank and Jerusalem with young people who were between the ages of eighteen and twenty-five years (including all the artists, activists, students, and youth/NGO workers but one). The interviews were open-ended and were conducted in classrooms, cafes, homes, youth centers, offices, and one by phone. While the focus group discussions were roughly evenly divided between male and female students, only eight of the interviews with activists and artists were with young women. This reflects the dominance of Palestinian hip hop by male artists as well as the preponderance of male activists in the West Bank, an issue that I discuss in the book. In contrast, there are many more female hip hop artists among '48 Palestinians—an issue I will return to later—so while I interviewed a much smaller number of '48 Palestinian youth, three of the six artists I spoke to were young women and the two youth activists I interviewed were both female. The interviews about '48 Palestinian hip hop were also open-ended and were conducted in person in Haifa and Jerusalem or by phone from the West Bank. I also did a focus group discussion with fifteen '48 Palestinian youth from a variety of locations in Israel at a youth forum organized in Nazareth by Baladna, a Palestinian youth organization based in Haifa. In addition, I shared the findings of my research and engaged in a discussion about these issues with '48 Palestinian youth at a talk in Haifa in the winter of 2013. I have had numerous informal conversations with many other young people—students, activists, and artists—and with older activists and artists, community members, and scholars about this topic, in the West Bank, Jerusalem, and in '48 Palestine.

I want to note that I include a discussion of my previous research on '48 Palestinian hip hop, even though it was partly conducted in an earlier moment, for two major reasons: first, '48 Palestinian youth were the pioneers of Palestinian hip hop and have inspired much of the hip hop movement in the West Bank, Gaza, and the diaspora, generating a transnational network of artists, and fans. This is an important context for the emergence of the Palestinian hip hop movement. Second, the interviews with artists and young activists in the West Bank underscored that many of them are committed to reconceptualizing the Palestinian national movement to include '48 Palestinians, and believe that hip hop and the youth movement are sites in which they are creating, or reviving, this unified identity. Thus, it seemed important that the project reflect the vision of a larger Palestinian geography articulated within this youth culture and movement and also provide a somewhat comparative perspective on these different sites. The research is not strictly comparative, however, and is clearly uneven in its empirical scope. The field work conducted in the West Bank was over a longer period of time, during ongoing residence in Ramallah, and included many more interviews with youth and activists in addition to hip hop artists, as well as attendance at performances and political events. The research on '48 Palestinian hip hop relied mainly on interviews with a few artists and analyses of their lyrics and music, which had to be conducted during short visits or by phone, as well as the focus group discussion. So the major focus of the research is clearly focused on the context of the West Bank and the youth movement that emerged in 2011, while situated in the context of a larger cartography of youth culture and politics in order to draw out some of the connections across borders. In mapping the range of sites in which the hip hop and also the youth movement has emerged, the book provides a window into some important, cross-cutting themes that resonate powerfully across different geographic sites as well as some notable differences in this emergent youth culture and politics.

Jil Oslo

My interviews and conversations with young people, artists, youth activists, scholars, and community members revealed recurrent debates and tensions that surfaced in nearly all discussions of Palestinian rap and the youth movement. There were three key themes that emerged from the research: 1) the search for an alternative politics in the post-Oslo moment in Palestine; 2) the definition of national culture and cultural authenticity, as it relates to Palestinian hip hop; and 3) the politicization of a new generation in the context of the youth movement and the Arab revolutions that began in 2011. The young people I spoke to had a range of views about these three themes but what emerged was a picture of hip hop firmly embedded in the larger political and historical context of this generation and in the political events of 2011-2013, during the time that I was conducting this research. The chapters that follow are organized around these core themes or debates, each of which troubles a certain consensus about national identity and national politics, producing what Jacques Rancière calls a dissensus—that is, challenging the boundaries of what is considered "proper" or "pure" politics and, in this case, constituting youth as political subjects.[36]

It was apparent that Palestinian hip hop is inextricably intertwined with politics and that these tensions, such as the concern with "proper" national culture and "proper" political identity, demand serious reflection and can not simply be dismissed as epiphenomenal to the music or subculture, just as cultural production is not epiphenomenal to politics. I argue that it is not just that hip hop is a window into these political debates on the ground, but that it is a site which itself constitutes these debates; that is, politics is not just something external that this youth culture comments on or reveals, but is constantly produced, negotiated, and challenged within youth culture itself. In this, I build on the work of the Birmingham School while pressing further on their analysis to consider the ways in which political resistance is in some cases waged in, with the help of, or despite youth cultural expressions. The cultural, social, and political anxieties, dilemmas, and aspirations of this generation of Palestinian youth in the West Bank and in '48 Palestine, as discussed by the young people I spoke to, are negotiated within and through hip hop and discourse about this youth subculture and what it represents. I should note that this project focuses on the production and reception of hip hop by young Palestinians, in order to understand its social and political significance in relation to youth activism, so it is not an ethnomusicological study focused on the musical form, though there is clearly more work to be done on this topic from a musicological perspective.

In the following chapter, I provide a sketch of the politics of jil Oslo and the search for an alternative political paradigm in the context of the evident disillusionment with existing political frameworks and the desire for a unified Palestinian identity. Chapter two discusses Palestinian hip hop as a musical genre and youth culture, and the ways in which youth understand Palestinian hip hop in relation to debates about national culture and national authenticity, grappling with the contradictions of what it means to be properly Palestinian in relation to new cultural expressions and global cultures. Discourses of "improper" social and cultural expressions, I found, were also deeply imbued with concerns about the boundaries of gendered and sexual behavior, and hip hop seemed to be a charged locus of some of these concerns in the context of post-Oslo social and class transformations. In chapter three, I focus on the youth movement of 2011-12 and its emergence in the context of the Arab uprisings and the Palestinian bid for statehood in the United Nations, exploring these protests as a site where the Oslo paradigm for national politics has been publicly challenged by youth. I discuss the engagement of young activists with boycott campaigns as a political strategy and their resistance to projects of normalization with Israel in a context where NGO activity has increasingly come to dominate the cultural as well as political spheres in Palestine. Chapter four focuses on issues of domestic repression, surveillance, and counter-surveillance in different geographic sites, including in Israeli universities where Palestinian students are mobilizing against militarization and racism. It explores the use of graffiti art to politicize public space and critique repression, as well as the ways in which issues of gender and sexuality infuse political activism and protest culture and constitute a feminist politics. The discussion in the book moves between an analysis of hip hop and youth culture and of youth activism and protest cultures, exploring the ways in which cultural politics infuse national politics, and vice versa, and demonstrating the ways in which the political vision articulated in hip hop, and the debates and contradictions that surround it, are integral to the politics of jil Oslo.

I want to point out that this book is not a primer on Palestinian youth nor does it contain an introductory discussion of Palestinian history and politics, as there is already a well-researched body of work that provides this information and analysis. Rather, it fills a gap in the scholarly literature by providing a discussion of a particular historical moment and political formation, specifically related to youth activism and youth culture produced by the Oslo generation. I have tried to present the perspectives and insights of the young artists and activists I spoke to, and to share their own words, because it is the perspectives of young people themselves that I found was missing in much of the literature as well as in larger discussions about these topics. These youth had astute theoretical analyses that I found illuminating, refreshing, and thought-provoking and so the theorizing in this book emerges largely through their reflections and observations. I am sure that the discussions in the following chapter will raise many questions, not all of which will be answered in this book, but I view this as the beginning of a conversation that I hope will continue in other works and in future discussions with, and political and cultural mobilization by, youth.

---

[1] "Palestinians Establish a New Village, Bab alshams, in Area E1." Popular Struggle Coordination Committee, http://popularstruggle.org/content/palestinians-establish-new-village-bab-alshams-area-e1.

[2] Ibid.

[3] Irene Nasser, "In Bab Al-Shams, Palestinians create new facts on the ground," *+972*, 3 May 2013. http://972mag.com/in-bab-al-shams-palestinians-created-new-facts-on-the-ground/64732/.

[4] "Area A" refers to the areas of the West Bank occupied by Israel that are putatively under the control of the Palestinian Authority. The video is at: http://www.youtube.com/watch?v=v1YJUs5Op8g.

[5] Popular Struggle Coordination Commitee, "Palestinians Erect New Bab al Shams Neighborhood as Obama lands in Israel/Palestine," *Mondoweiss*, 20 March 2013. http://mondoweiss.net/2013/03/palestinians-neighborhood-israelpalestine.html.

[6] I thank Mark Ayyash for some of these insights.

[7] Nouri Gana, "Rap and Revolt in the Arab World." *Social Text* 113 30 no. 4 (2012): 25-53.

[8] Linda Herrera and Asef Bayat, "Conclusion: Knowing Muslim Youth," In *Being Young and Muslim: New Cultural Politics in the Global South and North*, ed. Linda Herrera and Asef Bayat (New York: Oxford University Press, 2010), 355.

[9] See Sunaina Maira and Elisabeth Soep, "Introduction," in *Youthscapes: The Popular, the National, the Global* ed. Sunaina Maira and Elisabeth Soep (Philadelphia: University of Pennsylvania Press, 2005), xv-xxxv.

Introduction

[10] For example: Brian Barber, "Political Violence, Social Integration, and Youth Functioning: Palestinian Youth from the Intifada," *Journal of Community Psychology* 29 no. 3 (2001): 259-280; Salman Elbedour, "Youth in Crisis: The Well-Being of Middle Eastern Youth and Adolescents During War and Peace," *Journal of Youth and Adolescence* 27 no. 5 (1998): 539-557; Erica Frydenberg et al., "Coping with Concerns: An Exploratory Comparision of Australian, Colombian, German, and Palestinian Adolescents," *Journal of Youth and Adolescence* 32 no. 1 (2003): 59-66; James Garbarino, "Youth in Dangerous Environments: Coping with the Consequences," in *Social Problems and Social Contexts in Adolescence: Perspectives Across Boundaries* ed. Klaus Hurrelmann and Stephen Hamilton (New York: Aldine de Gruyter, 1996); Mohammed Shadid and Rick Seltzer, "Student-Youth Differences among Palestinians in the West Bank," *Youth and Society* 20 no. 4 (1989): 445-460.

[11] Khaled Furani and Dan Rabinowitz, "The Ethnographic Arriving of Palestine," *Annual Review of Anthropology* 40 (2011): 484.

[12] Ibid., 477.

[13] For example: John Collins, *Occupied by Memory: The Intifada Generation and the Palestinian State of Emergency* (New York: New York University Press, 2004); Jason Hart,. "Children and Nationalism in a Palestinian Refugee Camp in Jordan," *Childhood* 9 no. 1 (2002): 35-47; Ibid., "Dislocated Masculinity: Adolescence and the Palestinian Nation-in-Exile." *Journal of Refugee Studies* 21 no.1 (2008): 64-81; Michael I. Jensen, "Youth, Morals and Islamism: Spending Your Leisure Time with Hamas in Palestine," in *Youth and Youth Culture in the Contemporary Middle East*, ed. Jorgen B. Simonsen (Damascus: Danish Institute, 2005), 116-127; Daoud Kuttab, "A Profile of the Stonethrowers," *Journal of Palestine Studies* 17 no. 3 (1988): 14-23; Sylvie Mansour, "Identity Among Palestinian Youth: Male and Female Differentials." *Journal of Palestine Studies* 6 no. 4 (Summer 1977): 71-89; Mahmoud Mi'ari, "Self-Identity and Readiness for Interethnic Contact among Young Palestinians in the West Bank," *Canadian Journal of Sociology* 23 no. 1 (1998): 47-70; Viet Nguyen-Gillham et al., "Normalizing the Abnormal: Palestinian Youth and the Contradictions of Resilience in Protracted Conflict," *Health and Social Care in the Community* 16 no. 3 (2008): 291-298; Julie Peteet, "Male Gender and Rituals of Resistance in the Palestinian "Intifada": A Cultural Politics of Violence," *American Ethnologist* 21 no. 1 (1994): 31-49.

[14] For example: Camille Fronk, Ray Huntington, and Bruce Chadwick, "Expectations for Traditional Family Roles: Palestinian Adolescents in the West Bank and Gaza," *Sex Roles* 41 nos. 9/10 (1999): 705-733; Juliane Hammer, *Palestinians Born in Exile: Diaspora and the Search for Homeland* (Austin: University of Texas Press, 2005). Nadera S. Kevorkian, "Fear of Sexual Harassment: Palestinian Adolescent Girls in the Intifada," in *Palestinian Women: Identity and Experience* ed. Ebba Augustin. London: Zed Books, 1993); Ibid., "Trapped: The Violence of Exclusion in Jerusalem," *Jerusalem Quarterly* 49 (Spring 2012): 6-25.

[15] See, for example: Amber Fares, "Speed Sisters," *This Week in Palestine* 165 (January 2012): 38-41; Lana Shehadeh, "Football in a Refugee Camp," *This Week in Palestine* 180 (April 2013): 58-59; Jensen, "Youth Morals, and Islamism"; "Palestine Parkour: Gaza Free Running," 7 February 2011, at: http://www.youtube.com/watch?v=cSMbjuzhqiQ.

[16] Rebecca L. Stein and Ted Swedenburg, "Popular Culture, Relational History, and the Question of Power In Palestine and Israel," *Journal of Palestine Studies* 33 no. 4 (2004): 5.

[17] Ibid., 5.

[18] Ibid., 5-6.

[19] Ibid., 6-7.

[20] Ibid., 8.

[21] Gana, "Rap and Revolt in the Arab World," 26.

[22] Ibid. Rebecca L. Stein and Ted Swedenburg, ed. *Palestine, Israel, and the Politics of Popular Culture* (Durham: Duke University Press, 2005).

[23] Stuart Hall and Tony Jefferson, ed. *Resistance through Rituals: Youth Subcultures in Post-War Britain* (London: Hutchinson/Centre for Contemporary Cultural Studies, University of Birmingham, 1976).

[24] Maira and Soep, "Introduction."

[25] Asef Bayat and Linda Herrera, "Introduction: Being Young and Muslim in Neoliberal Times," in *Being Young and Muslim: New Cultural Politics in the Global South and North*, ed. Linda Herrera and Asef Bayat (New York: Oxford University Press, 2010), 8.

[26] Ted Swedenburg, "Imagined Youths." *Middle East Research and Information Project* 245 (Winter 2007): 6.

[27] Ibid., 7.

[28] Herrera and Bayat, "Knowing Muslim Youth," 356.

[29] Collins, *Occupied by Memory*, 13.

[30] Ibid., 16-17.

[31] See: http://www.reverbnation.com/egtya7 (accessed 25 September 2012).

Introduction

[32] Nguyen-Gillham et al., "Normalizing the Abnormal."

[33] The interviews were done variously in Arabic (with the help of a translator) or English.

[34] These focus group discussions are cited in the paper as groups 1, 2, and 3.

[35] The names of all interviewees, including young activists, have been changed here for reasons of confidentiality, except in the case of the artists, activists, or youth workers who were public figures and/or who were comfortable being cited by name. The focus group participants are all cited anonymously.

[36] Jacques Rancière, *Dissensus: On Politics and Aesthetics*. ed. and transl. Steven Corcoran (London and New York: Continuum Publishing, 2010), electronic edition.

Chapter 1

Jil Oslo: The Search for an Alternative Politics

The category of youth is often under-explored in academic as well as popular discussions of Palestinian politics and political movements at large, due to both the marginalization and exclusion of youth from official politics as well as the difficulty of recognizing them as political actors. The Arab revolutions and the Palestinian youth movement and protests of 2011-12 brought renewed attention to youth as a force of political change. The specter of youth, however, still retained its sedimented association with rebelliousness, activism "without ideology," malleability, irrational violence, and unruliness, and thus, the perception of the Palestinian youth movement was often ambivalent. Some of these persistent conceptualizations of youth may have contained kernels of truth in certain instances in Palestine. Still, the involvement of youth in these protests needs to be situated in the political contexts and material realities that generated what had been glossed as "alienation" or disaffection, and which propelled youth to take to the streets. While the category of youth, as discussed earlier, is generally intertwined with the notion of liminality or alienation from the existing social order, and an uncertainty about who youth will become in that order, it is clear that there are economic and political factors that drive youth to challenge this liminal status at certain moments. This is what is often coded as youth "rebellion."

In the case of Palestine, rebellion or resistance is often inextricably associated with the notion of "youth" for observers. There is a popular imaginary associated with the intifada that highlights the, by now, iconic images of (especially male) youth throwing stones at armed soldiers or facing off against tanks with slingshots. Behind these images of youthful uprising, which circulated globally during the first intifada, and were replaced somewhat by images of armed fighters and young martyrs during the second intifada, is a material reality of youth and their conditions that have shifted, often in depressing ways, over time.[1]

As elsewhere in the region, the Palestinian population in the West Bank, Gaza, and East Jerusalem could be described as "youthful," and those between the ages of fifteen and twenty-nine years represent almost a third (29.8 percent) of the population in 2011.[2] Among Palestinians in Israel (a population of approximately 1.3 million by the end of 2010), 25 percent are between fifteen and twenty-nine years of age.[3] A few points are worth highlighting here in terms of the general socio-economic profile of Palestinian youth in the West Bank, Gaza, Jerusalem, and inside Israel (each of these statistical findings is of course just the tip of the proverbial iceberg and there are many complex issues buried under the data). First, 44.7 percent of youth aged 15-29 years are enrolled in education in the West Bank, Gaza, and East Jerusalem and 8.6 percent of males and 11.1 percent of females between 15-29 years have a university degree; about thirty percent of youth in this group drop out or fail to attend educational institutions.[4] Among Palestinian youth in Israel, in the older age group of 25-34 years, 13.3 percent of males and 19.7 percent of females have a bachelor's degree.[5]

Economic pressures force many students in the West Bank and Gaza to drop out of college before graduation. There is also a general perception that Palestinian universities are failing youth not just due to financial constraints but due to an outdated educational model that does not fit with the economic and political realities of Palestine. In addition, youth who do not leave to study overseas often pursue certain fields due to financial constraints or family and social pressures. It must be noted, also, that Palestinian academics in the West Bank are poorly paid and in some cases have to go on strike just to receive their wages. In Israel, Palestinian youth study in segregated Arab high schools which have fewer resources than Jewish Israeli schools and if they manage to get in to an Israeli university, many face racism in institutions where, as one student said, "being an Arab is itself an obstacle."[6]

Second, unemployment is high among youth in the West Bank, Gaza, and East Jerusalem with 35.7 percent of 15-19 year olds reportedly unemployed in 2012.[7] According to one survey in 2011, unemployment ranges from 58 percent among 15-19 year olds to 40 percent among 25-29 year olds.[8] What is particularly striking is that half of those with graduate diplomas or more advanced higher education in the West Bank and Gaza are unemployed. Graduates of social and behavioral sciences have the highest unemployment rate of 60.1 percent.[9] The participation of women (over 15 years of age) in the formal labor force is very low in Palestine and was only 15.2 percent of the labor force in 2008; however, many women work in the informal sector, for example, as domestic workers.[10] As a result of the dire economic situation, many young

Palestinians from the West Bank or Gaza try to find employment in the Israeli labor market and those in Jerusalem often work for Israeli employers. Therefore, these young people also have to deal with systemic racial discrimination in the workplace. In Israel, nearly half of Palestinian youth enter the labor market while in high school, in a context in which Palestinian families are among the poorest in Israel. Thirty-eight percent of all poor families in Israel are Palestinian (54 percent of Palestinian families are below the poverty level) although Palestinians constitute only 17 percent of the Israeli population.[11]

While this crisis of employment and poverty is widely known, particularly in the case of the West Bank, Jerusalem, and Gaza, what is becoming more apparent is the growing debt crisis as banks have proliferated in the West Bank, in particular. Palestinians of all ages have begun relying on loans and easy credit to buy cars or homes and finance their education or consumption in an increasingly neoliberal economy. This shift, propelled by the availability of new loan systems and the rapid growth of Palestinian banks (including Islamic banks), has led to a situation in which 95 percent of youth (15-29 years old) in the West Bank and Gaza reportedly borrow from multiple sources (including friends and family). A full 46 percent borrow from banks and lending institutions, primarily to fund their education, help build homes, and support themselves.[12] This is also in a context in which young adults from this age group want to or are expected to get married, particularly women. Yet the dismal economic situation in Palestine makes this an ever more difficult prospect so the markers of transition to adulthood are destabilized.

Third, it is also apparent that after the Oslo Accords of 1993 and the establishment of the Palestinian Authority (PA), and with the profusion of local and international NGOs established in the West Bank, Gaza, and (less so) Jerusalem, the class schism has widened in these areas and new consumer lifestyles have emerged. The PA and the NGO sector are among the largest employers in the de facto capital of Ramallah in the West Bank , which has undergone a dramatic transformation from what was once a small hill town and summer resort. The city has witnessed a rapid expansion of a globalized consumer culture and a service-sector economy, with a profusion of upscale restaurants, cafes, and bars, while its class culture remains deeply stratified. Thousands of workers and employees come to Ramallah every day, and return after work to villages and towns because they cannot afford to live in the city where real estate and rent prices have skyrocketed since Oslo. The new lifestyle that has emerged in Ramallah, which some describe as a "five star occupation," has led to a sense of disconnection from the realities in the rest of Palestine—or even the daily reality at the Israeli military checkpoint just outside Ramallah.

The "Ramallah bubble," as it is critically described, shapes the contexts and possibilities of youth culture and youth politics as it has come to emblematize the contradictions of social and political life in the post-Oslo era. For example, Kareem Rabie writes:

> Even if some accounts of the bubble are based on
> certain assumptions of what Palestinianness,
> resistance, or forms of wealth should look like, it is
> clear that for some, the economic situation, and the
> idea of the bubble, is reconfiguring resistance. For
> others, it is "truly a bubble" that prevents resistance
> altogether, or it could be close to bursting, a "recipe
> for revolution" that results from unsustainable growth
> and the widening gap between a "new, highly
> educated, English-speaking class in Ramallah" and
> those classes most harmed by austerity measures.[13]

Underlying the discourse of the bubble, Rabie argues, is a more complex debate about the PA's state-building project and its neoliberal economic policies that have normalized Israeli occupation, replacing a discourse of resistance with new social practices and consumer lifestyles. All the while, the West Bank has remained a consumer market and labor market for Israel. But the point is also that there is a larger settler-colonial project underlying the contradictory economic and political landscape of the West Bank, Gaza, and Jerusalem, as well as the condition of Palestinians in Israel. The paradoxes of the post-Oslo moment are merely one phase of this ongoing colonial regime. Basel Abbas and Ruanne Abourahme, two young artists from Ramallah formed the multimedia performance collective Tashweesh with the rapper and music producer Boikutt (which evolved out of Ramallah Underground, a hip hop collective founded in Ramallah in 2003). They comment in their multimedia work, "The Zone:"

> In what would appear to us as one of the darkest
> moments in Palestinian lived history, a "dream-
> world" has somehow emerged in the West Bank: a
> host of commodified desires, semblance of normality,
> have been constructed atop the debris of political
> failure and collapse. Here, new lifestyles, desires,

> senses of self mingle and collide with a persistent
> denial of the disasters of Palestine's current
> situation. . . . in order for us to invest in this new
> dream we must somehow ignore the increasingly
> visible violence of the colonial situation, this
> dreamworld's increasingly dystopian wider
> environment.[14]

This is the historical context in which jil Oslo, or the Oslo generation, has come of age. Throughout Palestine, this generation has struggled with the political conjunctures of the first and second intifadas, the establishment of a virtual state or a state without real sovereignty, and the formation of separate political regimes governing the West Bank and Gaza after 2007.

Local Cosmopolitanisms

Ramallah encapsulates, more than any other site in Palestine, the political and cultural contradictions of the post-Oslo moment, the era of "normalization," and of incipient state-building without actual sovereignty. It represents for many the paradoxical state of living in a colonial present and with neoliberal capitalism that is described as the "Ramallah syndrome." Lisa Taraki and Rita Giacaman observe that Ramallah, a historically Christian city, has been transformed into a diverse (predominantly Muslim) "city of migrants and transients" that has come to represent "a space tolerant of differing ways of life"—what I would describe as a space of localized cosmopolitanism.[15] Taraki and Giacaman point out that Ramallah has a longer history of transnational migration and return migration to and from the United States, in particular, and has been reshaped by the influx of refugees after 1948. So this cosmopolitanism is not new if it still co-exists, sometimes uneasily, with local social networks and well-established older residents. However, since Oslo, Ramallah became the de facto capital city of Palestine, and the center of cultural production in public and "official" arenas.

The urban culture of Ramallah has thus been shaped by the influx of new residents working for the Palestinian Authority and the burgeoning of local and international NGOs. As Hafez, a young artist and activist who lives in Ramallah but is from a village near Nablus, said: "There is a problem of focusing on arts in Ramallah as if it is not just the capital, it is Palestine." The city has become a major site of Palestinian hip hop as well as the youth movement in the West Bank. But it must be noted that Palestinian rappers come from various towns and villages across the West Bank and that youth organizing occurs in multiple locations—some argue, in its most radical and militant forms outside Ramallah, where young people have been involved in ongoing resistance against the Wall and the settlements.

The notion of the Ramallah bubble as a lens into the political and social paradoxes of post-Oslo Palestine and the culture of normalization has been addressed by several artists in self-reflexive works in Ramallah. Yazid Anani, an artist and scholar from Ramallah, co-curated an exhibit about Ramallah ("Ramallah: The Fairest of Them All?") at the Ethnographic and Art Museum at Birzeit University and in public spaces around the city in 2010. This included his project on "The Ramallah Syndrome," with Alessandro Petti and Sandi Hilal, which examined "the new spatial and social order that emerged after the collapse of the Oslo 'peace process'" and the "'hallucination of normality,' the fantasy of a co-existence of occupation and liberty."[16] The artists hung posters in cafes and restaurants around the city that posed questions such as, "What's wrong about having a normal life in Ramallah?," "Is Ramallah New York?," and "Is Ramallah under occupation?," and requested that people share their responses, making use of the consumer culture in the city to stage a public art project.

Anani's work also focuses on the privatization of public spaces in Ramallah, pointing out that "political uncertainties and thriving neoliberalism have shifted the balance between economics and politics in the city, leading to [the] economization and politicization of public spaces and prohibiting their use for collective assembly, collective political exchange, accessibility, and self-criticism."[17] So while privatized public spaces, such as chic restaurants and cafes as well as new art galleries, have sprung up in Ramallah, many lament the shrinking of spaces for collective political resistance. There are also fewer spaces for collective cultural consumption, such as cinemas, nearly all of which have been torn down or converted into shopping malls as individuals increasingly retreat to private spaces of television viewing.[18] In the context of the PA's state-building project, the struggle over public space is part of the larger contest over public culture, and the boundaries of permissibility in public behavior, which also shape debates about hip hop and youth activism, as I will discuss later.

Taraki and Giacaman observe that in post-Oslo Ramallah, a "globalized and modernist urban middle class ethos has captured the imagination of the city's new middle class and is reflected in the sensibilities, dispositions, life projects, and practices of wide sections of the urban middle strata."[19] Consumption, according to Taraki, is the "overarching medium through which this new consciousness is expressed."[20] This is true not just of Ramallah, but also of middle-class families in other towns and cities, such as Bethlehem or Nablus, as well as in refugee camps who are also consuming images of what it means to be "global" or "urban," if in a less cosmopolitan environment. There is also exchange and traffic between cities, towns, and villages as people do indeed travel to Ramallah, including youth, despite restrictions on mobility in the West Bank. In addition, since the 1980s Ramallah has become a hub for youth who are not only interested in cultural consumption, but in political activity as well. This rang especially true when the city was an "important node in national politics" during the period of "mass resistance to the occupation," and for students at Birzeit University who socialize or live in the city as well as young people who move to the city to work.[21]

Furthermore, Taraki and Giacaman make the important point that the elites and the "new middle class" in the West Bank identify not just with Western urban spaces, but also with the "hybrid trans-Arab urban culture" that has emerged in cities such as Amman or Beirut.[22] In the everyday lives of Palestinian youth, hip hop coexists with a range of popular culture expressions, including Lebanese pop, Egyptian films, Turkish television dramas, and fashionable Muslim clothing styles for women imported from Turkey or the Gulf that shape youth culture. Therefore, hip hop cannot be compartmentalized as simply a "Western" cultural form as it interacts with and draws on diverse cultural expressions.[23] Hip hop culture has emerged from these historical shifts in urbanization and cosmopolitanism and this matrix of political, economic, and social forces that produced new subcultures in which youth mix, and recreate, multiple cultural idioms.

Thus, there is a local politics that embeds new forms of cultural consumption and production, and that defines what is possible and permissible for youth or artists in various locations. Ramallah's "modernity, dynamism, and diversity" is often contrasted with the social conservatism of other cities in the West Bank, particularly Nablus and al-Khalil (Hebron).[24] For example, Rajeh Dana, a rapper and student at Birzeit University from al-Khalil, remarked that Black Revolution's first rap performance was at the Jerusalem Festival in al-Khalil and he was "afraid" of the response because the city is a "closed society." But he was surprised that the young people in the audience loved the music, and were "clapping" and "screaming" because rap is a "common language" with which these youth identified. Salim, a theater artist who runs youth programs, including hip hop projects, at Yafa Cultural Center in Balata refugee camp in Nablus, commented that Nablus is "more conservative" and "traditional" than other cities. Yet he also spoke about the many collaborative projects that the center had done with Danish and Norwegian artists who came to Balata and worked with youth, suggesting the ways that the space of the camp is an increasingly internationalized one. Tina Sherwell of the International Academy of Art in Ramallah, who has been doing art workshops with youth in Shu'afat camp, said that it had become more difficult to have mixed-gender programs than in the past. She noted the prohibitions and regulations of visual culture, such as photography, due to what she describes as an increasing "conservatism" among youth, most of whom go to gender-segregated schools, noting, "the Ramallah bubble doesn't spread everywhere."

At the same time, there are many international projects and NGOs outside of Ramallah that have developed youth programs and arts projects in refugee camps as well as cities in the West Bank, introducing hybrid forms of cultural expression. The Yafa Cultural Center in Balata camp, for example, hosted a hip hop workshop for youth, teaching "resistance through the arts," in conjunction with a tour by well-known rappers from the United States and the UK, some of them Palestinian and Arab, including M1 of Dead Prez, Mazzi of Soul Purpose, Shadia Mansour, and Low Key. This became the basis of a film with the evocative title, "Hip Hop is Bigger than the Occupation." [25] MC Dave, a young rapper from Jerusalem, said that he participated in a workshop organized by Swedish artists at Dar al-Anadwa in Bethlehem, that included hip hop groups such as G-Town, the Outlaws, and DAM as well as Arab rock bands such as Hawa Dafi, from the Golan Heights, and Khalas, from Acca. It also included multiple dance genres, such as *dabke*, breakdancing, and modern dance. Palestinian Street participated in a music workshop for youth in Bethlehem's Dheisheh Refugee Camp, sponsored by Musicians Without Borders.

Refugee camps, as well as (certain) cities, have become the site of a cosmopolitan localism, or localized cosmopolitanism—a space where young people interact with people from diverse national and racial backgrounds, and where cultural imaginaries are shaped and transformed by diverse aesthetic traditions, if under conditions of confinement and uneven access to economic and educational resources. These transformations inevitably lead to tensions due to racialized and class-based hierarchies, as different world views or aesthetic imaginaries collide. These spaces of localized cosmopolitanism are clearly not without contradictions or conflict and there is an active and ongoing debate about the NGOization of popular culture and youth programs. Yet, it is striking that in the focus group interviews I did with youth in the West Bank, none of them spoke about foreign NGOs as a factor in the "Westernization" of

Palestinian culture or the entry of globalized cultural forms. A study of Palestinian youth activists and their engagement with local as well as global issues noted that the concept of "globalization" was not mentioned by youth in any of the interviews, even though it seemed to be a central factor in shaping their relationship with the larger world.[26] This absence of direct critique of globalization, or the related process of NGOization, of the cultural sphere is a point I will return to later in the book. Here, I want to highlight that popular culture is always a readily available site through which anxieties about national identity, class, gender, and sexuality are narrated, as is the case for Palestinian youth and the hip hop movement.

The Search for a New Narrative

One of the most striking, and persistent, observations made by the young people I spoke to, students as well as artists and activists, was that their generation of Palestinian youth wanted an alternative politics and that the pursuit of new cultural forms overlapped with their search for a new politics in the post-Oslo era. Basel said, "We were trying to give voice to an alternative art scene in Palestine, an alternative voice in Palestine that was trying to say something different and to find a different language." Young artists and activists of jil Oslo were thus engaged in this quest that drew on or revived, in many cases, earlier frameworks of Palestinian resistance or discourses of national identity while (re)creating new cultural idioms or political vocabularies. Yasmine, a young activist from al-Bireh, said eloquently that the independent youth movement's "aims were to go back to resistance and resuscitate the Palestinian struggle as a national movement," in the post-Oslo context of general depoliticization and demobilization. As Ahmed, a young activist from Ramallah, astutely observed, "Popular culture plays a massive part in building the national narrative, especially when there's a problem with that narrative."

This quest for a new narrative or alternative politics is situated in the post-Oslo moment which heightened for Palestinians, including youth, the contradictions of living in a state without sovereignty, in the West Bank and Gaza, and in an increasingly Judaized East Jerusalem. The youth of jil Oslo, particularly those who are in their late teens to mid-twenties today and were born just before or after the Oslo Accords of 1993, have come of age in a very different political reality than the previous generation. The supposed political withdrawal or apathy of youth has to be understood in a historical context in which youth are not represented in the "leadership and decision-making" of the Palestinian national movement, according to commentators such as Samir Seif.

However, as Seif adds, young people were "widely engaged in the organization and leadership of the [first] intifada, its striking forces, its popular committees," and "young people served in the unified leadership of the intifada."[27] The young people that I spoke to were also old enough to remember the second intifada, and to have been deeply affected by those memories of occupation, invasion, and resistance. Feryal, a young woman who was from Nablus and remembers living through the months of curfew, said that it was the "traumatizing experience" of the second intifada that motivated her political activism as it did for others to whom I spoke.

Fajr Harb, a young activist from Ramallah who is well known in the youth movement, observed thoughtfully:

> To understand Palestinian youth today, you have to understand the previous generation's politics and Oslo. During the first intifada, the enemy was in the streets. It was very clear who we had to fight. After Oslo, things changed and the Palestinian cause changed. The purpose of Oslo was to divide the West Bank from Gaza from Jerusalem—the purpose was to divide Palestine.

As the lines of national struggle became less clear after Oslo, Palestinians were also increasingly disconnected and divided from one another in the bantustans created by Israel's fragmentation of the West Bank, using the Wall and the settlements; in an encircled and increasingly peripheralized Jerusalem; and in a besieged and blockaded Gaza. In fact, many commentators observe that it is the Oslo agreements that gave "birth [to] what Jeff Halper has called Israel's 'matrix of control'" in Palestinian areas with the construction and expansion of the Wall, settlements, bypass roads, and checkpoints.[28] The colonial state apparatus generated ambiguous legal categories and forms of identity documentation for the colonized population and territories—differentiating between peoples and geographic spaces, for example, in Israel, East/West Jerusalem, Gaza, and West Bank Areas A, B, C. This is what Ann Stoler describes as the inherent blurring of rights and "epistemic murk" constitutive of the architecture of settler colonial states, an ambiguity that is core to imperial biopolitics and its construction of proliferating territorial and identity designations.[29]

The ambiguity of legal identities and the profusion of spatial categorizations has also generated hierarchies among Palestinians based on associated distinctions about who can live where, who can marry whom, or who can travel across which borders. For example, Nadera Shalhoub-Kevorkian addresses the divisions within families in East Jerusalem, some of whose members have Jerusalem identity cards ("blue IDs") and some of whom have the more restrictive West Bank identification; the fear and anxiety created by living in conditions of "illegality" in Jerusalem; and the ways that this has broken down social and family relations.[30] I heard stories of young people who were interested in a romantic relationship with someone who had a different identity category and chose not to pursue it because it would mean that they may not be able to live together due to Israeli laws regulating residence for Palestinians. One young woman interviewed by Shalhoub-Kevorkian offered an eloquent statement that captured the nature of colonial rule that permeates spaces of intimacy: "Their borders are in our homes, lives, bodies, and relationships."[31] Young activists from the West Bank and also 1948 Palestine have engaged in creative campaigns to challenge these Israeli laws that regulate residence, romance, and family life, as in the mock "weddings" near the Wall staged by the campaign "Love in the Time of Apartheid" in 2013.[32] Settler colonial rule permeates the most intimate of spaces, reshaping relationships of kinship, desire, marriage, and sociability, which is why it has been described as a form of sociocide in Palestine, a destruction of social relationships and the fabric of society and an assault on the social itself.

Parallel to the colonial partitioning of national space and management of bodies and affective lives, there has been a de-politicization in the post-Oslo moment, not just of youth but also of Palestinian society in general. This is the social and political context in which jil Oslo has come of age. Relative to the mass movements and intense mobilization during the first and second intifadas, there has been a demobilization of Palestinians who are still living under conditions of occupation, if in a different phase of colonial governmentality. Ruanne said incisively that, for Palestinian youth in the 1990s, "It was a moment when the revolutionary movement was, in a sense, dissolving after Oslo. I think probably young Palestinians started looking for something else to articulate their experiences, for they were still experiencing the full force of the racist state." By the time the Oslo Accords were signed in 1993, according to George Giacaman, "most parties, including those on the left, were quickly losing whatever mass base" they had during the first intifada." There was a decline in the hitherto energetic grassroots involvement of student groups, women's organizations, and popular committees throughout the West Bank and Gaza.[33] The Oslo Accords introduced a new paradigm for Palestinian politics but also precipitated a "crisis" for the Palestinian national movement, marked by "loss of a clear cause, lack of hope, and perception of the end of the national project."[34]

The youth of jil Oslo, then, have two major points of departure for their search for an alternative to existing political frameworks. First, youth in the West Bank and Gaza have experienced a restructuring of Israeli military control given that "the withdrawal of the IDF from the Gaza Strip and the removal of many of the internal checkpoints in the West Bank have created fewer arenas for direct confrontation with the Israeli enemy . . . . interest in traditional youth activism has dwindled and there are fewer sites of direct clashes."[35] As Ruanne observed, the fragile semblance of "peace" and the relative loosening of restrictions on movement and easing of checkpoints also led to fewer militarized encounters with Israelis that created a schizophrenic reality for this generation: "There is a classic colonial context of double consciousness. The more people here do not interact with Israelis as a colonial force, the more removed they are from that reality." Feryal said that what was "most depressing" after Oslo was that so little had changed and that "people lose track of why we did this [resistance during the intifadas] in the first place." The politics of normalization, or what Taraki calls the "new normal politics" of this period, was marked by a "deradicalized politics of normality" and a "new individualistic ethos" that distanced itself from collective struggle.[36]

The contradictory reality of this new phase of colonization is marked by the fact that the Palestinian Authority did not have full sovereignty after Oslo but became the subcontractor for the occupation, in a sense, managing security and repressing dissent through its own internal military and intelligence apparatus. Ramzy Baroud observes of the crisis in Palestinian politics since the concessions made in the Oslo agreements:

> . . . for a Palestinian leadership to be acknowledged as such by regional and international players, it has to excel in the art of "compromise". These carefully molded leaders often cater to the interests of their Arab and Western benefactors, at the expense of their own people. Not one single popular faction has resolutely escaped this seeming generalization. . . . This reality has permeated Palestinian politics for decades. However, in the last two decades the distance between the Palestinian leadership and the people has grown by a once unimaginable distance, where the

Palestinian has become a jailor and a peddling
politician or a security coordinator working hand in
hand with Israel.[37]

Echoing this view, Hafez was critical of the PA's willingness to comply with
externally imposed frameworks and "demands of self-governance" and the
"discourse of countering terrorism, according to Western agendas." Hafez, and
many other young (as well as older) activists with whom I spoke, view the PA as
a "comprador regime serving Western interests" that has undermined genuine
grassroots or mass-based collective resistance.

As Ruanne observed, the search for an alternative politics in her generation
had begun before Oslo, but it took a while for the implications and "disasters" of
the second intifada to crystallize into a new political moment, in which
Palestinians had to grapple not just with the Israeli regime but also with the
Palestinian "security apparatus and their training with the Israelis and the CIA."
Thus, the Tashweesh collective's project, "The Zone," is an investigation of "the
transformation of the PLO into an 'authority' and eventually a 'security' regime"
and "the way in which this new regime displaced the old collective 'dreams' and
gave birth to new political discourses and desires largely centered on
consumption."[38] Ruanne and Basel describe this, eloquently and also critically, as
the production of a "dream-image situated in a kind of neo-liberal creed [that] is
being projected in the public spaces of West Bank cities," and as an illusion of
consumerist freedom that masks projects of neoliberal economic restrictions and
repressive securitization which has replaced collective political struggle and
discourse.[39] Salim, a young theater artist from Balata, observed that for youth, "It
is hard to understand why so much money is put into security, not education"
and why the Palestinian security forces have attacked young protesters in Nablus
or Ramallah. It is in this context that young activists experience surveillance and
repression by a regime that—if it is not quite a police state, given that it is not yet
even a state—has created a climate of fear and insecurity that underlies some of
what is glossed as youth "apathy" in the West Bank.

Giacaman has observed that on the one hand, Israel ensured that "the
Palestinian Authority [PA] play a policing role among its own population
without regard to civil and human rights."[40] On the other hand, he made a
prescient observation that if the Palestinian people largely perceived the Oslo
agreements to be undermining their national interests, then the PA's
commitment to an unpopular political framework meant that it would eventually
"come into conflict with its own population on issues related to national rights

and national future."[41] These observations were borne out more than ever by the protests and the youth movement that emerged in 2011-12, among other events that have challenged the PA's policies and its security and economic agreements with Israel. But if aspects of the occupation have been outsourced to the Palestinian regime under Oslo, then clearly a new political framework for resistance is needed to focus on both national liberation and building a democratic society. Political resistance at this moment has to challenge the degraded sovereignty of the virtual state created by Israel, through Oslo and with the support of Western powers, and oppose the creation by imperial and settler colonial powers of forms of partial or deferred sovereignty and their attendant illusions of "democracy" and "self-governance."[42]

The second major feature of this post-Oslo politics is the disillusionment with existing political frameworks and party structures, which affects Palestinian youth in the West Bank and Gaza as well as those living in Israel. One study of Palestinian youth politics in the West Bank and Gaza notes, "Palestinian youth have largely exited from politics, prioritizing personal affairs (family and job) when considering the current situation and their future."[43] As Fajr observed of youth in the West Bank, "There has been a de-politicization of the population. My generation was not expected to understand anything about politics but just be interested in daily life." In other words, the modicum of economic stability available after Oslo, especially in the West Bank, was expected to divert youth from political mobilization, if not to pacify them. Ramallah Underground's song, "*Min El Kaheff*" ("From the Cave") eloquently captures the paradoxical political moment facing youth living with the poisonous facade of "democracy" and desiring a "normal life." It depicts youth struggling with the lure of a "politics" seemingly distant:

> And Arab leaders let us down
> Abandoned us, fled to our enemies
> Because they couldn't infect us with their cowardice
> They promised the future and look what they got us
> into
> 2007: the world's moving ahead and they blow us up,
> Starve us, they wanna forget us
> We spent years building and they came suddenly led
> us on,
> Threatened and frightened us
> Poisoned us with democracy
> Wouldn't let us have a normal life

They set us right on line of fire, they ruined us,
destroyed us, dried up our blood
All that and still they couldn't finish the job
I am trying not to care anymore, but politics pulls at
me
I say, leave me alone
She says, I am part of your life
You won't be able to resist me.[44]

This song poetically evokes the specter of a politics (gendered female) for a generation that is seemingly apathetic and indifferent, but in actuality disappointed and betrayed by their cowardly leadership that has "dried up their blood." Politics, in this song, is something other than what these leaders represent, inescapably a part of life. It is this (re)conceptualization of politics as something other than what exists, as sanctioned, official politics, that some in jil Oslo are trying to produce. Ahmed, who was involved in the youth movement in the West Bank in spring 2011, recollected that when he returned to Palestine after studying abroad in 2009, he was "shocked by the lack of political involvement of youth," including among college students; he realized that they were "fed up" with the existing "political culture" which is "very alienating." But a growing segment of youth, of diverse class backgrounds, in the West Bank, Gaza, and '48 Palestine, became increasingly dissatisfied with existing structures and paradigms for politics, and began rethinking the "political" itself.

As Salim commented, "We don't know why we should fight [for Palestinian liberation]. We don't know where we're going, and what's the vision." This frustration exists was expressed by all the young Palestinians to whom I spoke, not to mention others. A young man from Gaza states, "We have no unified strategy for the struggle. We are busy with the Fateh and Hamas division today. We will wake up one day surprised by the presence of one million settlers [in Palestine]."[45] This disillusionment with the political leadership and the (lack of a) national movement is a pervasive, daily refrain among Palestinians, including many youth. As Ruanne remarked, "This is an interesting moment for the younger generation because they are political but not connected to any political party. Young people today reject that party structure completely. That is new." She noted that many young hip hop artists speak critically about the *Sulta* (the PA) and the "failure of the political process marked by Oslo. They are looking for a new politics." But as she also added, "There is no particular organization or movement."

A swathe of youth opinion polls and surveys conducted in the West Bank and Gaza consistently report a pattern of rising skepticism and distrust in existing political factions, a sense of disappointment in and betrayal by established or formal political movements, and a fear or ambivalence about public forms of political activism. This has coincided with what has been commonly viewed as a "retreat" from the political arena among jil Oslo, also documented in numerous youth studies. For example, Sharek Youth Forum reported that in a survey of youth in the West Bank and Gaza in 2009, 70 percent of youth "described themselves as politically inactive" and 52 percent "do not trust any political faction existing in the Palestinian arena."[46] By 2011, Sharek's poll of youth in the West Bank, Gaza, and Jerusalem reported that a clear majority (62 percent) did not trust any political factions and 48 percent of youth "support a national unity government of all factions."[47] In 2013, 73 percent of youth surveyed said that they do not belong to any political faction, 39 percent saying this was due to their "lack of confidence" in these parties.[48] While quantitative findings must be considered very carefully—and the profusion of opinion polls about Palestinian youth often do not share information about how respondents were contacted or selected, what questions were asked, or how concepts were defined in the questionnaires—it is apparent that there is a general consistency among these surveys of major trends among Palestinian youth. However, I argue that among youth there is not necessarily a withdrawal from politics—and certainly not for all youth—but a reshaping of the political and a reinvestment in other, informal, grassroots, autonomous, or new forms of politics.

The disillusionment with established political factions, including left factions, which had historically provided established youth wings that were the basis for campus politics, increased in the wake of the second legislative elections in 2006 and the subsequent violent conflict between Hamas and Fateh. A large majority (76 percent) in Sharek's 2013 youth survey also thought that student clubs, which are generally affiliated with factions, represent the political agendas of those parties and not the actual concerns of students and youth.[49] Feryal, who studied at an-Najah University in Nablus, recalled that nearly all students were "affiliated with one faction or another," but that the elections were basically a contest between Fateh and Hamas candidates, the two dominant parties. She commented that, for some, participation in these political activities was "for the fun of voting and having a day off" for elections. While some genuinely were politically involved, others voted because they were given "money or phone credit."

At al-Quds University in East Jerusalem, I noticed the campus would be plastered with flags of a different political faction every other week, sometimes with posters honoring prisoners from that faction and generally with political slogans raised at rallies on the plaza which always seemed to feature male speakers (never female). The corruption and constriction of student politics has led to the widespread cynicism and presumed political apathy among youth. According to former Birzeit University student and political journalist Ihab Al-Jariri, "the Palestinian student movement . . . is in disarray," holding strikes and raising slogans but "ineffective in the face of developments on the ground."[50] A young man who studies at Birzeit, Mahmoud, said that among Palestinian youth there is "frustration" with political leaders, as well as young activists: "They talk and talk but they don't do anything . . . People who join these parties do so for self-interest."

Many young people also spoke about the fear of reprisals and imprisonment for political engagement, both by Fateh in the West Bank and by the Israeli intelligence and security apparatus, that underlies the hesitation among many youth about public political involvement.[51] Mahmoud thought that hip hop artists such as Black Revolution were careful about public engagement with political activism probably because they were "frightened" of being imprisoned or even killed, either by Israel or the PA. This was poignantly brought home to me when one young activist, affiliated with the Popular Front for the Liberation of Palestine (PFLP), who had been imprisoned more than once, was hesitant to meet with me at any public place other than two or three specific restaurants in Ramallah. Later I learned that this was because he was afraid of the presence of PA intelligence agents at other venues, underscoring the depth of fear and anxiety about surveillance and repression under the PA. Two young activists who had been involved in the hunger strike in Ramallah in March 2011 told me that they even knew the PA security agents who surveilled them by name. Israeli surveillance is very much a part of life for Palestinian youth, as demonstrated by Shalhoub-Kevorkian's research in the greater Jerusalem area where "the everydayness of surveillance practices, both technological (such as video cameras and recording devices) and physical (Israeli guards, checkpoints, and the Wall), has heightened the sense of being trapped and suffocated."[52] These issues of the fear, and intimacy, of the intrusion of surveillance into the crevices of everyday life, and into popular culture, emerged repeatedly in the interviews with youth.

The political critique of dominant or acceptable political frameworks is evident among '48 Palestinian youth who are also evidently dissatisfied with established party politics and partisan divisions in Palestinian politics in Israel. A study by Baladna, a youth organization in Haifa, found that "partisan activism was criticized by young people" because, as some respondents observed, the parties "do not care about the people" but only about building their own strength. Only 5 percent of the youth surveyed belonged to political parties.[53] Other '48 Palestinian youth commented that these political groups do not participate in protests or activities if they are not sponsored by their own party. In addition, this territoriality and narrow vision is part of a political culture in which party loyalty is associated with families, as is also the case in the West Bank. As one young woman at Birzeit University (focus group 2) pointed out in discussing the limited political engagement at the university, "People just follow parties that their parents do." One young '48 Palestinian woman commented, echoing a common observation among youth in the West Bank as well: "This means that if your parents are affiliated with this party, the children should follow their path . . . If you don't, the whole family will ask, what happened? What is wrong with you? I realized that political parties don't lead us anywhere, and that political and social activism should not only be through political parties."[54]

In addition, for '48 Palestinian youth, there is the question of whether or not to support parties who want representation in the Israeli government and run for election to the Knesset. The parties claim that they want to change policies from within the framework of the state, even if some parties reject the presumptions of Israeli "democracy." Maisa Daw, a young woman from Haifa, is a vocalist who belongs to the reggae-rap-dub group, Ministry of Dub-Key. When I met her in February 2013, she said, "Many youth are not affiliated with parties. In the last elections, many people did not vote, like me. First of all, it is not going to change anything. I saw this quote which I like: if voting brought about change, it would be illegal. Second, voting is for the Knesset, and I do not support the Knesset and I also do not support any of the parties." Ministry of Dub-Key, and other young Palestinian musicians and artists from '48 Palestine, are involved in local protests as well as in cross-border political movements involving groups in the West Bank. One example is the Freedom Bus tour sponsored by the Freedom Theater in Jenin, which does community theater and music events in villages and towns in the West Bank to support resistance against the Wall, settlements, and land confiscation.

While Palestinian student movements and youth organizing in Israel is relatively weak and generally "limited to demonstrations," according to the Baladna study, "some young people attempted to establish nonpartisan independent frameworks that bring together society's different segments." There is a youth movement that has emerged in places such as Jaffa and also in the Galilee region, in northern Israel, that is focused on mobilizing and educating youth around "national identity" as well as social issues.[55] Many are also involved in mobilizing with other '48 Palestinian youth through groups such as Baladna in Haifa, Baqaa and Haq in Nazareth, and Khoutwa in Lid. This is important "especially in a society where parents warn their children not to be politically active when they go to universities," given the repression of and reprisals against Palestinian activists in Israel, an issue I will discuss in chapter four.[56]

A third issue to be considered in contextualizing the politics of jil Oslo and the protests of 2011-12 is that unemployment is very high among youth in the West Bank and Gaza, as noted earlier. This is a significant source of frustration and anxiety for this generation. For example, a survey of Palestinian youth in the West Bank and Gaza in 2012 by the Arab World for Research and Development (AWRAD) found that a large majority consider "corruption in public institutions" (78 percent) and unemployment (72 percent) a very important concern, which is echoed among other youth surveys, and a majority (62 percent) "believe that their needs and priorities are not integrated in public policies and decisions."[57] Another (qualitative as well as quantitative) study reported that youth in the West Bank were more confident of their economic and career prospects than those in Gaza—not surprising, given the economic blockade and siege on Gaza; however, young people in both regions believe that to get a stable job in the public sector, "you need *wasta*" or political connections —what is humorously referred to as the magic "vitamin W."[58] In addition, party factionalism has also shaped employment prospects to the degree that youth feel that "belonging to the 'wrong' political faction makes it hard to get work"—that is, belonging to Hamas in the case of the West Bank or Fateh in the case of Gaza.[59] A 2010 poll of youth in the West Bank reported that 83.5 percent believed "to a very high degree or to a high degree that people get away with things through nepotism and cronyism."[60]

These observations and feelings of frustration about possibilities for education and work in the post-Oslo moment was a refrain among most of the youth with whom I spoke. Hussein, a student at Birzeit University who said he did not want to be affiliated with either Fateh or Hamas, remarked, "There are no opportunities here, no possibilities. There are limitations also on what we do, what we can study." For middle-class youth, such as Hussein and many of the students I interviewed in the West Bank, there is still a great deal of economic uncertainty and anxiety about the future. Don Bassa, a rapper who is studying hospitality/hotel management and works at a Jewish-owned restaurant in

Jerusalem, talked about how Palestinian workers in restaurants are underpaid and in some cases, not even allowed to touch the stoves in the kitchen due to "kosher laws that mean only Jews can work as higher-paid chefs." In addition to racial discrimination in the Israeli labor market, he also pointed out that Palestinians in East Jerusalem pay high (Israeli municipal) taxes but do not receive adequate social services from the state: "The government doesn't spend it on fixing our streets, they spend it on West Jerusalem."

The Ramallah "bubble" of neoliberal development has clearly not benefited everyone and has indeed enlarged the class schism in the post-Oslo period. As Fajr observed, "There are people who are benefiting from the status quo, in real estate and telecommunications, while others are struggling." Al'aa, a young activist, remarked, "Oslo was also a re-organization of classes; it widened the gap between the rich and the poor." He added, "Our generation has been smacked by globalization. But people are stuck in their jobs, they are really unhappy. Neoliberalism is going to make things explode; it is a bubble. There are 40,000 PA employees and 40,000 NGO employees in Ramallah. When the funding gets cut, it's going to collapse." So, as Taraki observes, the post-Oslo moment was a period of "transformations in the class structure" in the West Bank, including the "consolidation of a new and aspiring modernist middle class" and the consumer culture that attended this shift.[61]

At the same time, across the Green Line, '48 Palestinian youth also struggle with limited economic opportunities due to racial discrimination in the mainstream labor market in Israel and inadequate training and preparation in Arab schools. In the film *Slingshot Hip Hop*, Abeer, a young female rapper from Acca, talks about how she was fired from a McDonald's in Israel for speaking Arabic, after working there for three years.[62] Racial discrimination against Palestinian students in Israeli universities is a major impediment to their enrollment in higher education, according to 40 percent of youth surveyed by Baladna, and as one young Palestinian said "being Arab is itself an obstacle." Only 11 percent of undergraduates and 7 percent of master's students in Israeli universities are Palestinian, and many youth end up leaving to study in Jordan or Europe, while some go to the West Bank.[63] Palestinian students in Israeli universities have to deal with a host of repressive policies that prevent them from organizing events and hosting speakers about Palestine, commemorating the Nakba on campus, and in some cases, even running for election as president of the student union.[64]

Palestinian youth are ill-equipped to enter the Israeli labor market due to their lack of appropriate specializations and a lack of professional counseling and educational resources in underfunded Arab schools that are often criticized for offering inadequate academic skills.[65] Furthermore, Israeli military service is sometimes the basis for discrimination against Palestinians, who generally do not serve in the military. In addition, the Palestinian labor market is restricted, which particularly impacts young women, who often end up working in Palestinian villages and towns.[66] While young Palestinian women in Israel have a higher rate of participation in the formal labor market than young men, it is also the case that fields of work are gendered, with the majority of Palestinian women in education, social work, and health services, while most Palestinian men work in construction or industry in Israel.[67] DAM's song, "*Muwatin Mustahdaf*" ("Targeted Citizen"), produced in 2010 for a film by Adalah (The Legal Center for Arab Minority Rights in Israel) with the same name, offers an incisive commentary on discrimination in employment facing Palestinian youth in Israel:

> My story begins in school
> The lesson was done before roll-call had begun,
> 41 kids in a class and the light of knowledge
> burned out on the shelf. Our parents asked,
> "Why"? They said, "Budget cuts."
> Another education lost.
>
> I took things in my own hands
> And went looking for some manual work.
> Found a job that didn't require army service.
> They asked, "Name?" I said, "Mahmoud."
> They said, "Change it." I said, "Request denied."
> They said, "Job denied."[68]

"We Want a Generation of Giants"

Palestinian youth culture and youth organizing has emerged from specific political and material conditions at this historical moment, as demonstrated by findings from existing studies. It is in this context that Palestinian youth have turned to political movements or attempted to engage in political activism outside of established party and factional structures after Oslo, particularly in the aftermath of the Hamas-Fateh clashes, and produced new cultural expressions of political identity. For '48 Palestinians, the politicization and radicalization of youth was intensified in the wake of what is known as Black October. Thirteen young Palestinians were killed by Israeli police within a two-week time period in October 2000, during demonstrations and acts of civil disobedience that broke out in support of the second intifada and that galvanized political resistance among a younger generation of '48 Palestinians.

Inas Margieh, who grew up in Nazareth and has worked with Baladna in Haifa, notes that Black October was "a turning point" in the political discourse for '48 Palestinians and for youth, in particular, who saw young Palestinians being shot dead by live bullets in Nazareth. She recalls, "Literally, there was a war in Nasra [Nazareth]. . . One youth said, 'All of a sudden, I knew I was in a battlefield.' ... Young people who were six or seven at the time were born into a reality with no illusions. This experience would always stay with them, this is why there was a change in political identity for this generation."[69] Duaa, a young woman who has been engaged with political activism at Haifa University and Hebrew University, observed that Palestinian flags were only raised on Israeli campuses by students after 2000 and since the second intifada. As Ruanne observed, '48 Palestinian hip hop is embedded in the politicization of young people since 2000 and grew out of that political moment: "DAM expressed what a lot of young people inside were experiencing as they were becoming politicized, and they were expressing that feeling during the second intifada." It is this moment that helped seed the Palestinian rap that later burgeoned into the larger Palestinian hip hop movement.

DAM's internationally famous first single, "*Meen Irhabi*" ("Who's the Terrorist?"), marking their maturation as political rappers, was released during the second intifada and was reportedly downloaded more than one million times from their website until 2008.[70] The song layers Arabic rap over female vocals in Arabic and concludes with the voices of older Palestinian men lamenting the destruction of their olive trees. In the powerful video for the song, produced by Jackie Salloum and circulated on the Internet via YouTube, DAM raps over images of the occupation and the intifada:

> Who's a terrorist?
> Me, a terrorist?
> How am I a terrorist
> When you've taken my land?
> You're the terrorist!
> You've taken everything I own while I'm living in my
> homeland.

You want me to go to the law?
You're the witness, the lawyer, and the judge.
I'll be sentenced to death,
To end up the majority in the cemetery.
. . .

You attack me but still you cry out,
When I remind you it was you attacked me
You silence me and shout,
"Don't they have parents to keep them at home?"[71]

The lyrics challenge the Zionist doctrine that underwrites the very foundation of the Israeli state, pointing out that Palestinians inside are living in a homeland that was occupied by settlers, where they will eventually become the majority despite plans for their expulsion (euphemistically called "transfer"), only in the cemetery.[72] The song, as well as the images from the video, powerfully challenge Orientalist and racialized notions of terrorism ascribed to Palestinians, Arabs, and Muslims, by pointing to daily and dramatic episodes of state terror. This colonial violence is obscured by the reversal of victimhood as well as the notion that Palestinian youth are inherently violent, raised to become militants by uncaring parents, both tropes that are challenged in DAM's song. While these tropes are enduring in Zionist discourse about Palestinian youth, the events of 2000 and the second intifada galvanized a generation that had grown up listening to the sounds of hip hop and compelled them to use a new cultural idiom to convey their predicament to a larger, increasingly global, audience.

Tamer Nafar of DAM says the song, "*Meen Irhabi*," was inspired by the Western media's distorted coverage of the second intifada: "Back in the year 2000, Israeli police and army murdered more than a thousand Palestinians. And the world stood still, didn't do nothing. And a few months later, a Palestinian guy got into Tel Aviv, and he committed a suicide bombing which led to twenty-one victims, young kids who were also killed. Twenty-one versus thousands of Palestinians, and suddenly the world says, 'Let's stop the war, and let's stop the murder. Let's stop the terror!' And we saw that as an unfair thing, to shut down one eye and to open the other one, and to … legitimize the killing of Palestinians."[73] "*Meen Irhabi*" also astutely critiques the notion of legal justice and the official claim that Israel is a democracy with equal rights for all its citizens, by pointing out that there is no neutral arbiter of justice in a state where discrimination is built into citizenship and the law itself.[74]

The events of October 2000 deeply affected what Dan Rabinowitz and Khawla Abu-Baker call "the Stand-Tall Generation," whose politics are powerfully expressed in the rap that emerged in '48 Palestine at the same moment.[75] In DAM's song "*Mali Hurriye*" ("I Don't Have Freedom," *Dedication*), they rap:

> We want an angry generation
> To plough the sky, to blow up history
> To blow up our thoughts
> We want a new generation
> That does not forgive mistakes
> That does not bend
> We want a generation of giants . . .[76]

This generation of Palestinians, who are the grandchildren of the generation that experienced the Nakba and the children of those who mobilized the Palestinian minority in Israel in the 1970s and 1980s, is assertively challenging the fundamental definition of Israel as "the state of the Jewish people." Many are demanding full citizenship and equality, building on the new phase of the Palestinian national movement within Israel that has been developing since the 1990s.[77] Palestinians in Israel are discriminated against, directly and indirectly, in the provision of social services by the state and there have been significant legal and political battles to fight for equality, including by college students. At the same time, many in this generation reject the illusion of civil rights and citizenship as promised by the Israeli state. For example, Saz, an MC from Ramleh, raps: "The authorities give you freedom of expression? No!/Are you an Israeli citizen? Of course not!/It's about time we faced the facts/We deserve equal rights, lift your head up, *stand tall*" (emphasis mine).[78] In August 2005, I participated in a rally in Nazareth with many '48 Palestinian youth protesting the killing of four Palestinians by an Israeli soldier on a bus in Shefa'amr, in northern Israel. Young Palestinians waved flags in the center of the city and the crowd energetically chanted slogans against "Israeli fascism" from "Jenin to Shefa'amr," also making references to the Palestinians killed in Black October. The bold display of Palestinian flags (previously illegal in Israel) and slogans at the protest underscored what Inas at the time hoped would be a moment in the building of a unified youth movement.

It is important to note that the notion of a "generation of giants," standing tall, does not imply that previous generations of '48 Palestinians laid low. Rather, DAM and Saz are calling for their generation to take up an ongoing struggle while standing on the shoulders of giants who went before, and to engage with the current phase of a growing nationalist movement, using a cultural idiom that resonates with their peers and with youth globally. In fact, some hip hop artists are linked to '48 Palestinian nationalist groups, such as Tajammu, according to Lara, a student at Birzeit University who is from Nazareth and who had seen a performance by two male and two female rappers involved with youth programs organized by Tajammu.[79] Political parties who attempt to engage with youth may end up supporting youth cultural expressions such as hip hop, especially when there is a shared political critique across generations, so this is not a stark intergenerational divide or opposition between formal/electoral and informal politics. However, it is also apparent that there are grassroots expressions of politics that are not contained by the boundaries of formal political structures. DAM has for several years been doing educational workshops on history, politics, and identity for Palestinian youth in Israel, as have other '48 Palestinian hip hop artists. During the focus group discussion in Nazareth at the Baladna youth conference in 2005, one young '48 Palestinian woman said, "I think we talk a lot about making youth 'aware.' A lot of youth organizations focus on 'awareness' and 'activation,' but what we need is a youth movement"—an aspiration that was borne out by the youth organizing that was to expand in subsequent years.

In the film, *Slingshot Hip Hop*, rapper Mahmoud Shalabi of MWR from Acca says of the predicament of '48 Palestinian youth, "There are no youth centers or places for youth here to hang out in . . . They have no goals because they feel lost." Another young woman I spoke to in the focus group in Nazareth said, "I did not know anything about my Palestinian identity growing up till I finished high school, I just knew I was 'Israeli.'" This observation was echoed by another young woman, who reflected, "For us, there is a conflict of identity because we are Palestinian but when we go through education in Israel, and we open the textbooks, what we see is nothing about our identity, our culture." Rap has become a pedagogical medium to address the absence of Palestinian history and culture in the Israeli school curriculum, not to mention mainstream Israeli media and discourse. This critique of the Zionist emphasis in education, which has been deepened by the Israeli Ministry of Education during the Netanyahu regime,[80] is expressed in DAM's song, "*Gareeb Fi Bladi*" ("Stranger in My Country"), from *Dedication*:

> 'Cause it's denying my existence
> Still blind to my colors, my history and my people
> Brain-washing my children

> So that they grow up in a reality
> That doesn't represent them
> The blue ID card worth nothing to us
> Let us believe we are a part of a nation
> That does nothing but makes us feel like strangers
> Me?? A stranger in my own country!!!

Safa Hathoot from Acca, who formed Arapeyat with Nahwa Abed Alal in 2001 and went on to become a solo rapper, reflected on the ways that rap has provided a context for the formation of Palestinian identity for youth in her generation:

> For young people, it is hard to know your identity. . .
> In schools, they do not teach us about [Mahmoud]
> Darwish or about Palestine. They do not teach us
> about our history, we do not know it, so we teach
> youth through our songs. When I was in school, I did
> not know about Darwish or about Palestinian history.
> Through hip hop, I came to know and became
> *wataniya* (politically conscious/patriotic). Identity is
> our number one issue, and hip hop is our tool of
> education.

So the politics of this generation has been deeply infused by youth culture and new forms of cultural expression have in turn inflected the emergence of new, and revived, forms of political discourse.

In fact, it is apparent that the political critique waged through '48 Palestinian hip hop offers a direct critique of the paradoxical citizen-subject created by the Israeli state, what Magid Shihade and I have described elsewhere as a "present/absent" subject produced by settler colonialism.[81] Palestinians in Israel, some of whom are classified by the state with the oxymoronic label "present absentees," occupy the paradoxical position of being designated by the state as citizens without a "nationality," which is reserved only for those who are Jewish. '48 Palestinians are not just second- or third-class citizens who are discriminated against in multiple realms and whose identities and histories are subjected to erasure, but in effect, citizens without full citizenship living in a liminal state of an ever present absence. In the documentary film, *Saz*, about Samih Zakout's life and music, the young MC articulates a deeply skeptical view of the exclusionary inclusion of Palestinians in the Israeli state as it is constructed via the designation "Israeli Arab:" "I do not consider myself Israeli, I do not have a relationship with

Israel. What is Israeli citizenship to me? My blue ID?"[82] In the film, Saz reflects, "As time goes by, I realize I have nothing to do with this country. I have nothing here, but the land is mine. The police, the school, nothing is mine, nothing belongs to me."

Everyday experiences of racism, particularly by Palestinian youth in urban areas in Israel, lead them to directly confront the racist nature of the state and its institutions, as well as the racial logic of securitization that constructs Palestinians as immanent threats. Shalabi raps: "Every time I speak Arabic, I get stopped by a cop. He stops me and demands to see my ID . . . 'You searched my bag upstairs, and you searched it downstairs!' It's about racism and hatred."[83] For Saz and others of his generation, "the state of Israel has failed and it is now their turn to put it on probation" till it offers them "genuine equality, including the recognition of collective rights and the rectification of past wrongs. Until then, they see the state as a mere provider of services, not a locus of true affiliation. . . Their point of departure—a clear sense of not belonging—is their first step toward emancipation."[84] This sense of radical alienation from Israeli citizenship and also identity is apparent among some in this generation of '48 Palestinian youth, who reject the deliberate absenting of their Palestinian identity in the state's label, "Israeli Arabs," and of their history in the Zionist school curriculum.

The last decade, in fact, has been described as a period of "unprecedented" activism among Palestinian youth in Israel that some note has been marked by a change in discourse and political consciousness that has "surpassed" organizing by political parties and led to the emergence of a "cross-partisan, local, and regional youth politics."[85] For example, a scene from *Slingshot Hip Hop* shows DAM speaking at a rally for youth and calling out to the crowd, "Do we want home demolitions? Do we want police here? Do we want to mobilize?" These political issues and the call for collective mobilization are highlighted in DAM's video for their famous song in Arabic and Hebrew, "Born Here" (directed by the late Juliano Mer-Khamis), featuring the female rapper Abeer.[86] After Israeli police and soldiers search young Palestinian males in the "ghetto" of Lid (Lod) and bulldozers destroy homes in a poor Palestinian neighborhood, where children sit next to the railway tracks, the rappers and youth take to the streets to protest "ethnic cleansing" and the "separation wall," exhorting the crowd with the chant, "No fear!"

Geographies of Hip Hop

It is significant that DAM's pioneering music played a significant role in the development of Palestinian hip hop in the West Bank in the early 2000s, sparking interest in rap for many youth as they were grappling with the second intifada and the contradictions generated by Oslo. MC Don Bassa, from Jerusalem, says that he was inspired by MWR and was a "big fan" of DAM, who performed in Jerusalem in 2005. He went on to perform with DAM at a concert in Ramallah. Bassa, who started rapping when he was fifteen, said that he was "looking for music to convey" the problems facing Palestinian youth in his "hood" of East Jerusalem, such as crime, drugs, and gang violence, which were exacerbated after the expansion of the Wall and increasing poverty and unemployment in some neighborhoods, such as Eizariya. Mohammed of Palestinian Street, from Dheisheh refugee camp near Bethlehem, also says he and others were inspired by DAM and other '48 Palestinian MCs: "We started to connect with Saz and Wlad el 7ara, and it changed us, our way of thinking." He added, "Rap was a tool to get out of this bubble we're in now." The bubble is thus not just a phenomenon of de-politicization confined to Ramallah alone, but encapsulates the larger situation of post-Oslo politics and for this generation.

So while the political circumstances of Palestinian youth in Israel and the West Bank, as well as in Jerusalem, are clearly different, for both '48 Palestinian youth and youth in the West Bank and Jerusalem the emergence of hip hop converged with a challenge to the existing or sanctioned forms of political discourse, a frustration with the manifestations of colonialism in the 21st century, and a critique of what was considered acceptable "politics." On all sides of Israeli borders, youth were rethinking the political by building on the work and ideas of previous generations. It is important to note that this is not a sharp rupture in political discourse but that youth culture, such as hip hop and other cultural forms, has provided a generational idiom for expressing politics. It has also connected different groups of youth who were physically divided and spatially disconnected, given that youth find it difficult to travel to other parts of Palestine, especially those from the West Bank and Gaza who are not allowed in Jerusalem or inside Israel without Israeli permits, which are very difficult to obtain. Kanaan, of the rap crew PR from Khan Younis in Gaza, says, "Being denied the chance to see our own country is the hardest part of not having freedom."[87] For some Palestinian rappers or break dancers, the Internet is the primary medium where they can connect and see or hear one another virtually. For example, Camp Breakerz, the b-boy crew from Gaza that conducts breakdance workshops for youth across Gaza, became famous through YouTube videos.[88] The film *Slingshot Hip Hop* illustrates how rappers from Gaza and '48 Palestine forged friendships using the Internet and mobile phones and shared videos of their performances and music.

Rappers, breakdancers, DJs, and graffiti artists are part of a larger artistic community that increasingly connects Palestinian youth from various locations. Hip hop artists and fans from across Palestine and the diaspora congregate at music concerts and hip hop "battles" in Ramallah, at cultural festivals in Jerusalem or Taybeh, and at hip hop and music workshops across the West Bank. A crew of young breakdancers from Balata, which formed roughly four years ago, for example, has participated in breakdance competitions in Ramallah, and '48 Palestinian youth, in particular, increasingly travel to attend hip hop shows in Jerusalem and the West Bank, as I found at concerts I attended. It is apparent that this is a subculture that crosses the colonial borders and the Wall that have fragmented Palestine. This unified vision was, in part, succinctly illustrated on the T-shirt of a young Palestinian activist from '48 Palestine, who was also involved with the youth movement and protests in Ramallah, and whom I saw at a political concert by youth groups in Ramallah in October 2012. The T-shirt (which was designed in Haifa) bore the slogan: "48+67=1," with the root sign above "48+67." That is, Palestinians within the '48 and '67 borders share a common root, in the vision of these young activists and artists, and are part of an indivisible Palestinian entity that includes also East Jerusalem and the diaspora. The insistence that any vision of the Palestinian nation and the national movement has to include those in the West Bank, Gaza, East Jerusalem, '48 Palestine, and the diaspora, in defiance of the Oslo framework, was one of the important features of this hip hop movement and the larger youth politics in which it is embedded.

This credo of hip hop artists and of the youth movement reflects an attempt to undo the lack of knowledge or understanding of the lives of other young Palestinians in the fragmented nation. This disconnection is true for all groups of youth, on both sides of the Green Line, who have few opportunities to meet one another in person. Safa recalls that before she became engaged with hip hop, she did not know much about the lives of youth in Jerusalem, the West Bank, or Gaza, but became connected to other rappers, such as PR in Gaza, via the Internet. As I will demonstrate in the following chapter, one of the political interventions waged through Palestinian hip hop is to connect different groups of youth who are dissected by the colonial fragmentation of Palestinian geography and to directly challenge the feelings of distrust or suspicion that further divide

Palestinians. Rajeh commented, "'48 Palestinians are pure Palestinians, they support us. We share the same language, the same feelings, the same identities." While this observation invokes a notion of cultural purity, which I discuss in greater depth in chapter two, it challenges the perception that '48 Palestinians are somehow culturally inauthentic for living in Israel and also suggests that there is a shared subjective and also political experience across colonial borders. Palestinian hip hop has multiple audiences—local, national, and global—and, like other genres of popular culture, travels across social and national boundaries, even as hip hop has traveled to Palestine and becomes transformed. This is, precisely, the point and the allure of underground rap for Palestinian youth, that it can travel across borders when bodies cannot. Sound, and also images, can move across checkpoints, walls, and colonial boundaries with the help of technology and so hip hop has become a de-territorialized space where spatial fragmentation is being challenged in this generation.

The experience of disconnection has also become increasingly acute for youth from East Jerusalem who are cut off from other areas in the West Bank as Jerusalem has become encircled by the apartheid wall and proliferating Jewish settlements, and as entry into Jerusalem for other Palestinians is regulated and restricted by Israel. This peripheralization has strangled the Palestinian economy and choked cultural life in East Jerusalem due to "Israeli policies of encirclement and siege since the early 1990s."[89] For example, the MC Maqdsi says that the rap produced by Egtya7 Underground from Jerusalem offers a medium to speak about "holding on to Jerusalem" and resisting "Israeli policies of Judaization of the city" in the context of home demolitions, assaults by soldiers and settlers, and security searches. Bassa and MC Dave both spoke about how Palestinian youth cannot move around Jerusalem without being stopped by Israeli police and soldiers; Bassa noted, somewhat wryly, "Every five minutes, every five meters, you have to show your ID to them. They think all Arabs walk around with knives or guns, so they throw you against the wall and start searching you." Shalhoub-Kevorkian describes the ways in which the "mundane power of the architecture of surveillance and colonial rule" creates a sense for youth in Jerusalem of living in a "prison" and in "multiple unending traps" of surveillance and control that affect their "bodies, daily movements, and actions," due to "Israel's policies of ethnic cleansing."[90] As Sherwell eloquently observed, with the growing encagement of Palestinian youth in spaces such as Shu'afat camp in East Jerusalem: "There isn't a horizon: it's the shrinking of Palestine."

It is in this context that hip hop, and also other forms of art and popular culture, offers a way to enlarge the cultural horizon for young people in the shrinking cultural and political geography of Palestine. Bassa, who in 2007 founded the website www.palrap.net, the first Palestinian hip hop website (in Arabic, which is no longer active), said that the Internet site not only helped share music and news in the burgeoning "rap scene" in Palestine but also created a network with rappers from Egypt, and other Arab countries who helped "bring the rap culture from their countries" into Palestine. In addition to the linkages forged in cyberspace, there are also projects involving collaboration between Palestinian and other Arab rappers. For instance, in October 2012, I attended a rap concert organized by the curators of The River Has Two Banks, an artistic project focused on connecting Palestinians on both sides of the Jordan River, and Palestine with Jordan. The show, which was held in a cobble-stoned plaza in the old town of Birzeit, featured El Far3i, a Palestinian rapper and percussionist from Amman (whose mother is from Jenin), who says his name means "the branched . . . the non-main or the 'sub'-anything" and "comes from the idea that the branch expands outwards to see, learn, extend, grow and discover *only* if they are still attached to the roots. It's that conditional state where ... it is about being different and open to things, without loosing your self."[91] El Far3i began the show by playing guitar while rapping and then performed songs about the boycott of Israel. He criticized the Jordanian regime as well as the PA and did not spare then Prime Minister Salman Fayyad. The young people in the crowd clapped and waved kaffiyehs, and the older Palestinians watched intently. The show concluded with an improvised session with Boikutt and a couple of other local, young male rappers, on the small stage erected between the old stone houses.

Rap is a medium that links Palestinian youth with one another and with other Arab youth, and it also connects them to a larger, global geography of youth culture and politics. It is apparent that the experiences of youth growing up in Jerusalem, in camps and urban ghettoes, underlies their identification with rap produced by urban youth of color in the United States. Ruanne, who grew up in Shu'afat, reflects that youth from Jerusalem could relate to the experience of "ghettoization" that was expressed in African-American rap and that this resonance was part of the identification with hip hop for youth. She says that rap was "huge" in Jerusalem while she was growing up, with many young people listening to black MCs such as Tupac Shakur and identifying with "black struggles." For Maqdsi, who began rapping at the age of seventeen with two other young men, DAM was an inspiration but so were African-American rappers, particularly "old school" artists who spoke on issues of "poverty, oppression, and injustice."

The identification with African-American youth resisting racism, police brutality, poverty, and invisibilization is what kindled the early flame of '48 Palestinian rap. Tamer says he was inspired by African-American rappers such as Tupac Shakur, who spoke about the poverty and racism affecting inner-city youth that he, too, experienced growing up in Lid: "My reality is hip hop. I listened to the lyrics and felt they were describing me, my situation. You can exchange the word 'nigger' with 'Palestinian.' Lid is the ghetto, the biggest crime and drug center in the Middle East."[92] 'Adi Krayem, who is from a village near Nazareth, formed the rap group Wlad el 7ara (Children of the Neighborhood) with two other young men from Nazareth after attending a DAM concert in 2001. He had also watched rap videos featuring images of African-American youth being attacked by the police which resonated with his own experience of growing up Palestinian in Israel.[93] Similarly, Safa said she was drawn to hip hop at the age of ten because she identified with the "racism and deprivation" critiqued by black rappers. She says, "We are from Acca, it hurts us to see young people doing drugs, not studying." Palestinian youth from Israel resonate with the experiences of ghettoization, poverty, violence, and problems with crime among urban African-American youth, as do rappers from Jerusalem, refugee camps, or on the other side of the Wall. Black Revolution commented, "Rap was established by black people who have been suffering from racism. It is about fighting problems, it is a strong medium to express our message."

For 'Adi, rap's linkage to African poetic and musical traditions is also a connection to Africa via Arab communities in Africa, for he pointed out that Arabs can also be African. He situated Palestinians and Arabs in this larger geography and connected Palestinian hip hop to its diasporic cultural forms, as part of the Black Mediterranean and Afro-Arab histories. Maqdsi had an even broader internationalist vision as he identified with other groups around the world struggling against US imperialism and with "rappers from Latin America, Puerto Rico" who are in "a similar colonial situation." After DAM released their second album, *Dabke on the Moon* (*Nudbok al Amar*) in 2013, Tamer reflected that DAM had toured around the world and were "exposed to a lot of people with different stories," concluding that "the world is not Palestine. Palestine became part of the world. And the struggle became part of the international struggle." For him, the album's message to its listeners is "uniting minorities around the world. And showing them that minorities are 90 percent of this earth."[94] These young people use the language of racism and colonialism to describe the historical experience of Palestinians, a vocabulary that connects them with other groups of youth and geographies of imperialism and resistance, even as they inflect it with local concerns and musical idioms. Palestinian hip hop emerging in different sites is deeply infused by an anti-colonial and anti-racist politics and has become a medium, as well as a subculture, through which and in which young people grapple with questions of cultural and national identity, about what it means to be Palestinian and their relationship to national as well as global struggles.

---

[1] For example, Brian Barber found in a study of Palestinians who participated as adolescents in the first intifada that while most felt that they had matured and discovered a sense of identity during this struggle, many questioned the value of their political involvement later and variously reported feelings of depression or uncertainty about the future; Brian Barber, "Focus on the New Generation: What Has Become of the 'Children of the Stone'?" *Palestine-Israel Journal of Politics, Economics, and Culture* 4 (January 2000): 7.

[2] Palestinian Central Bureau of Statistics (PCBS), "On the Eve of International Youth Day 12/8/2011: Press Release" (Ramallah, Palestine: Palestinian Central Bureau of Statistics, 2011); Sharek Youth Forum, "The Status of Youth in Palestine—2013: The Future is Knocking" (al-Tireh, Palestine: Sharek Youth Forum, 2013), 33.

[3] Baladna: Association for Arab Youth, "Palestinian Youth Affairs in Israel" (Field Research Conducted by Mtanes Shihadeh and Himmat Zu'bi) (Haifa: Baladna, 2012), 6.

[4] PCBS; Sharek Youth Forum, "The Status of Youth," 68.

[5] Baladna, "Palestinian Youth Affairs in Israel," 9.

[6] Ibid., 22.

[7] Sharek Youth Forum, "The Status of Youth," 20.

[8] Report by Fafo, cited in NOREF (Norwegian Peacebuilding Resource Centre), "Palestinian Youth and the Arab Spring" (Publication by Mona Christopherson, Jacob Hoigilt, and Age A. Tiltnes), February 2012, 5. http://www.peacebuilding.no/Regions/Middle-East-and-North Africa/Israel-Palestine/Publications/Palestinian-youth-and-the-Arab-Spring/%28language%29/eng-US (accessed 5 September 2012).

[9] Sharek Youth Forum, "The Status of Youth," 21.

[10] Cited in Natalie K. Jensen, "Mobility Within Constraints: Gender, Migration, and New Spaces for Palestinian Women," Unpublished Doctoral Dissertation, Geography, University of South Carolina, 2011, 157.

[11] Baladna, "Palestinian Youth Affairs in Israel," 7.

[12] Sharek Youth Forum, "The Status of Youth," 25.

[13] Kareem Rabie, "Ramallah's Bubbles," *Jadaliyya*, 18 January 2013. http://www.jadaliyya.com/pages/index/9617/ramallah%E2%80%99s-bubbles

[14] Basel Abbas and Ruanne Abourahme, "The Zone," *Artterritories*, http://www.artterritories.net/designingcivicencounter/?page_id=633.

[15] Lisa Taraki and Rita Giacaman, "Modernity Aborted and Reborn: Ways of Being Urban in Palestine," in *Living Palestine: Family Survival, Resistance, and Mobility under Occupation*, ed. Lisa Taraki (Syracuse, NY: Syracuse University Press, 2006), 34-35, 42.

[16] From catalog for exhibit, "Ramallah—the Fairest of Them All?" Ethnographic and Arab Museum, Birzeit University, Birzeit, Palestine, 2010.

[17] "Interview with Yazid Anani, by Shuruq Harb," *Artterritories*, 7 September 2010. http://www.artterritories.net/?page_id=889.

[18] Inas Yassin, "Projection: Three Cinemas in Ramallah and al-Bireh," *Jerusalem Quarterly* 42 (Summer 2010): 49-60.

[19] Taraki and Giacaman, "Modernity Aborted and Reborn," 27.

[20] Lisa Taraki, "Urban Modernity on the Periphery: A New Middle Class Reinvents the Palestinian City," Social Text 95 vol. 26 no. 2 (Summer 2008): 64.

[21] Jensen, "Mobility Within Constraints"; Taraki, "Urban Modernity on the Periphery," 66; Taraki and Giacaman, "Modernity Aborted and Reborn," 25-26.

[22] Taraki and Giacaman, "Modernity Aborted and Reborn," 27.

[23] Tony Mitchell, 2001. "Another Root: Hip-Hop outside the USA," in *Global Noise: Rap and Hip-Hop outside the USA*, ed. Tony Mitchell (Middletown, CT: Wesleyan University Press), 1-38; Halifu Osumare, "Beat Streets in the Global Hood: Connective Marginalities of the Hip Hop Globe," *Journal of American and Comparative Cultures* 24 nos. 1-2 (2001): 171-181.

[24] Taraki and Giacaman, "Modernity Aborted and Reborn," 50.

[25] The film is produced by Existence is Resistance and directed by Nana Dankwa (2011). See trailer at: http://www.youtube.com/watch?feature=player_detailpage&v=PGvP0OREI2E.

[26] Rajaa Barghouthi, *Local to Global: Palestinian Youth Issues and Concerns* (Ramallah: Bisan Center for Research and Development, 2007), 6.

[27] Samir Seif, "Youth in the Palestinian National Movement: Painful Truths," *Palestine-Israel Journal of Politics, Economics, and Culture* 4 (January 2000): 20.

[28] Sherene Seikaly and Noura Erekat, "Tahrir's Other Sky," in *The Dawn of the Arab Uprisings: End of An Old Order?* ed. Bassam Haddad, Rosie Bsheer, and Ziad Abu-Rish (London: Pluto 2012), 275.

[29] Ann L. Stoler, "Intimations of Empire: Predicaments of the Tactile and Unseen," in *Haunted by Empire: Geographies of Intimacy in North American History*, ed. Ann L. Stoler (Durham and London: Duke University Press, 2006), 8-9.

[30] Shalhoub-Kevorkian, "Trapped."

[31] Ibid., 7.

[32] Jessica Purkiss, "Love in the Time of Apartheid," *Palestine Monitor*, 11 March 2013. http://palestinemonitor.org/details.php?id=0n14spa3075yzmzibxc08.

[33] George Giacaman, "In the Throes of Oslo: Palestinian Society, Civil Society and the Future," in *After Oslo: New Realities, Old Problems*, ed. George Giacaman and Dag J. Lonning (London: Pluto Press, 1998), 8.

[34] Giacaman, "In the Throes of Oslo," 4.

[35] NOREF, "Palestinian Youth and the Arab Spring," 9.

[36] Taraki, "Urban Modernity on the Periphery," 65, 69.

[37] Ramzy Baroud, "The Unity Charade and Prisoners' Intifada," *Ma'an News*, 17 January 2013. http://maannews.net/eng/ViewDetails.aspx?ID=557063.

[38] Abbas and Abourahme, "The Zone."

[39] Ibid.

[40] Giacaman, "In the Throes of Oslo," 13.

[41] Ibid.

[42] Ann L. Stoler and Carole McGranahan, "Introduction: Refiguring Imperial Terrains," in *Imperial Formations*, ed. Ann L. Stoler, Carole McGranahan, and Peter Perdue (Santa Fe, NM: School for Advanced Research, 2007), 3-44.

[43] NOREF, "Palestinian Youth and the Arab Spring," 1.

[44] From album compiled by *Shahadat: Exploring Popular Literature Series – Hip Hop* (New York: ArteEast, January 2012). http://issuu.com/arteeast/docs/shahadatwinter2012.

[45] Sharek Youth Forum, "The Status of Youth," 57.

[46] Sharek Youth Forum, *Palestinian Youth and Political Parties: From a Pioneering Engagement with Political Parties to Fear and Disappointment* (Al-Tireh: Sharek, 2010), 5.

[47] Sharek Youth Forum, *Situation Report: Winds of Change . . . Will They Break Down the Walls of Oppression?* (Al-Tireh: Sharek, 2011), 10.

[48] Sharek Youth Forum, "The Status of Youth," 52.

[49] Ibid., 52, 55.

[50] Ihab Al-Jariri, "The Palestinian Student Movement After Oslo," *Palestine-Israel Journal of Politics, Economics, and Culture* 4 (31 January 2000): 32.

[51] Ibid., 9.

[52] Nadera Shalhoub-Kevorkian, "E-Resistance and Technological In/Security in Everyday Life: The Palestinian Case." *British Journal of Criminology* 52 (2012): 62.

[53] Baladna, "Palestinian Youth Affairs in Israel," 53.

[54] Cited in Baladna, "Palestinian Youth Affairs in Israel," 53.

[55] Baladna, "Palestinian Youth Affairs in Israel," 51-52.

[56] Rabi' Abed, "Youth and Students: The Youth Movement 'Inside' and the Horizon Envisioned." 15 November 2011. www.arabs48.com (accessed 25 April 2012).

[57] AWRAD (Arab World for Research and Development), "Results of a Specialized Opinion Poll Among Palestinian Youth," (Ramallah: AWRAD, February 2012), 2. Available at: www.awrad.org.

[58] NOREF, "Palestinian Youth and the Arab Spring," 6.

59 Ibid., 8.

60 Palestinian Center for Research and Cultural Dialogue (PCRD) (in cooperation with the Hans Seidel Foundation), "Poll On Youth (18-30 Years) in the West Bank" (Bethlehem: PRCD, 2010). http://www.pcrd-pal.org/opinion_polls.php (accessed 5 September 2012).

61 Taraki, "Urban Modernity on the Periphery," 62.

62 *Slingshot Hip Hop* (dir. Jackie Salloum, 2008).

63 Baladna, "Palestinian Youth Affairs in Israel," 17, 22, 56.

64 Sawsan Khalife, "Palestinian Students 'Surrounded by Guns' at Israeli Universities," *Electronic Intifada*, 22 February 2013. http://electronicintifada.net/content/palestinian-students-surrounded-guns-israeli-universities/12215.

65 Baladna, "Palestinian Youth Affairs in Israel," 17.

66 Ibid., 23-31.

67 Ibid., 7, 11.

68 See: http://www.youtube.com/watch?v=EhXa_luFgZQ.

69 Interview with authors, December 2010.

70 Dan Charnas, "Review of DAM's 'Dedication.'" *Washington Post* (9 January 2008) C04. Posted at http://www.kabobfest.com/search/label/music (accessed 30 January 2008).

71 See: http://www.youtube.com/watch?v=ZqbDiN2uYcQ.

72 Nur Masalha, Expulsion of the Palestinians: The Concept of "Transfer" in Zionist Political Thought 1882-1948 (Beirut, Lebanon: Institute for Palestine Studies, 1992.); Ibid., A Land Without A People (London: Faber and Faber, 1997); Joseph Massad, The Persistence of the Palestinian Question: Essay on Zionism and the Palestinians (London and New York: Routledge, 2006); Ilan Pappe, The Ethnic Cleansing of Palestine (London and New York: Oneworld, 2006).

73 Interview with Tamar Nafar of DAM. Television broadcast of "Democracy Now." 15 May 2008. http://www.democracynow.org/2008/5/15/slingshot_hip_hop_palestinian_rap_group (accessed 17 May 2010).

74 Uri Davis, *Israel: An Apartheid State*, (London, UK: Zed Books Ltd, 1987); Sabri Jiryis, *The Arabs in Israel*. (Beirut, Lebanon: The Institute for Palestine Studies, 1969); Nimer Sultany, *Citizens Without Citizenship: Israel and the Palestinian Minority 2000-2002* (Haifa, Israel: Mada-Arab Center For Applied Social Research, 2003).

75 The label is drawn from Samih al-Qasem's poem, "Standing Tall (Muntasib al Qama)": "Standing tall I march/My head held high/An olive branch held in my palm/A coffin on my shoulder/On I walk." Dan Rabinowitz and Khawla Abu-Baker, *Coffins on Our Shoulders: The Experience of the Palestinian Citizens of Israel* (Berkeley: University of California Press, 2005), 2.

76 All translations of the lyrics of DAM's songs from Dedication are from the CD liner notes.

77 Amal Eqeiq, "Louder than the Blue ID: Palestinian Hip-Hop in Israel," in *Displaced at Home: Ethnicity and Gender among Palestinians in Israel*, ed. Rhoda A. Kanaaneh and Isis Nusair (Albany, NY: State University of New York Press, 2010), 53-71; Rabinowitz and Abu-Baker, *Coffins on Our Shoulders*, 2-3.

78 From the film *Saz*, dir. Gil Karni, 2006.

79 *Al-Tajammu al-Watani al-Dimuqrati*, or the National Democratic Assembly (NDA), is a Palestinian political party that was formed in 1996, after the Oslo Accords, and has called for equality and collective rights for the Palestinian citizens of Israel.

80 "Palestinian Hip Hop vs. Israeli Educational System." *Alternative News*, 1 April 2012. http://www.alternativenews.org/english/index.php/component/content/article/28-news/4253-palestinian-hip-hop-vs-israeli-education-system.

81 Sunaina Maira and Magid Shihade, "Hip Hop from '48 Palestine: Youth, Music, and the Present/Absent," *Social Text* 112, 30 no. 3 (2012): 1-25.

82 See Magid Shihade, *Not Just a Soccer Game: Colonialism and Conflict Among Palestinians in Israel* (Syracuse, NY: Syracuse University Press, 2011).

83 In *Slingshot Hip Hop*.

84 Rabinowitz and Abu-Baker, *Coffins on Our Shoulders*, 137.

85 Abed, "Youth and Students."

86 "Born Here," 2006. http://www.youtube.com/watch?v=zIo6lyP9tTE

87 In *Slingshot Hip Hop*.

88 "Made in Gaza: Camp Breakerz Crew, 2013," http://www.youtube.com/watch?v=OFNwr9r3GZM. Also, on the youth workshops: http://www.youtube.com/watch?v=s8j1zYwANYw

89 Taraki and Giacaman, "Modernity Aborted and Reborn," 3, note 1.

90 Shalhoub-Kevorkian, "Trapped," 8, 12.

91 Personal communication, May 2013.

92 Cited in Taleed El-Sabawi, "Palestinian Conflict Bounces to a New Beat," *AngeLingo* vol. 2(2) (2005): http://angelingo.usc.edu/issue03/politics/a_palhiphop.php (accessed 4 February 2007).

93 Interview with author, April 2011.

94 "DAM"s new album, 'Dabke on the Moon': an interview with Tamer Nafar," *Electronic Intifada*, 9 January 2013. http://electronicintifada.net/blogs/nora/dams-new-album-dabke-moon-interview-tamer-nafar.

Chapter 2

Palestinian Hip Hop: A Different Kind of Map

On 2 October 2012, I attended a concert featuring several hip hop performances at the Oktoberfest festival in Taybeh, a small village located atop of the hills of the West Bank. This annual event is sponsored by the only Palestinian beer brewery, Taybeh, named after the ancient village in which it is located and is a two-day cultural and music festival, promoting Palestinian products, that draws large audiences. There are a range of performances at the festival each year and it has become something of a major venue where Palestinian rappers from across Palestine perform in public. The 2012 program included folkloric dance troupes as well as several hip hop groups, such as DAM, Egtya7 Underground, and OC Soldiers (from Jerusalem), in addition to bands such as the popular reggae-rock group Toot Ard (from the Golan Heights). The performances were staged in the grounds of the municipal office building in the center of the village, where a diverse crowd had gathered by evening, including Palestinians of all ages and some foreigners. Following a performance by a Palestinian rock band from Jerusalem, there was a *dabke* (Palestinian folk dance) performance of the Funnounyat dance troupe from Taybeh, which included a rousing song celebrating the recent Palestinian bid for statehood at the United Nations, accompanied by the waving of Palestinian flags by the young dancers.

As OC Soldiers came onstage, the MC for the rap performances, wearing an oversized black T-shirt and baseball cap, ran around the stage energetically and roused the crowd. Several young people from the audience began moving toward the stage and some burst into a frenzy of breakdancing, somersaulting, and popping. OC Soldiers, consisting of two male rappers, performed some songs about café culture, as the audience members waved their hands in the air. Some young men were hoisted by others on their shoulders, and were bouncing and clapping their hands above the crowd. Meanwhile, in the middle of the audience, a small group of teenage boys broke into agile breakdance moves, one of them sporting spiked hair and the other with a baseball cap. The audience was by now excited and energized. While some might assume that only youth would respond to hip hop and adults, especially outside the Unites States, would be uninterested or possibly turned off by rap, I noticed that some of the older adults in the crowd were also listening intently to the young rappers. A middle-aged woman draped in a kaffiyeh swayed to the music on one side of the crowd.

A rap duo from Jerusalem came on next, but their lyrics were barely audible over the loud beats pumping out from the sound system and their music was rather lackluster. The crowd began to get palpably impatient, clearly wanting more than just entertainment, and began yelling for DAM to come on stage. The two rappers looked quite chastened, realizing the audience was disappointed in their performance. But DAM was nowhere to be seen, and so the festival organizers asked a DJ to spin some music and then a young man to placate the crowd with an Arabic pop song. The audience became more restless and started yelling, "*Yalla* (come on), do something!" An ensemble of traditional musicians was brought onstage and one of them started playing the *darbuke* (goblet drum or tabla), but then all of a sudden, the lights went off. The festival was in the dark. The disappointment and intensified frustration of the audience was palpable. I left after waiting for some time for DAM to appear and I am not sure if they ever did. However, what was striking about this rather anticlimactic performance was that it was very apparent that this was an event that had drawn youth who were familiar with hip hop, quite critical in their tastes and assessments of musical quality, and even involved in breakdancing. The festival was a venue where this subculture, if small, could be constituted and where the performance and consumption of rap and break dance could take place along with "traditional" forms of Palestinian music and dance.

The hip hop performances were not just on the official stage, in other words, but also in the audience. In many ways, the teenagers who created their own stage in the audience to dance, or to respond to the rappers, were demonstrating their own cultural and performative knowledge. It was also apparent that Palestinian hip hop had now become part of the repertoire of Palestinian popular culture, perhaps even national culture, at festivals and showcases such as this one where "traditional" music was interspersed with rap, and *dabke* and breakdancing were performed in the same space. This is not to overestimate the popularity of hip hop, for, as I found in my research, it is a contested cultural form in Palestine and among youth, but to indicate the ways in which the definition of Palestinian popular culture has shifted and collided with new forms of youth culture. Hip hop, I would argue, has come to represent an aspect of national culture, if a contested one, and is part of a broader articulation of a new political language by youth, in the West Bank, Jerusalem, and also in '48 Palestine, as I will discuss in this chapter.

Palestinian Hip Hop

Hip hop was created by African-American, Caribbean, and Latino (Puerto Rican) youth in New York in the late 1970s to address everyday experiences of exclusion, criminalization, and impoverishment. Marginalized and invisibilized youth in the South Bronx responded to urban restructuring, de-industrialization, poverty, and racism by producing a new cultural expression that required few economic resources and that claimed the streets as a public stage.[1] This youth subculture consists of several elements, musical and visual as well as kinesthetic: rapping (MCing), deejaying, producing the beats (music), graffiti art, and breakdancing. Hip hop is thus more than just a musical form, and more than just rap. To many, it expresses a worldview or political stance. Tricia Rose describes hip hop as a hybrid cultural form that mixes Afro-Caribbean and African-American musical, oral, visual, and dance practices with contemporary technologies and urban cultures to create a "counterdominant narrative."[2] The "heavy reliance on lyricism" makes hip hop a genre that can be powerfully used for social and political commentary by layering poetry over beats, with rappers described as poets or MCs.[3]

Since rap has its roots in an oppositional subculture in the United States, it has lent itself to protest music, particularly in its manifestation as "progressive" or "conscious" rap, sub-genres which depart from mainstream or "gangsta" rap.[4] It is an appealing form for subaltern youth globally because its emphasis on lyrics allows it to serve as a mode of narrating personal or collective experiences, particularly those that are suppressed in the mainstream public sphere. Rap has become the basis for a global youth subculture and musical form that crosses national, racial, and religious boundaries. Hip hop has not been simply adopted or reproduced but also recreated and indigenized by young people around the world, who have used it as a medium for commentary on a range of political and social issues.[5] Palestinian rappers have used this idiom to translate their experiences to other marginalized and minority groups and to speak to global publics, largely via the Internet but also to some extent through performances. However, the increasing mainstreaming of hip hop as a global rite of passage into being "young" or "cool" has been accompanied by its hyper-commercialization and depoliticization, with politically progressive rap an increasing marginal genre in the United States.[6] It is in this context that the growth of Palestinian rap is significant, and illuminates a range of possibilities and also contradictions as a genre that remains somewhat marginal, or represents an "alternative" subculture, within various locations in Palestine.

The genre of Palestinian hip hop emerged after the late 1990s, most famously when a group of three young men from Lid in Israel (Tamer and Suhell Nafar and Mahmoud Jreri), calling themselves DAM (or Da Arabian MCs; dam also means "persisting" in Arabic and "blood" in Hebrew and Arabic), began doing underground rap in Arabic and released their first single on the Internet in 2001. Their music quickly went viral and inspired other Palestinian youth in Israel and increasing numbers of youth from the West Bank, Gaza, and Jerusalem as well as in the diaspora to produce rap in Arabic.[7] It is striking that the early pioneers of Palestinian hip hop and the most well known Palestinian and Arab hip hop artists rap about political themes that could be described as variously progressive or left in orientation. In fact, Iron Sheik, a pioneering Palestinian American rapper whose family is from Nazareth, suggests that the "message rap" produced by Arabs/Palestinians and Arab/Palestinian American MCs has reinvigorated the progressive potential of hip hop, commenting: "I feel ambivalent about what hip hop has become in the United States and I'm happy to see messages in rap again."[8] As the genre has gained popularity within Palestine, however, Palestinian rap that is mainstream and less politicized than underground rap has also emerged. I found in my conversations with Palestinian youth that hip hop is inevitably embroiled in debates about the meaning of the "popular" and always intertwined with the politics of national identity in youth culture. It is in this context that I discuss the questions that bind the "youth movement" to the burgeoning "hip hop movement" among young Palestinians.

The Palestinian hip hop movement includes a growing number of young '48 Palestinian artists, such as Saz, Abeer, Arapeyat, MWR, Wlad El 7ara (also known as We7), and Dmar; Palestinian Street, Rami G.B., Boikutt, and Stormtrap in the West Bank; PR (Palestine Rapperz) and MC Gaza in Gaza; and G-Town, OC Soldiers, and Egtya7 Underground from Jerusalem. Many of these rappers belong to what could be called a "second generation" of young rappers who have followed in the wake of early MCs such as DAM, Abeer, and PR.[9] In addition, there is a growing, transnational Arab hip hop movement spanning the Arab world with well-known rappers such as El Général from Tunisia; M.B.S., Lotfi Double Kanon, and S.O.S. in Algeria; Haked and Soultana from Morocco; Fareek al Atrache (Edd Abbas), Aksser, El Rass, Rayess Bek, and Malikah in Lebanon; Ramy Donjewan, Mohammed El Deeb, MC Amin, and Arabian Knightz from Egypt; Ibn Thabit from Libya; El Far3i and Khotta (Plan) B from Jordan. MCs in the larger Arab diaspora include, for example, the Philistines in the United States; Narcicyst in Canada; MC Solaar, IAM, and La Caution in France; Shadia Mansour and Lowkey in Britain, and Isam Bachiri of Outlandish in Denmark, who increasingly collaborate and perform with one another.[10] There are also performance poets, such as Suheir Hammad and Remi Kanazi in the United States, who often travel to Palestine and who are part of this Arab hip hop subculture. Palestinian hip hop is, thus, part of a global Arab hip hop movement that is diverse and has evolved differently in various geographic and cultural sites, and it is also part of a transnational Palestinian youth subculture and political movement.[11]

Palestinian hip hop in the West Bank has emerged and is performed in different spaces, in cities as well as camps, but major rap concerts and hip hop/breakdancing "battles" are staged in Ramallah, considered a liberal social space, as well as at the annual Oktoberfest in the Christian village of Taybeh and sometimes in Jerusalem or Bethlehem. I found that hip hop is generally viewed as a marginal cultural genre in the West Bank, in contrast to *musika sha'bi* or popular music. But it is also apparent that rap has increasingly crossed class boundaries and is popular in refugee camps as much as in cities and towns of the West Bank and Gaza and among Palestinian youth in Israel, even those in villages.[12] So while hip hop may be intertwined with urban modernity, in the popular imagination, it is not necessarily rooted only in urban spaces in Palestine. There is a pervasive experience of racism and unemployment that is shared among Palestinian youth in Israel, in cities as well as villages and smaller towns, where young people are similarly exposed to rap through films, television, and the Internet. It is also important to keep in mind that most Palestinian villages in Israel are in the vicinity of Jewish towns and cities, which are more affluent and receive more state services, and so can be understood as the external ghettos, or slums, of these cities. It is these experiences, as discussed in the previous chapter, that underlie the identification of Palestinian youth from cities, camps, and villages with the cultural and political imaginaries of hip hop.

However, there is clearly a mapping of hip hop onto urban space and onto youthfulness that lingers in images of Palestinian hip hop, despite its appearance in a range of locations, from Jenin and Dheisheh in the West Bank to Nazareth and 'Iksal in Israel. The conflation of rap with the urban, the global, and the "Western" means that it is inextricably intertwined with deeper concerns about shifts in local culture and national identity. These anxieties are justifiable in light of the changes wrought by globalization and the impact of transnational media and new commodities on Palestinian society, in the West Bank, Jerusalem, as well as Israel. Hip hop thus becomes a cultural site in which these anxieties are expressed and notions of Palestinian identity, urbanity, and modernity are negotiated by youth.

If hip hop was famously described as "the Black CNN" by the African American rapper Chuck D of Public Enemy, suggesting its role as a tool for sharing news of the social and political realities of urban, disadvantaged youth of color in the United States, it is conceivable that hip hop has become the "Palestinian Al Jazeera," as observed by Tamer Nafar of DAM.[13] In other words, Palestinian rap in its political variant is a popular expression of the concerns, experiences, and critiques of this generation of youth. For example, Bad Luck Rappers from Dheisheh Refugee Camp in Bethlehem told me they changed their name to Palestinian Street because they felt they were using rap, ultimately, to represent the street or the views of ordinary people. The "street" or "the underground" indexes a notion of everyday experience, and in some instances its own cultural authenticity, that has always been key to the allure of rap.[14] Palestinian hip hop artists are rarely signed onto record labels (hence they are generally "underground" rappers) but they have used new media such as Myspace, YouTube, and Facebook to disseminate their music and connect with local as well as global publics. In 2003, We7 established the Underground Studio (literally, in a basement) in Nazareth, and launched the Under-Stood-Yo record label, becoming a home for Palestinian rap and rappers from across Palestine.[15]

Palestinian hip hop is one current in the larger globalization of hip hop culture that has, in various national locations, gone beyond a simple adoption of American rap and drawn on "local musical idioms and vernaculars to produce excitingly distinctive syncretic manifestations of African American influences and local indigenous elements."[16] In Palestine, hip hop artists use colloquial Arabic and local dialect, sampling and producing electronic or dance music as well as Palestinian and Arab music and poetry, and using the sounds of traditional Arab instruments such as the *darbuke, nay,* or oud. There are, of course, multiple musical forms in the Arab world that are hybrid in style and instrumentation—such as *rai* in North Africa—and a long history of sonic experimentation, including among artists situated in the global north who have drawn on sounds from elsewhere, including from Arab music.[17] This complicates the model of "center" and "periphery" in the diffusion and recreation of music cultures that suggests that popular culture only flows from the "West" to "other" places.[18] It is worth pointing out here that Arabic rap emerged first in Algeria where hip hop was Arabicized, and there is also a flourishing French-Arabic hip hop movement produced by Maghrebi youth in France where it is part of a musical environment that includes *rai* as a popular protest music that has flowed from North Africa to France and throughout the world.[19]

It is also important to highlight that Palestinian hip hop is situated in a much longer genealogy of protest music and poetry within Palestine, not to mention a long and rich history of oppositional artistic practices more generally. For example, Joseph Massad situates the political rap produced by Palestinian youth in a longer tradition of revolutionary, underground Arabic music and political songs that have supported the Palestinian liberation movement since the 1950s and that mixed nationalist poetry with hybrid Arab/Western musical instrumentation.[20] Poetry and music, and the arts in general, have always been part of national politics in Palestine and the diaspora; they have also been used by Palestinians in Israel to maintain Palestinian and Arab language and identity in the face of Israeli policies of erasing Palestinian identities and histories.[21] Music and poetry have also provided an archive of collective memory that has memorialized events such as the massacres of Deir Yassin, Kafr Qassim, and Land Day; the 1967, 1973, and 1982 wars; and the killing of '48 Palestinian demonstrators in October 2000. In fact, Amal Eqeiq suggests that '48 Palestinian hip hop is continuing in a tradition of *'amudi*, or social realist poetry, that developed after the Nakba, and "earlier forms of Palestinian oral narrative."[22] It is not surprising that this musical form lends itself to adoption by Palestinian youth, who have grown up with forms of improvised and folk poetry such as *zajal, mawwal (mawwaliya)*, and *saj'*, and bring the percussiveness and lyricism of Arab music to their own genre of Arab rap.[23] The figure of the poet/singer who improvises commentary on social and political issues, as well as call-and-response in music, has been central to Palestinian community events and resistance movements well before the emergence of intifada songs. Palestinian rappers are thus responding to the global popularity of hip hop as well as engaging with Arab musical and poetic traditions that they have grown up with and are incorporating into a new cultural form. Graffiti artists and breakdancers, too, draw on local practices of street art, music, and dance, so this is a highly experimental and syncretic subculture.

I should note that I largely focus on a textual analysis of hip hop as a cultural form, given the importance of poetry (rap) to the genre of hip hop and my interest in the discursive construction of national imaginaries and identities, as well as an analysis of hip hop performances and graffiti art. In drawing on interviews with a range of young people, including those who were not artists and in some cases not even fans of hip hop themselves, this research goes beyond a narrow focus on hip hop to situate this youth culture in the politics of everyday life and in the context of mobilization by Palestinian youth. This is one of the contributions of the study to the existing literature on Palestinian hip hop, which has not always offered a nuanced contextualization of the music and a broader analysis of the historical moment in which young people are constructing and contesting national politics.

Defining National Culture and Identity

One of the striking refrains that emerged from the interviews, especially with youth who were not themselves rappers or artists, was the concern with the place of Palestinian or Arab rap within national culture. This was a persistent leitmotif in conversations with young people and the lens of cultural authenticity seemed to be one of the most salient in viewing hip hop. A major topic in my discussions with college-age youth was whether it was even possible to conceive of conjoining the words "Palestinian" and "hip hop" and if so, what that meant for the definition of what could be considered "Palestinian music." That is, could Palestinian rap in Arabic be considered a genre within the repertoire of Palestinian music and Palestinian culture? During the first focus group discussion I held with a group of undergraduate students at Birzeit University, I asked the students what they generally thought about Palestinian rap and they immediately erupted into a vigorous debate about how to define Palestinian hip hop in relation to Western and Arab/indigenous cultures. One young woman (group 1) remarked, "It's a form of American colonization. And it's too loud!" But another young man retorted, "Rap is good music, even if it's Western. But some who have adopted it here have not done it well," suggesting that the criterion for assessing hip hop should not be its cultural provenance, but its quality. Echoing this view, a young woman commented, "If it's good quality music, it does not matter if it's Western or not."

Underlying this contentious exchange among the students were differences in opinion about whether Palestinian hip hop was "good" music, aesthetically but also politically. One young woman (group 1), who knew the rap group G-Town personally from Shu'afat Refugee Camp, added, "Rap allows us to reflect on our situation." Another young woman said she knew DAM and described their music as "social and political," while a young man claimed that DAM's music was of much better "quality" than G-Town's. Some youth insisted that it was not an appropriate element of Palestinian popular culture because it was originally Western or American; others argued that what mattered was that it was a vehicle for political expression and that some rap could be judged as better, aesthetically, than other rap music. Rappers themselves, of course, had a very different take on this and argued for a more expansive definition of hip hop as not just an "American" cultural form. Don Bassa pointed out that his last show included breakdancing and the Brazilian martial arts/dance form capoeira as well as *dabke*, commenting that "hip hop culture is not only American." Bassa's friend, MC Dave from Jerusalem, argued that hip hop, like other artistic production, crosses national and racial borders, saying: "Art is not just for one nationality or race."

A young woman at Birzeit University (group 1), who was from Jerusalem and was studying classical music at the Al-Kamandjati music school in Ramallah, touched directly on the issue of the representativeness of music for national identity and politics, commenting: "I do not think rap should represent the Palestinian issue, there are other forms of art that should do that. Rap may twist people's ideas about our society and make them think we are too modern." She went on to observe, "I think it's annoying and it's not good musically, like classical music. It's not Beethoven, it's not Fairuz." Her comments expressed an interesting contradiction, for she rejected rap as "annoying" and unrepresentative of Palestinian music and simultaneously claimed that a European (classical music) composer, such as Beethoven, was more acceptable. There seemed to be a concern here, too, with discerning "classical"/high culture from popular or mass/low culture, and with the hierarchies that define taste for "proper" kinds of music, including that of the iconic Lebanese singer, Fairuz.

This young woman also critiqued rap for creating an image of Palestinian society as too "modern," invoking a binary of traditional/proper versus "modern" Palestinian culture and identity. There seemed to be an unease among youth about the meaning of modernity—tied to a worry about the representation of Palestinian society. Other students were concerned about hip hop as an improper, inferior form of music or culture associated with inappropriate social behavior. One young man said, "Rap is too distant from our culture," while a young woman observed that hip hop fans were "too Westernized," based on how they dress (group 3). Another young man (group 3) said, "People who listen to hip hop are freaks. They like vulgar language, they want to dance in funny ways." A couple of the young women from the first discussion group remarked that the "image of rap fans is not positive, they are loose," and that "rap concerts are not decent parties. Those who go are not interested in music or issues, it's more about dancing. It's a chaotic scene." So parties featuring hip hop are associated by some youth with indecent behavior and immoral social spaces, in a context in which dance parties are generally viewed with some suspicion, and there are no official nightclubs in Ramallah.

However, the binary, and moral hierarchy, of Western (bad/corrupting) versus indigenous (good/proper) dissolved somewhat in other conversations with youth. One of the ways in which young people seemed to resist this dichotomy was by juxtaposing the perceived impropriety of a Westernized form of popular culture, associated with immoral ("loose") behavior, with the propriety and justness of political struggle. In other words, commitment to nationalist politics often trumped anxiety about cultural hybridity—the binary of Western/indigenous or global/local was not completely undone, but it was viewed as irrelevant by some. Given that the hip hop artists who spearheaded Palestinian rap have consistently injected strong political critiques of Israeli occupation, colonialism, and apartheid into their music, and speak directly to the construction of a Palestinian national identity and to social issues affecting youth, it was seen by some young people as a cultural expression committed to the national struggle and thus a viable, if not compelling, genre of Palestinian popular culture. As one young woman (group 1) said, "I might not like it but if it supports my cause, I'm fine with it. Like in Egypt, they used music and hip hop in the revolution and I'm fine with that." A female student (group 3) who had participated in the youth movement protests in the West Bank in spring 2011 commented, "It may be different but it's associated with something political, with how young people think." Another young woman from the same group observed, "They [hip hop artists and fans] want some alternative," while a young man commented that in contrast to the political consciousness associated with hip hop, "youth at Birzeit do not know about anything," a remark that triggered a vigorous debate, with some attributing the decline of political engagement to the "context of the PA" and to "globalization."

For these youth, the politics of national and anti-colonial struggle—and in some instances, also the aesthetic quality of the music—was the single most important reason for hip hop's allure and also its significance for youth. That is, the commitment to national politics superseded a politics of cultural authenticity that would mark hip hop as a Western imposition. For example, Maqdsi, a rapper with the (former) group Egtaya7 Underground from Shu'afat Refugee Camp in Jerusalem, who had participated in the youth protests in Ramallah in spring 2011, has written songs about issues of political injustice, including "holding on" to life in Jerusalem and women's rights. He recalled that when he was on a local radio show, a young woman from Nablus called in to say, "You are ruining our culture! The Israelis are taking our culture and representing it as their own on the outside, and what are you doing with our culture?" Maqdsi responded incisively to this accusation of national betrayal, saying: "You are not more committed than me based on what you must be wearing. And it's about building consciousness, it's not about identity." He pointed out, "What's not Western today? Look at our clothes!" Implying that the young woman was herself likely wearing trousers or jeans, or some item of Western clothing that was not in any sense "traditional," he also overturned the central assumption that political commitment rested on a narrow definition of national identity or cultural authenticity and not on a deeper political consciousness.

Maqdsi (left) in performance, East Jerusalem, May 2013.

It is true, of course, that hip hop is American in its origins, even if it is by now a global youth subculture and musical form, but this provenance had different meanings for youth and was viewed through different ethical lenses. For a young leftist activist from the West Bank who was involved with the PFLP, hip hop was a "tool of colonialism" but he acknowledged it could "be used for good or for evil. It can be used for rebellion, as was obvious in the Arab revolts. But when disorganized it can be problematic, like all tools. This is the dialectics of culture, as [Frantz] Fanon said." This dialectical approach to culture shaped some of the more critical views expressed by young people about hip hop's role in Palestinian youth culture and politics.

In the context of these debates about what constitutes Palestinian popular culture, I asked the young people in my discussions at Birzeit what they thought of Arabic pop, which is a deeply hybrid musical form and if they would also describe it as "Westernized." The students were ambivalent, with one young man (group 1) saying unequivocally that Arabic pop was "bad music," while a young woman (group 1) said, "Not all pop is crap. It's not more Arabic necessarily, but it's older." Another young woman (group 3) remarked, "The subjects of hip hop are different from [Egyptian pop idol] Amr Diab's music. It's not just love and romance." This echoed the comments of yet another female student (group 3): "Hip hop is more expressive than other music we listen to. It has a better message, it's a political message." Arabic pop, while very popular among youth, was viewed as being simultaneously apolitical and "bad" musically, yet more embedded in regional and local culture and hence more acceptable than rap. There seemed to be no gender differentiation in these young people's views of hip hop, nor did it seem to matter whether the young women were wearing "Western" clothes or "Islamic" attire and hijab; for example, one young *muhajibi* woman said of rap, "The music could be loud but it expresses our anger and frustration, due to our oppression." The expressiveness of rap as a medium conveying young people's critiques of political issues and oppression was a major reason why many young people respected Palestinian hip hop, even for those who were not fans of the music themselves.

What was striking throughout these conversations was the ways in which hip hop was a lightning rod for deeper debates about cultural authenticity—debates that are, of course, not to be taken lightly in the context of Israeli policies of suppressing and censoring Palestinian identity and national culture and an ongoing struggle against occupation, displacement, and colonization. For some Palestinians, folkloric forms of music and performance are a sturdy defense against the threat of cultural annihilation. Rajeh, who said that his group Black Revolution were the first rappers from al-Khalil (Hebron), commented, "People are fighting us because they say it's [hip hop is] a foreign culture and the whole world is against our culture. You should be doing *dabke*, folklore." Yet it is also interesting that the boundaries of "proper" national culture are often ambiguously defined, and that they overlap with the boundaries of appropriate social behavior in constituting moral-political identities for youth.

If defending national culture is a moral issue, then the regulation of social morality infuses the construction of national identity, as is the case across many national contexts and particularly in conditions of colonialism. Yet the problem is that this "national culture" is not a natural, pre-given entity but is always defined, (re)invented, and managed by a web of forces embedded in class, gender, and in some cases, ethnic or racial hierarchies. Cultural authenticity is a deeply ideological notion, and it is understandably guarded with passion and policed with vigor, particularly by subjects under colonial rule. The problem is that the patrolling of cultural borders misses the larger issue of the question of colonial oppression and national liberation itself. My conversations with these young Palestinians revealed that the struggle over "proper" culture was deeply intertwined with the struggle over national identity and, as I will discuss later, with the national political sphere as it is being redefined by youth who are challenging the definition of what is "proper" politics.

The Struggle Over Representation

My discussions of hip hop with different groups of youth in the West Bank and East Jerusalem raised the thorny question of what, and who, should represent Palestinian identity. The politics of national culture was part of a complex struggle about representation, in different spaces within and beyond Palestine, and in music, culture, and politics. Basel thoughtfully observed: "Across the Arab world, there is this problem of East versus West. So oud and *dabke* is national, it belongs to us. Everything else is Western, it does not belong to us. Anything Western is entertainment, it's for kids." Basel astutely pinpointed two important implications of the regulation of the boundaries of "Western" versus "Eastern" music and dance. First, the issue of cultural ownership of national "folklore" can be embedded in Orientalist binaries of "East" and "West" that are themselves imbricated with colonial imaginaries of and investments in "authentic" and static traditions. As Edward Said argued, this is a historical process in which the cultural imperialism of dominant Western forms that circulate globally is twinned with the imperial culture of mapping, saving, and commodifying local "traditions."[24] Second, Basel also suggests that the problem is that if hip hop is seen as primarily and always a "Western" genre, it is also inevitably associated with mass culture and commercialized "entertainment." This means that it is not just foreign but tainted by its association with commodification and the "popular." This is, of course, what Stein and Swedenburg argue is one of the paradigms that has traditionally inflected the literature on Palestinian popular culture.[25]

Basel went further to reflect on the debate about the place of hip hop in Palestinian national culture and critique hierarchies of "high" and "low" culture that underlie the definition of cultural "tradition":

> It's about high art, and the traditional and the sacred,
> and the symbol of the nation. [Renowned Arab
> singers and musicians] Fairuz, Um Kulthum, and
> Ziad Rahbani also used Western instrumentation. So
> how exactly is that different from hip hop? It's elitist,
> in fact, and classical music is not just Western, but
> imperial.

The music of Fairuz and the Rahbani brothers, Um Kulthum, and indeed much popular Arab music since the mid-twentieth century that addressed pan-Arab nationalism and Palestinian liberation, was "heavily influenced by European functional harmony, orchestral setting, and other non-indigenous styles and practices."[26] In fact, some ethnomusicologists observe that the "Palestinian music of struggle and resistance" since the 1960s and 1970s has "been created with substantial musical borrowings from non-indigenous traditions" and argue that the "incessant search and struggle for stylistic innovation" should be understood not within the standard frame of "musical modernization and Westernization" but within a colonial context of struggle and resistance.[27]

Palestinian musicians and poets have, of course, continually engaged in aesthetic experiments and artists who were part of the national struggle have developed new cultural idioms that did not exist before. Nasser Al-Taee, for example, cites the music of the Palestinian group, Sabreen—which developed modern Palestinian music drawing on local as well as international sources—to argue that "stylistic newness is often conceived as a new means for struggle" and that "transnational and global" elements of music are often deployed as "artistic weapons."[28] Al-Taee's critique of music is interesting for it relates the question of aesthetic experimentation to political experiments in resistance, suggesting that the dynamism of popular culture is dialectically related to the dynamism of political struggle. This reframes the question of cultural authenticity and opens up the question of how conservatism in cultural innovation, or even social mores, is situated in relation to the evolution of political movements.

DAM directly addresses the question of hybridity and tradition in their song, *Hibuna Ishtruna* ("Love Us and Buy Us"), from the album *Dedication*:

> "Who was your influence?" I'll tell you who

> I'm like Sinbad, I'll reach every land
> With my flying carpet—the mic [mike], I'll open
> every secret door.
> "How do you know the password?" Well, I grew up on
> Ali Baba
> And using foreign tradition, I'm bringing us back to
> our tradition.

The song wittily makes the point that in sampling Arab music and using Arab instrumentation in their rap music, DAM's hip hop is actually returning to "tradition." In their music, DAM samples the sounds of traditional Arab rhythms, instruments such as the *nay* (Arab flute), poetry (such as that of Tawfiq Zayyad), as well as electronic beats. This eclecticism is very common in Palestinian hip hop that draws on a range of artistic as well as political sources. For example, DAM notes that its diverse influences are: "Jamal Abdel Nasser, Naji al-'Ali, Ghassan Kanafani, Fadwa Tuqan, Tupac Shakur, Toufiq Zayyad, Malcolm X, Marcel Khalife, Fairuz, El Sheikh Imam, The Notorious BIG, George Habash, Edward Said, Nas, and KRS One."[29] Boikutt noted of Ramallah Underground's music: "We made it a point to only sample from Arabic records. We were making a statement that this is something not imported."

This view of Palestinian hip hop as a genre that breaks down the boundaries of Western/indigenous or traditional/modern, while highlighting the specificity and salience of local cultural forms, was expressed by many artists who were experimenting with Arab music in rap. Maisa Daw, who is a singer, said that her group, Ministry of Dub-Key (a play on *dabke*), mixes reggae and jazz with *dabke* music and hip hop. Rami GB, a hip hop artist from Ramallah, founded a virtual record label for hip hop as early as 2002, called Microphone Min Dahab (MMD); he recalled that he was invited to perform at a concert in Jenin in 2003 featuring traditional Palestinian music and *dabke*. He was worried because he assumed the audience would not like hip hop. At the time he thought, "I'm screwed, they'll hate me!" When he came on stage to perform, he told his friend to "loop eight chords" and play the *darbuke* while he rapped. Soon older men in their sixties and seventies who were in the audience were clapping and others at the show "started drumming and playing oud."

In Rami GB's view, "The old guys loved it because it's very close to *zajal*." As he pointed out, free style poetry in hip hop is similar to the improvisational flow that is the essence of *zajal*, a traditional form of oral poetry in colloquial dialect, in addition to the play of competitive jousting with one's musical interlocutors and other poets. Rami GB said that his special talent was free style rapping which he could do for up to three hours, improvising over beats and expressing himself "from the heart." He commented, "My music is simple, our roots in music are beautiful," comparing rap to *zajal* and the poetry from "the street" where people "say what things are." In a scene from the documentary film about Palestinian music, *Checkpoint Rock: Canciones desde Palestina*,[30] Suhell Nafar of DAM raps as an older Palestinian musician does *zajal*, underscoring the continuities between these old and new genres. Rami GB also samples music from a range of "traditional" and "classical" genres, from South Asian music, including *qawwali* music by Nusrat Fateh Ali Khan, and from Chopin, suggesting a broader conception of the "global" that extends beyond "the West."

While cultural hybridity makes hip hop suspect for some Palestinian youth, particularly in the context of charged national politics under a colonial regime, the politics of representation through music take a different form in the diaspora. As Basel observed, the question of cultural authenticity bedevils hip hop in performances outside Palestine, where the reverse problem sometimes emerges. That is, Palestinian hip hop actually becomes emblematic of Palestinian national identity. Palestinian rap, which is largely politicized and progressive, is often staged globally—particularly in the US and Europe—in the context of Palestine solidarity events which, Basel said, are "celebrating Palestinian culture or the cause." But this has also meant that hip hop performances would often, according to Basel, "be followed by belly dancing and falafel outside" the concert. In his view, apart from the symbolic and perhaps problematic staging of "Arab culture," the issue of artistic development and aesthetic quality sometimes fell by the wayside.

Tamer also expressed ambivalence about being restricted in the content of music and by the expectations that DAM only perform anthems for the Palestinian struggle. He said, "*Yanni* (you know), sometimes I feel selfish but it's not always about Palestine . . . It does not make you feel like an artist, singing the same thing."[31] DAM's success, particularly with their early single, "*Meen Irhabi*," meant that fans have often wanted them to sing this song at every performance (as I can testify from concerts I have attended in the United States), but they have increasingly diversified the content of their lyrics and also their musical style. Their second album (*Dabke on the Moon/Nudbuk Al Amar*), according to Tamer, was produced by "creating stories that reflect reality . . . but not just sitting and documenting like [the] news," and draws on reggae, *rai*, oud, and Arab jazz.[32] There is a tension in the notion of Palestinian hip hop as the alternative *Al Jazeera*, that Tamer himself suggested in an earlier moment, and that artists grapple with over the course of their careers. There is no inherent contradiction between "art" and "politics," but a tension between them has long been experienced by "committed" artists who are part of the global movement of Palestinian resistance art and who continue to use literature, music, film, visual art, and theater for "the cause." For the visual artist and activist Hafez Omar, this issue was clarified by the famous Palestinian writer, Ghassan Kanafani, whom he quoted, saying, "If an artist is not a revolutionary, then he is not an artist."

Many hip hop artists grappled with the burden of representation and the fetishization or reductive performance of Palestinian culture in the West that positioned them first and foremost as cultural ambassadors or political activists and only secondarily, as artists. Tamer said, "Palestinians in the United States get very excited to see us, it's like bringing sons from Palestine. But they do not get the whole metaphor, it's not just about Palestine, it's about creative lyrics, but for them it's [representing the] geographic, the local."[33] As Basel said wryly, critiquing this politics of national representation, "I'm not the Ministry of Culture." So the anxiety and unease about, if not criticism of, Palestinian hip hop as inauthentic and globalized within Palestine is twinned with the consumption of hip hop, among other forms of popular culture, as "authentic" and "local" outside Palestine. This is an interesting paradox that means that Palestinian rappers are forced to always engage with the discourse of in/authenticity, and also political representation, in different geographic contexts even while they may try to resist this in their music. Both within and outside Palestine, existing paradigms of national identity and political mobilization demand, and stage, a particular kind of performance of national culture and regulate what is "good" or proper Palestinian identity and politics.

It must be noted that a politics of authenticity has always been constitutive of hip hop as a musical genre in which "realness" or "keeping it real" is used as an axiom to legitimize hip hop performers.[34] As a genre that emerged from urban, economically marginalized youth of color, questions of race, class, and credibility "on the street" have long been part of contentious debates about who authentically belongs to the "hip hop nation." While this is a different politics of authenticity, like all communities envisioned in the form of a nation, there are hierarchies and exclusions; some hip hop artists have tried to envision an "alternative community of belonging" or "(post)nation" resisting dominant or imperial nationalism, as Sohail Daulatzai argues Muslim and African American rappers have attempted to do in crafting a "Muslim International" through hip hop that links "African Americans to the Arab and Muslim Middle East."[35] In the context of Palestinian rap, there is a double—or triple—layer in these debates about authenticity in hip hop, for there is the question of cultural/national and political authenticity as well as local credibility reflecting specific geographic sites.

If Palestinian hip hop has come to represent national culture, and a particular kind of national politics, *outside* Palestine, it is apparent that it is also in certain spaces becoming a representation of a new, youthful Palestinian culture *inside* Palestine, despite ongoing and intense contestations of its legitimacy. This is partly because the global has already intruded into the local in Palestine, given the (historic) ties of international movements to the Palestine national struggle, global migration and return migration, and the influx of "internationals" to the West Bank, especially to cities such as Ramallah and Bethlehem. Hip hop has, in some sites, increasingly become part of the encounter with "Palestinian culture." For example, the Palestinian Street MCs, who have been supported by the Ibdaa Cultural Center in Dheisheh Refugee Camp, are often asked to meet with foreign visitors and, in a sense, they have become one of the faces representing the camp. They do many interviews, as they did with me in the rooftop cafeteria in the Ibdaa Cultural Center, and have learned enough English to be fluent and articulate spokespersons for visitors who want to learn about the camp, Palestinian life, and Palestinian youth. There are also many hip hop workshops in refugee camps, such as in Balata, Dheisheh, and Shu'afat, which bring together artists and youth of diverse backgrounds.

So on the one hand, it is very possible that hip hop artists now represent a "modern," globalized Palestinian youth culture that, for some, is positive and worth showcasing. This may also be why Rajeh mentioned that Black Revolution actually received some funding from the Ministry of Culture to produce their album, *One Revolution*. He noted that a Palestinian minister attended their concert at the al-Kasaba theater in Ramallah (although he commented wryly that he was closing his ears). While national leaders or politicians from an older generation may not personally enjoy rap, some may be conceding that it is a growing youth culture and also an effective political medium for representing the nation—as modern, cosmopolitan, or liberal/progressive—in a global context in which Palestinian/Arab culture and Islam is often marked as anti-modern, regressive, or insular.

On the other hand, this staging of hip hop as representative allows some youth to challenge other layers of cultural or political authenticity, from within, as it were. There are several tensions at work in these struggles over representation. For example, hip hop has been very popular among youth in refugee camps who, as the Palestinian Street MCs observe, are generally seen as "troublemakers, not proper" subjects by Palestinians from cities. Salim commented that some people in Nablus have such a "negative" view of Balata camp that they "die without ever having entered the camp," underscoring the social segregation that many observe exists between camps and other spaces. Salim also noted that many youth from the camp are frustrated, confined, and struggling for better educational and economic opportunities. It is in this context that he noted that the Yafa Center's program on "hip hop and the arts has become an outlet" for cultural expression and also for producing a different image of camp youth.

Hip hop has become a medium to perhaps renegotiate, if not challenge, the negative image of the camp as a space of disorder, violence, and backwardness— yet a space that is also generally romanticized and reified as "the authentic heart of the Palestinian community-in-exile" and of national resistance.[36] This is partly because refugee camps symbolize the displacement of the Nakba and represent "the embodiment and expression of the right of return," according to Alessandro Petti, a political principle which is a touchstone of Palestinian national politics.[37] As Khaldun Bshara writes, "social, anthropological, spatial, and geographic values elevate the status of the camps to heritage . . . for Palestinians searching for identity and for tangible reminders of their displacement."[38]

Youth from the camps, including young artists, engage in a self-reflexive critique of these images of "proper" or authentic political subjects and "improper" social subjects. Refugee youth who participate in the Campus in Camps, an alternative educational program based in Dheisheh Refugee Camp, observed at a public presentation I attended in January 2013 that the camp is exceptionalized within Palestinian and also global discourse—not just as a legal state of exception, in Giorgio Agamben's terms—but as an exceptionalized symbol of victimhood and poverty that bears the burden of representing the national question.[39] Some of these youth from the camps had worked as tour guides in Dheisheh and began rethinking their own participation in the production of static and humanitarian discourses about refugees, through various kinds of artistic and social projects in the camp. So in a sense, the interventions of youth or the work of hip hop artists that redefine representations of the camp reconfigure camp tourism and the tropes of refugee youth as simultaneously heroic nationalists and disorderly *ibn mukhayamat* (children of the camps).

These new performances and cultural practices are perhaps one instance of what Petti describes as the camp as "a counter-site for emerging political practices and a new form of urbanism."[40] I view hip hop produced in camps as one of the expressions of the ways in which, as scholars such as Petti and Sandi Hilal observe, "the refugee camp has been transformed from a marginalized holding area to an interconnected center of social and political life," yet "this radical transformation has not normalized the political condition of being exiled."[41] For example, I spoke to a group of young teenage males in Balata Refugee Camp, sitting in the Yafa Center office under an old, sepia photo on the wall of Palestinian refugees in tents. Each of them introduced themselves to me as coming from the village from where their family had been displaced during the Nakba (a common practice among refugees of all generations). They went on to talk about how they liked hip hop because they could "use it to deliver stories," reflecting on their concerns about doing well in school, limited employment opportunities, and the confined and crowded space of the camp.

Hip hop has also been used to produce and comment on self-representation by Palestinian youth from urban areas such as East Jerusalem, who are also sometimes associated with youth deviance. Young people from neighborhoods suffering from poverty and unemployment have been increasingly drawn into drug use, gang-related violence, and criminalized activities. Don Bassa, who has lived in Eizariya and the Mount of Olives, said that he used rap to address the "problems of my 'hood," such as drugs and gun violence, but some people refused to believe that these issues existed among Palestinian youth and said that these are "from America . . . it does not exist" in Palestine. Usama Kahf observes that Palestinian hip hop artists, such as Khalifa E., address issues of drug use that many want to deny, and that '48 Palestinian rappers such as DAM have also confronted through their music. Thus hip hop offers a critique of an existing reality on the streets that troubles notions of what is "authentically" Palestinian culture. Palestinian hip hop engages with and critiques the politics of national and cultural authenticity for youth who are seen as "not proper" social subjects and, in the case of youth from refugee camps, at the same time as essentially "proper" Palestinian national subjects.

Cultural Promiscuity and Gender/Sexual Politics

In discussions of hip hop with youth in the West Bank, there was an ambivalence about the penetration or absorption of "foreign" cultural forms, that were viewed as inauthentic, decadent, and corrupting of Palestinian society.

There was also some unease with local or urban spaces which were seen as problematic sites of cultural production or consumption, because they were too "Western," and it became apparent that this critique had a sharply gendered edge. The criticism of hip hop shows as "chaotic" and involving "loose" behavior seemed to underlie the moral approbation about hip hop as a genre that was not just culturally promiscuous, but also a site of promiscuous social behavior. This view was also associated with generational distinctions that are not uncommon across the world in discussions of hip hop or other forms of youth culture. One student at Birzeit (group 1) thought it was mainly urban youth who liked rap and that older people did not. A young woman said to me after our discussion that her father would not approve if she listened to hip hop. Rajeh commented that it was "more fun" for Black Revolution to perform at Birzeit University than at the al-Kasaba Theater in Ramallah because the audience on campus was younger and knew and enjoyed the music. However, it is also striking that some in the older generation, including the parents of several well-known (male) rappers, are supportive of this new music, as illustrated in a poignant scene with Tamer and Suhell Nafar and their parents, clearly proud of their celebrity sons, in *Slingshot Hip Hop*. While the film also depicts how difficult it is for female rappers to get support from their families, the larger issue is that hip hop—as elsewhere— remains a genre that is associated with youthfulness and with urban youth cultures, and thus with all the tensions and anxieties surrounding this generational and spatial location.

For example, in Ramallah, many people I talked to (of various ages) viewed with disapproval venues such as Beit Aneeseh, an upscale restaurant that hosts concerts by young musicians and is known for drawing a youthful, mixed-gender crowd. The restaurant is one of many trendy cafes and bars that have sprung up in Ramallah and that serve alcohol, but it is also just one of a few where young people can dance. On warm evenings, people sometimes even dance outdoors in the garden, behind the high picket fence that surrounds the restaurant. There was a perception among some in the city that Beit Aneeseh was the site of "wild" parties with promiscuous "women from '48 [Palestine]," a hedonistic and morally corrupt place. I was told by youth that, at demonstrations in Ramallah, some PA security would try to delegitimize young activists by commenting that they were part of the "Beit Aneeseh crowd." One young male activist said that progressive youth avoided the restaurant because they were concerned about having their reputations smeared or even being blackmailed if security agents saw them there.

Beit Aneeseh, Ramallah.

Many other restaurants and cafes in the city also cater to an upwardly mobile, Westernized, mixed-gender clientele, and feature events with rock music and DJs—such as Snowbar, Café La Vie, Andareen, and, previously, Lawein. However, it is striking that this cloud of suspicion and moral approbation centered primarily on Beit Aneeseh, a venue that hosts hip hop artists. It is also worth noting that the restaurant draws many '48 Palestinians and youth from Jerusalem, a point I will return to later. One of the owners of Beit Aneeseh, who is a well-known visual artist, commented to me that the moral panic about the venue, and the rumors that it was even a brothel, rested in part on its name, which means House of Aneeseh (it is the former home of a Palestinian woman teacher). He observed insightfully that the gendering (female) of the venue's name is perhaps what has provoked a suspicion that has not to the same degree been pinned onto other venues in Ramallah that cater to a similar clientele and also feature music events or are associated, according to some, with the consumption of soft drugs. In fact, in 2013, this rumor-mongering reached new levels when an international media report alleged that Beit Aneeseh was actually a house of "ill repute" where "Palestinian women are being exploited and ruined, with no hope of being accepted back into society."[42] The article, which was ostensibly about the trafficking of Palestinian women, cited unnamed

"Palestinian officials" who claimed that Beit Aneeseh "is one of more than seven brothels operating clandestinely in Ramallah and East Jerusalem since 2002."

While such wild allegations caused the owners of this venue much angst, it is apparent that these sensationalist rumors arise in a context in which the shifting gender, sexual, and class politics of youth culture, and public culture more generally, are being negotiated daily and where there are highly charged battles about social norms, religiosity, and secularity. These debates center not just on the suspicion of hip hop per se, but on concerns about the drinking, dancing, gender mixing, and female behavior and dress that presumably accompany the youth culture of which hip hop is one element, and of which religious and social conservatives disapprove. For example, some young male activists apparently choose not to go to Beit Aneeseh largely because they are worried that they might be associated with a space viewed as problematic by feminists or morally decadent by others. Yet, the restaurant, which is housed in an old Palestinian home, is adorned with old PLO and Palestine solidarity posters, has progressive political graffiti on the walls outside, and hosts many political arts events, including hip hop shows. In October 2012, I saw DAM perform in the garden with El Far3i, as young people danced and drank on the lawn at night.

The overtly politicized aesthetic of Beit Aneeseh coexists with an unease about the promiscuity of particular musical genres (such as rap) and female bodies (particularly of '48 Palestinian women) that are assumed to be "loose," both of which are presumably tainted by hybridity and inauthenticity.[43] Youth cultures that are hybridized are often censured through a sexualized and gendered discourse that is intertwined with the policing of female bodies and the regulation of "proper" social behavior and national identities, as I found in my previous research on bhangra remix music and youth culture produced by Indian youth in the diaspora.[44]

Female bodies and female behavior is a primary locus of this scrutiny and surveillance in contexts where the defense or preservation of national culture is seen as of paramount importance, as in colonial or diasporic contexts, as well as in social milieux shaped by competing views about Islamicization and cultural conservatism, national identity, and globalization.[45] This social monitoring and policing, I should note, does extend to masculinities as well but it occurs in contexts where the regulation of activity and discourse is largely dictated by men. Michael Jensen, in his research on young men in Hamas-affiliated sports clubs in Gaza, discusses the concern about properly Islamic masculinity and the sense of "moral crisis" created after Oslo when Palestinians who returned from exile brought social and cultural practices viewed as "alien" and contributing to a perceived "moral crisis" in Palestinian (Muslim) society.[46]

Given the assaults on Palestinian society and Zionist attempts to erase Palestinian identity and history over decades, the anxieties about embodied cultural inauthenticity are not inexplicable. What is striking is that, as in other social contexts, cultural purity has an enduring association with sexual purity, so that behaviors associated with the "foreign" are viewed as morally corrupting of women and youth through their tainting by the other/colonizer. As is often the case, the anxiety about the promiscuity/immorality of Westernized or hybrid culture is pinned onto the presumed promiscuity/immorality of social spaces through these circuits of surveillance and scrutiny. While Ramallah may represent a cultural "bubble" or epitomize liberal decadence to some in Palestine, it is not devoid of colliding views and sometimes sharp tensions about gender segregation, alcohol consumption, female clothing, religious piety, and the presence of women in public space. These issues are charged in contexts of an ongoing threat to the national community posed by occupation and colonialism and where social norms or class relations are in flux, as in the post-Oslo, urban context of the West Bank. As Penny Johnson and Annelies Moors observe in their study of Palestinian Muslim youth and marriage, gendered and sexual "sites of moral danger" are often points of condensation of larger "fears about 'dissolution' to the social and political order," in a "colonial present marked by spatial segregation, insecurity, and social and political fragmentation."[47] I argue that hip hop is one site associated with "moral danger" in which these anxieties about an unstable or shifting social and political order are expressed, negotiated, reinscribed, and contested.

Young people's concerns about gender, sexuality, and female behavior cropped up in many conversations about the resistance to, as well as appeal of, hip hop. It was notable that while there were no female rappers who were known as public performers in the West Bank, there are several female MCs who have been part of the Palestinian hip hop scene in Israel since its inception, including a few who have collaborated with DAM. Although these young women's entry into hip hop was not necessarily easy in all cases, as documented in the film *Slingshot Hip Hop*, there are also newer female Palestinian rappers in Israel such as the young duo, Dmar, from Nazareth, and artists who perform with reggae-rap groups such as Maisa Daw from Haifa. Yet it is interesting that the femininity of '48 Palestinian women is considered dubious by some in the West Bank. The cloud of suspicion that seemed to perpetually hover over venues such as Beit Aneeseh was associated with Palestinian women, and artists, from Israel and from Jerusalem, and it was tinged with allegations about the presumed sexual promiscuity of these women.

Much of this suspicion arises from the perception that '48 Palestinians, both women and men, are Israelized and not fully authentic Palestinians, and that their identities, and moralities, have been corrupted by Israeli and Jewish social norms antithetical to Palestinian tradition. As one young woman from Ramallah observed, "'48 women are seen as corrupted because of the same notion that sees foreign women as 'loose,' since Israel is seen as a 'loose' and sexualized society." While it is evident that colonized and racialized minorities are forced to grapple with the culture of the colonizing group on a daily basis, and are influenced by it in a range of ways which are varied and nuanced, it is also evident that the perception of cultural and national inauthenticity is deeply imbued by a gendered and sexual imaginary.

These imaginaries also arise in spaces that are viewed as liminal or border zones and new youth cultures emerge in spatial locations that straddle different cultural (colonizing/colonized) worlds. Johnson and Moors observe that Jerusalem's increasing segregation from the West Bank and its isolation from Palestinian governance has made it a "border zone," which people imagine as a site of "improper" sexual relations and un-Palestinian marriages, particularly in schools, universities, and poor communities in the Old City.[48] Women who are seen as "flaunting" improper Palestinian behavior or who have grown up in Israel, or cultural spaces which are seen as Westernized and morally degenerate, are also border zones—viewed as neither fully Palestinian nor fully something else—and hence create unease, including among youth.[49] Zones of liminality, whether legal or social, are often associated with sexual promiscuity because these states of ambiguity create anxiety—for those outside as well as inside—about a presumably unstable social order. Precarity and promiscuity are thus often in bed with each other.

Johnson and Moors astutely suggest that moral anxieties about new forms of (Islamic) marriage are linked to the conditions of entrapment, statelessness and "social and political fragmentation" in Jerusalem.[50] Yet the cultural and political context of Jerusalem is clearly different from that in '48 Palestine, if increasingly Judaized and segregated from the rest of the West Bank. In the case of the hip hop subculture in Jerusalem, it seemed that young women were not as publicly involved as in '48 Palestine. I was told that there were some female rappers from East Jerusalem, but none of the hip hop artists I spoke to had heard of them and it seemed, at the least, that they were not well known. While two of the MCs I spoke to from Jerusalem mentioned a female rapper who used to perform with G-Town, they also observed that young women tended to perform during hip hop workshops, and not at public events. On the one hand, hip hop in the United States was in its early years also very male dominated. On the other hand, it is also apparent that everyday social restrictions on young women and on mixed-gender events in the West Bank and Jerusalem have made this a cultural genre which is not considered "proper" for females or highly contested, at this point.

As Bassa remarked, "There are fewer females in rap [in Jerusalem] because families will not let girls on stage if they are not open minded." This gendered sanctioning seemed to be directed at hip hop, in particular, more than other kinds of music or performance. As MC Dave said, "It takes a lot of power for a girl to go on stage and kick it." The Palestinian Street MCs talked about their hip hop workshops with girls and boys in Dheisheh and their fears about what people in the camp would say about these mixed gender events. Yet they recollected that when the Ibdaa Cultural Center's dance troupe started performing *dabke* in the camp, there was also some criticism from conservative quarters because it, too, was a mixed group, even if it was for folkloric dance. The MCs told me they "took the risk" and worked with four girls and eight boys, eventually staging a rap concert with the children. They said, "We were surprised, people came and the response was positive and they responded positively to girls rapping too."

It is important to acknowledge, especially given this context of gender representation, that Palestinian male rappers have explicitly addressed sensitive questions of gender and sexuality in their music; for example, Palestinian Street has done a song, "We are all Gaza," about the rape of women in Gaza, and DAM produced a song about feminism and liberation, "*Al Huriye Unt'a*" ("Freedom for My Sisters"), in collaboration with the female rappers Arapeyat. The Arapeyat duo, Safa Hathoot and Nahwa Abed Alal, performed at a music concert at the Ramallah Cultural Palace that I attended in April 2013, and performed this rap song as well as a couple of other songs about violence against women and men who behave as "players." What was apparent in this performance is that female rappers performed a femininity that would challenge local codes of conventional femininity and female behavior. Safa, in particular, made boisterous jokes and ran energetically around the stage, loudly exhorting the crowd to respond and participate. She was wearing androgynous hip hop gear—a puffy yellow jacket, baggy sweatpants, and sneakers—a look that defies the ultra-feminine, sleek, primped style of most young Palestinian women in West Bank cities, who tend to wear lots of make-up, skinny jeans, and high heels in public, whether or not they are covered in various ways. So in certain cases, hip hop performance can also become a space in which to trouble gender and sexual ideologies and challenge the policing of social behavior. Interestingly, Rajeh commented that Black Revolution's fans, largely teenagers, included more girls than boys, "perhaps because we are all guys." In fact, Black Revolution's performance style is in some ways that of a boy band, playful and macho. So while the group is not necessarily subverting dominant gender codes, it is evident that Palestinian hip hop in general is part of a youth culture in which issues of gender and sexuality are being publicly aired, if not critiqued, despite attempts to regulate or contain them.

The gender (and sexuality) question in Palestinian hip hop came to a head in 2012 with the controversy about DAM's song (in Arabic), "If I Could Go Back in Time," from their second album. The video for the song featured the Palestinian singer Amal Murkus and was produced by Jackie Salloum (director of *Slingshot Hip Hop*) and supported by UN Women (United Nations Entity for Gender Equality and the Empowerment of Women). Feminist scholars Lila Abu Lughod and Maya Mikdashi lambasted DAM for what they critiqued as an Orientalist and depoliticized video endorsing a UN-sponsored framework for "honor crimes" against Muslim and Arab women, writing: "Given DAM's unapologetic and sophisticated political positions, it is surprising that when they decide to champion women's rights, they succumb to an international anti-politics machine that blames only tradition for the intractability of (some) people's problems."[51] This criticism provoked a flurry of responses, including a detailed article based on research on violence against Palestinian women in Israel by Palestinian feminist scholar-activists, Nadera Shalhoub-Kevorkian and Suhad Daher-Nashif, which stated "that both DAM and Abu-Lughod and Mikdashi are making clear interventions in addressing the criminalization and politicization of Palestinian women by their family members." Their essay argued for using the term "femicide," rather than honor killing, so as to reject the framework of "honor" used by both Palestinians and the Israeli legal and welfare system.[52]

DAM responded to the US-based feminist scholars' criticism, pointing out that some murders of women by their families had occurred in their own hometown of Lid, and stated:

> To claim that we were seduced by Western
> propaganda is a cheap shot. DAM's song was written
> in Arabic, for an Arab audience, followed by
> workshops in the same areas in which these murders

occurred. We have a strategy that we are
implementing. We see the risks in singing about Arab
social and political issues. Opportunistic actors can
co-opt and manipulate these messages. But this is not
the case for us. . . . We are part of a new artistic
movement in Palestine that is secure enough to take
on occupation and domestic violence, racism and
sexism. We will not shy away from engaging our
society's taboos. We believe we can, and we must,
tackle these issues with openness, bravery, and
honesty.[53]

DAM's argument for a "new artistic" movement that addresses social as well as political issues, and can do so unapologetically, is important, because it emerges from a persistent debate about how to define "legitimate" (possibly authentic) political issues that can be addressed by Palestinian artists who are committed to the national struggle but are also concerned with social issues and problems "internal" to the national community—and who defines this. DAM also pointed out that the song was "one chapter" in their compilation and had to be situated in the context of other songs in their new album addressing a range of political issues. MC Dave said that while many Palestinian rappers focus on the occupation, "We should also face our problems and change ourselves. . . . We should start with our streets, our schools, our families." These young artists challenge the notion that the only "proper" subjects of political critique are the "external" threats to the nationalist movement, rejecting the either/or binary and burden of representation that weighs heavily on artists in all contexts of colonial violence and racial subjugation. In other words, the discussion about DAM's video was not a new debate but its particular inflections in the context of Palestinian hip hop were illuminating of these deeper concerns about gender, nation, and representation.

DAM also emphasized that they managed to produce the album while refusing funding from Israeli state institutions and honoring the cultural boycott, noting that DAM is itself boycotted by Arab music companies, such as Rotana. Thus, they highlighted some of the complex contradictions of their work as "politicized artists living as an indigenous population" in Israel, complexities largely overlooked in Abu-Lughod and Mikdashi's critique, even if the music video had its weaknesses.[54] While the criticism of the DAM video spoke to the politics of Islamophobia and Orientalism within a US and Western context, an issue not to be taken lightly, DAM's response, and also that of Shalhoub-Kevorkian and Daher-Nashif, illuminated a different politics, one grounded in a local, if highly fraught, Palestinian context. In addition to these nuanced issues of audience, political context, and musical production, what seemed to be missing from this scholarly debate was a reflection on the attempt by a new generation of Palestinian men, and also women, to articulate and enact a feminist politics through youth culture and music, with all its contradictions—which is what I see enacted in DAM's music video. The video raised for me questions that have been underexplored, such as: What does it mean to perform a feminist (Palestinian) masculinity within a particular cultural, visual, and musical genre, such as hip hop, which has its own generic codes? What does it mean for a youth culture form such as hip hop, bedeviled by accusations of misogyny and depoliticization in the US context, and associated primarily with nationalist politics in the Palestinian context, to take on the question of femicide in the colonial present?

These questions have also been inadequately addressed in most of the literature on Palestinian hip hop, which if addressing issues of masculinity tends to rehearse rather familiar arguments. For example, Ela Greenberg suggests that the subgenre of gangsta rap, in particular, has been adopted by young Palestinian men to reclaim their masculinity in response to the emasculating practices of the colonial regime.[55] She argues that while the young male rappers in G-Town, from Shu'afat Refugee Camp, may rewrite some of these gendered codes, they ultimately reassert a "tough" masculinity associated with and required of camp males. It is indeed apparent that the violence and racism of the Israeli regime rests on clearly gendered processes of humiliation, sexual abuse, misogyny, and homophobia that deeply affect young Palestinian men, as well as women, and that there are also powerful gender and sexual ideologies that prevail within Palestinian communities.[56] However, analyses such as that of Greenberg evade the ways in which these performances of gender (and sexuality) by Palestinian rappers are deeply intertwined with a politics of nationalism and, especially, race, in response to the colonial power of an apartheid regime. They offer an alternative political expression for young people, that may still be rife with social contradictions.

In using the single lens of gender—and specifically a particular, reified understanding of "camp masculinity"—to understand the appeal of hip hop, such research misses the complex working of gender and sexual politics within a colonial and racial context as it infuses hip hop.[57] Greenberg's analysis also underestimates the ways in which Palestinian youth, such as G-Town, are intervening in gender and sexual politics to address sensitive issues of domestic violence against women, for example, or how young artists may evolve and take different positions over time. In fact, Rayya El Zein highlights the feminist critique produced by Arab male rappers in general, something which is also true of well-known Palestinian MCs, who consistently resist the misogyny and vulgarity of gangsta rap: "Particularly noteworthy (not because of their ethnic or religious background, but because of the history of hip hop and rap in the West) is how adamantly young, Arab, male MCs eschew and challenge misogyny in both their content and performances."[58]

Palestinian hip hop provides a space to negotiate multiple axes of identity—including gender, sexuality, nationality, race, and class—and, like all forms of popular culture, to variously assert, challenge, or subvert social and political norms. I would like to suggest that the ambivalence about hip hop among Palestinian youth is in part due to anxieties about shifts in culture and class on the ground that are the result of a range of processes in the post-Oslo moment, including migration and global capitalism, gender and sexual politics, religious politics and the rise of Islamist movements, and the dissolution of the national movement and collective resistance in the Oslo era. These issues and concerns are not always directly addressed in hip hop or youth culture but often erupt through discourses that are more familiar or more sanctioned, such as those about cultural or national authenticity, religious piety, and proper gendered and sexual behavior. These debates are also rife in the context of the urbanization of public culture and rapid shifts in cultural consumption and production in cities, such as Ramallah or Bethlehem, as well as in the public culture of refugee camps.

(In)Authentic Identities and '48 Palestinian Youth

All the artists I interviewed spoke of the freedom they felt in rap to express their views and to reject hierarchies of cultural authenticity. Yet as with the issue of gender, the question of authenticity in Palestinian hip hop is often not understood in complex ways in popular discussions and even in the existing research, and the case of '48 Palestinian hip hop brings this to light most clearly. For some scholars such as Usama Kahf, Arab hip hop artists are actually creating new hierarchies of music by rejecting "traditional forms of expression that are propagated and maintained by [the] status quo as official and authentic."[59] Kahf claims that these artists are "de-authenticating everybody else's experiences," including traditional forms of resistance music, through their claims to marginalization and the authentic voice of the "Palestinian 'street.'"[60] He acknowledges that Palestinian hip hop artists, in particular, have expressed a meaningful critique of social and political issues, and have faced "strong resistance from various cultural forces" and critics of "anything that sounds western" as well as from those who resent "hip hop's criticism of their way of life."[61] For example, Hamas supporters apparently stoned a rap performance in Gaza by PR (Palestinian Rapperz) at a rally in 2005, objecting to the mixed-gender audience.[62] Yet Kahf's study goes so far as to claim that Palestinian rappers are using the "same logic of victimhood that the Israeli government and army speak with" in trying to establish credibility for themselves, and for Palestinians in general, as the "real" victims and in critiquing the Israeli state's label of "terrorists."[63] Providing no political context or discussion of the conditions of military violence, siege, subjugation, racism, and terror that Palestinian youth have experienced, Kahf concludes that Palestinian hip hop is discursively oppressive for indulging in a rhetoric of "victim makes right" which is akin to Zionist victimhood. With this rhetorical sleight of hand, the victims of occupation and colonialism become akin to the perpetrators due to their production of anti-colonial political critique through hip hop.

This troublingly misplaced reading of the question of authenticity in Palestinian rap is in part a response to the rapid development of a new genre of Palestinian resistance music that has become globally popular and to the strong critique that Palestinian rappers have waged, discursively and sonically, to Zionist narratives about Palestine and Palestinians. For example, Kahf cites DAM's by now classic single, "*Meen Irhabi*" ("Who's the Terrorist?"), as an example of the rewriting of narratives of "terrorism," viewing it as a rhetorical strategy of claiming the "authenticity" of their victimhood and of hip hop as a vernacular expression of resistance. For some scholars, such as Stein and Swedenburg, DAM both reproduces and refutes the "canonical logic" of Israeli and Palestinian nationalisms, by critiquing "hegemonic notions" of Israeli national identity, on the one hand, and challenging "traditional registers of Palestinian protest," on the other hand, since they rap in Arabic, English, as well as Hebrew and mix musical idioms.[64] In my view, however, it is not just that DAM is repossessing "Israeli-Jewish culture" while trafficking in a dominant Palestinian nationalism.[65] I argue that they are actually challenging the core definition of the Israeli state and rejecting Zionist mythologies of settler colonialism, but also pressing further on Palestinian nationalist discourse by articulating a definition of the Palestinian nation that includes Palestinians inside Israel. The issue here, then, is not authenticity, but something else—a different politics produced through a new medium.

'48 Palestinian hip hop thus offers a dual political critique, of Zionism *and* of dominant Palestinian national discourse that focuses primarily on the West Bank, Gaza, Jerusalem, and the diaspora. However, this double move is not an easy one to make. Arguably, the politics of cultural authenticity is the most charged for Palestinian youth who are viewed as tainted by Israeli citizenship and Israeli society. As discussed earlier, the suspicion that Palestinians from Israel are not fully Palestinian underlie the stereotypes about '48 Palestinian women as having an "improper" (un-Palestinian/Arab or un-Muslim) femininity. The assumption that '48 Palestinian youth were somehow less authentic, in their cultural identity and their national politics, and the ambivalence about their Palestinian-ness, surfaced in several of the conversations I had with youth in the West Bank. For example, in one discussion at Birzeit University (group 1), an intense exchange erupted among the students (whom I label here for the sake of simplicity as F [female] or M [male]):

> F1: Some '48 [Palestinian] youth are conservative and some are committed, some are Israelized and have lost their identity.
> F2: They are much more pressured in '48 [Palestine], they are more restricted. Let's not be fooled by the image that Israel gives! It's more difficult to study there, to build homes there.
> F3: It's the opposite, they have citizenship. They go to the army.
> F2: It's not true!
> M1: Only 1 percent go to the army.
> M2: There are two groups, they are more patriotic than us. People in Um al-Fahm are more politicized than us!

I cite this discussion at some length in part because it was particularly heated, especially during the debate about Palestinians serving in the Israeli military (in fact, only Druze and Bedouin Palestinians are conscripted into the Israeli army), and partly because it revealed the polarized view of the identity of '48 Palestinians among youth in the West Bank. On the one hand, '48 Palestinians are seen by other Palestinian youth as inauthentic ("Israelized") or disloyal; on the other hand, some view them as more patriotic, particularly in areas such as the "triangle" of Palestinian villages in northern Israel (which includes Um al-Fahm), while one student saw them as mixed in their relationship to Palestinian nationalism. The binary of politically and culturally inauthentic or hyper-authentic thus seems to always entrap '48 Palestinian youth—who are, of course, also always improper citizens for Israel—situating them in an essentialized framework of what it means to be a proper Palestinian national subject.

One of the central paradoxes created by the settler colonial state for '48 Palestinians is that their citizenship in Israel makes them suspect for other Palestinians and Arabs, yet their identity as Palestinians is erased and suppressed by Israel.[66] DAM directly challenges the perception in their song "*Ghareeb Fi Bladi*" ("Stranger in My Country") from their album *Dedication*:

> And our Arab roots are still strong
> But still our Arab brothers are calling us renegades!!??
> Noooooooooooooooooooooooo
> We never sold our country,
> The occupation has written our destiny
> Which is, that the whole world till today is treating us
> as Israelis
> And Israel till tomorrow will treat us as Palestinians.

Interestingly, one of the students who participated in the focus group discussions at Birzeit University was Lara, a young woman from Nazareth, who commented on how "everyone thinks that '48 Palestinians have forgotten about our case [as Palestinians], but that's not true." Lara said she always felt in Israel like "a guest in our home" and so wanted to come to the West Bank to study. She had been listening to African American rap since she was in the ninth grade, and became a fan of DAM after hearing them on the Internet and seeing them at a concert in Um al-Fahm. She said of DAM: "They represent our thoughts, our belonging." Lara commented, "Maybe we think differently [than Palestinians in the West Bank] because we have to live with Jews . . . even though they deal with them at the checkpoints," noting that this is why "it's our cause to want to be free from Israel." Lara's poignant reflections highlight the ways in which the experience of being Palestinian and the daily confrontation with the Israeli state, which is not confined to checkpoints or military encounters as it is for youth in the West Bank or Gaza, is more complex than the polarized perception of the identity of '48 Palestinians that exists among some youth in the West Bank.

I would argue that this complex, colonial predicament is precisely why rap exploded first among Palestinian youth in Israel, whose own ambiguous status within Palestinian nationhood was echoed in the "inauthentic" sounds of hip hop and who used this music to assert their struggle to be Palestinian within the settler colonial state.[67] The group, Wlad El 7ara, rap in their song, "Why Do They Say That About You, Rap?:"

> So we're always going to be grateful to rap, cuz it gave
> us the voice
> To be the advocates of freedom, to put an end to
> hatred,
> And to represent the voices of the marginalized
> minority. . . .
> They reacted against it and said it was wrong, and that
> it doesn't belong to us and shouldn't be among us.
> They said that rap is harming us,
> But we said that rap has crossed the border just to
> reach us,
> Even though it didn't come to life or start on our soil
> and under our sky. . . .
> Because the map is full of thick lines, and when rap
> saw that even the word "Arabic" is sick and wounded,
> with fire in its heart,
> It was rap that came to heal those wounds, and to
> recollect the letters of the Arab identity.[68]

Hip hop by youth from '48 Palestine addresses the central paradox of the "present absent" which evokes the ambivalent existence of a colonized "minority," present yet absent within Palestinian national politics, threateningly visible yet politically invisible within the (Israeli) state and (Palestinian) nation. They are simultaneously viewed as Arab yet not Palestinian, Israeli yet not Jewish, loyal yet disloyal, indigenous yet not authentic.[69]

Safa, who is from Acca, described to me the political reality of '48 Palestinians through the profound metaphor of an internal or "inside war" that is less tangible and more difficult to confront than the military occupation in the West Bank. She said: "The war is not visible, you cannot do anything about it. But you always feel you are Arab, everywhere, in schools, at work. We wish we could do something. People in Ramallah and in the West Bank, they can do something. But here we live with it everyday, it's an inside war, it's harder." Just one example of the repressive measures created by the Israeli state that makes Palestinian resistance to Zionist policies difficult and risky, and that absents Palestinian history and identity, is what is known as the Nakba Law. Passed in 2011, the law authorizes the Israeli government to cut funding from any entity that commemorates the Nakba. The very event that displaced and expelled Palestinians is itself displaced and erased, making it an offense to confront settler colonialism, let alone engage in national resistance. Yet, '48 Palestinian youth are increasingly engaged in public protests, not just commemorating the Nakba on Israeli campuses such as at Haifa University and Tel Aviv University, but also occupying destroyed ancestral villages and participating in protests with youth from the West Bank, as I will discuss in the following chapter. There is an increasing public and creative expression of political identity among '48 Palestinian youth, some of whom are publicly adopting symbols of Palestinian resistance and mixing this with hip hop style, such as T-shirts or jewelry displaying Palestinian artist Naji al-Ali's iconic figure of Handala (a youth with his back turned to the observer, another symbol of the present/absent).

'48 Palestinian hip hop articulates the connections between different forms of colonization, across borders, in Palestine. As Safa's critique suggests, it also articulates a more complex form of resistance in an invisible war inside the settler colony, offering an immanent analysis of visible and invisible checkpoints, walls, and barriers "inside" and "outside." The discursive critique of settler colonization and apartheid produced through hip hop becomes a way of making this invisibilized war visible, and this absented colonization present. This music is concerned with history, but not through static notions of "tradition," and it articulates national identity, but not based on identitarian exclusion. The musical epistemology offered in the rap of groups such as DAM, Arapeyat, Saz, Wlad el 7ara, and others, should not be romanticized or considered utopian; however, in its emphasis on the paradoxical presence/absence of '48 Palestine, it grapples with key contradictions of twenty-first century colonialisms and Western modernity, using new forms of cultural resistance to old-school oppression. This '48 Palestinian hip hop connects the issues of occupation and settler colonialism to the condition of exile, linking '48 Palestine with the West Bank, Gaza, and the diaspora. This linkage, and rejection of the fragmentation and cantonization of Palestine, is one of the key precepts of the youth movement that emerged in various sites in Palestine since 2011, as I discuss in the chapter that follows, and that has attempted to materialize its political imaginary through new forms of cultural production as well as cultures of protest.

[1] Juan Flores, *From Bomba to Hip-hop* (New York: Columbia University Press, 2000).

[2] Tricia Rose, *Black Noise: Rap Music and Black Culture in Contemporary America* (Hanover, NH: Wesleyan University Press of New England, 1994), 82.

[3] Will Youmans, "Arab American Hip-Hop," in *Etching Our Own Image: Voices from within the Arab American Art Movement*, ed. Anan Ameri and Holly Arida (Newcastle, UK: Cambridge Scholars Publishing, 2007), 42.

[4] Jeff Chang, *Can't Stop, Won't Stop: A History of the Hip-Hop Generation* (New York: St. Martin's Press, 2005).

[5] Mitchell, "Another Root."

[6] Osumare, "Beat Streets in the Global Hood."

[7] Sunaina Maira, "'We Ain't Missing': Palestinian Hip-hop—A Transnational Youth Movement," *The New Centennial Review* 8 no. 2 (2008): 161-192.

[8] Interview with author, 2008.

[9] See *Nafitha Hip Hop*, dir. Suha Ayyash, 2012 (http://www.youtube.com/watch?v=f9bqHVtwcbs). It should be noted also that hip hop crews shift and dissolve so by the time of writing this, some of these collectives may no longer exist; for example, Egtya7 Underground had dissolved by the time I finished writing this and saw them perform in Jerusalem in May 2013.

[10] See: Joan Gross, David McMurray, and Ted Swedenburg, "Arab Noise and Ramadan Nights: Rap, Rai, and Franco-Maghrebi Identities," in *Displacement, Diaspora, and Geographies of Identity*, ed. Smadar Lavie and Ted Swedenburg (Durham: Duke University Press, 1996), 119-155; Maira, "'We Ain't Missing.'"

[11] Hisham Aidi, "Jihadis in the Hood: Race, Urban Islam and the War on Terror," *Middle East Report* 224 (2007) www.merip.org/mer/mer"+/"+_aidi.html; H. Samy Alim, "A New Research Agenda: Exploring the Transglobal Hip Hop Umma," in *Muslim Networks from Hajj to Hip Hop*, ed. Miriam Cooke and Bruce B. Lawrence (Chapel Hill: University of North Carolina Press, 2005), 264-274; Davey D., "Fear of an Arab Planet: Hip-hop is Everywhere," The Hip-hop Cosign, *Breakdown FM*, November 2007; Youmans, "Arab American Hip-Hop."

[12] Eqeiq, "Louder than the Blue ID," 54.

[13] Cited in Rachel Shabi, "Palestinian political rap attracts growing crowds," *Common Ground News*, 8 January 2007. http://www.commongroundnews.org/article.php?id=20160&lan=en&sid=1&sp=0.

[14] Forman, Murray. *The 'Hood Comes First: Race, Space, and Place in Rap and Hip-Hop*. (Middletown, CT: Wesleyan University Press, 2002).

[15] "We7 (Wlad El 7ara)," Arabic Hip Hop Headz, 17 May 2009. http://hharabe.blogspot.com/2009/05/artists-we7-wlad-el-7ara.html.

[16] Mitchell, "Another Root," 3.

[17] Ted Swedenburg, "Islamic Hip-Hop vs. Islamophobia," in *Global Noise: Rap and Hip-Hop outside the USA*, ed. Tony Mitchell (Middletown, CT: Wesleyan University Press, 2001), 57-86.

[18] For example: Thomas Burkhalter, "World Music 2.0: Between Fun and Protest Culture," *Art and Thought/Fikrun wa Fann* 96 no. 21 (2011): 10-17; Sanjay Sharma, John Hutnyk, and Ajay Sharma, eds. *Dis-Orienting Rhythms: The Politics of the New Asian Dance Music* (London: Zed Press, 1996).

[19] See Gross, McMurray, and Swedenburg, "Arab Noise and Ramadan Nights."

[20] Joseph Massad, "Liberating Songs: Palestine Put to Music," in *Palestine, Israel, and the Politics of Popular Culture*, ed. Rebecca Stein and Ted Swedenburg (Durham, NC: Duke University Press, 2005), 175-201.

[21] Ahmad Sa'di and Lila Abu Lughod, *Nakba: Palestine, 1948 and the Claims of Memory* (New York: Columbia University Press, 2007).

[22] Eqeiq, "Louder than the Blue ID," 56. For more on this long and rich history of oppositional music, see Massad, "Liberating Songs," and other essays in Stein and Swedenburg's *Palestine, Israel, and the Politics of Popular Culture*, among other works.

[23] Youmans, "Arab American Hip-Hop," 46-47.

[24] Edward Said, *Orientalism* (New York: Vintage/Random House, 1978; 1981 ed.).

[25] Stein and Swedenburg, "Popular Culture, Relational History."

[26] Chuen-Fung Wong, "Conflicts, Occupation, and Music-Making in Palestine," *Macalester International* 23 (2009): 269.

[27] Ibid., 271.

[28] Cited in Wong, "Conflicts, Occupation, and Music-Making," 271.

[29] See: http://www.myspace.com/damrap (accessed 2 February 2007).

[30] Canciones desde Palestina (English title: Checkpoint Rock), dir. Fermin Muguruza, 2009.

[31] Interview with author, 2007.

[32] Nora Barrows-Friedman, "DAM's New Album 'Dabke on the Moon': An Interview with Tamer Nafar," *Electronic Intifada*, 9 January 2013. http://electronicintifada.net/blogs/nora/dams-new-album-dabke-moon-interview-tamer-nafar

[33] Interview with author, 2007.

[34] Usama Kahf, "Arabic Hip Hop: Claims of Authenticity and Identity of a New Genre." *Journal of Popular Music Studies* 19 no. 4 (2007): 359-385; Forman, *The 'Hood Comes First*.

[35] Sohail Daulatzai, *Black Star, Crescent Moon: The Muslim International and Black Freedom beyond America*. (Minneapolis: University of Minnesota Press), 90, 108.

[36] Jason Hart, "Dislocated Masculinity: Adolescence and the Palestinian Nation-in-Exile," *Journal of Refugee Studies* 21 no. 1 (2008): 64-8., 76.

[37] Alessandro Petti, "Architecture of Exile," Campus in Camps, January 2013. http://www.campusincamps.ps/en/architecture-exile/.

[38] Khaldun Bshara, "Jalazone Refugee Camp," in *Re-Walk Heritage* (Ramallah: Riwaq), 2012, 107.

[39] Giorgio Agamben, *State of Exception*, transl. Kevin Attell (Chicago and London: University of Chicago Press).

[40] Petti, "Architecture of Exile," Campus in Camps, January 2013. http://www.campusincamps.ps/en/architecture-exile/.

[41] Alessandro Petti and Sandi Hilal, "Beyond the Public, a Common Space in Faawar Refugee camp," *Theatrum Mundi/Global Street*, 4 March 2013. http://theatrum-mundi.org/reflections/beyond-the-public-a-common-space-in-fawaar-refugee-camp/#more-1512.

[42] "No Escape for Palestinian Women Forced into Prostitution," *Independent European Daily Express*, 12 May 2013 http://www.iede.co.uk/news/2013_1828/no-escape-palestinian-women-forced-prostitution

43 One young woman from Haifa who has been to Beit Aneeseh commented that during the war between Hezbollah and Israel in 2006, when many Palestinians from Israel came to Ramallah and the West Bank to escape the crossfire, there were rumors that '48 Palestinian males and females were kissing in the street outside of Beit Aneeseh—a cause for public consternation.

44 Sunaina Maira, *Desis in the House: Indian American Youth Culture in New York City* (Philadelphia: Temple University Press, 2002).

45 See, for example: Floya Anthias and Nira Yuval-Davis, eds. *Woman, Nation, State* (New York: St. Martin's Press, 1989); Kumari Jayawardena and Malathi de Alwis, *Embodied Violence: Communalising Women's Sexuality in South Asia* (London: Zed Books, 1996); Joanne Kadi, ed. *Food for Our Grandmothers: Writings by Arab-American and Arab-Canadian Feminists* (Boston: South End Press, 1994); Deniz Kandiyoti, "Identity and its Discontents: Women and the Nation," in *Colonial Discourse and Post-Colonial Theory: A Reader*, ed. Patrick Williams and Laura Chrisman (New York: Columbia University Press. 1994), 376-391; Jasmin Zine, "Between Orientalism and Fundamentalism: The Politics of Muslim Women's Feminist Engagement," *Muslim World Journal of Human Rights* 3 no. 1: 1-24.

46 Jensen, "Youth, Morals, and Islamism," 121.

47 Penny Johnson and Annelies Moors, "Strange to Palestinian Society? Young People and Men of Religion Talk about Urfi Marriage, Moral Dangers and the Colonial Present." Unpublished paper (cited with permission of author).

48 Ibid.

49 Manal Shalabi observes that sexuality is a neglected area of research in studies of Palestinians in Israel and has also not been adequately addressed by the '48 Palestinian feminist movement, in her view, with the obvious exception of queer Palestinian groups such as Aswat and, more recently, Al Qaws. For a thoughtful discussion of sexual politics from the perspective of '48 Palestinian women, see Manal Shalabi, "The Sexual Politics of Palestinian Women in Israel," in *Displaced at Home: Ethnicity and Gender among Palestinians in Israel*, ed. Rhoda A. Kanaaneh and Isis Nusair (Albany: SUNY Press, 2010), 153, 167. Also, see Rhoda A. Kanaaneh, *Birthing the Nation: Strategies of Palestinian Women in Israel* (Berkeley: UC Press, 2002).

50 Johnson and Moors, "Strange to Palestinian Society?"

51 Lila Abu-Lughod and Maya Mikdashi, "Tradition and the Anti-Politics Machine: DAM Seduced by the 'Honor Crime,'" *Jadaliyya*, 23 November 2012. http://www.jadaliyya.com/pages/index/8578/tradition-and-the-anti-politics-machine_dam-seduce.

[52] Nadera Shalhoub-Kevorkian and Suhad Daher-Nashif , "The Politics of Killing Women in Colonized Contexts," *Jadaliyya*,
17 December 2012. http://www.jadaliyya.com/pages/index/9061/the-politics-of-killing-women-in-colonized-context.

[53] Tamer Nafar, Suhell Nafar, and Mahmood Jrery, "DAM Responds: On Tradition and the Anti-Politcs of the Machine," *Jadaliyya*, 26 December 2012. http://www.jadaliyya.com/pages/index/9181/dam-responds_on-tradition-and-the-anti-politics-of.

[54] Ibid.

[55] Ela Greenberg, "'The King of the Streets': Hip Hop and the Reclaiming of Masculinity in Jerusalem's Shu'afat Refugee Camp," *Middle East Journal of Culture and Communication* 2 (2009): 231-250.

[56] Hart, "Dislocated Masculinity"; Penny Johnson and Eileen Kuttab, "Where Have all the Women (and Men) Gone? Reflections on Gender and the Second Palestinian Intifada," *Feminist Review* 69 (2001): 21-43; Shalabi, "The Sexual Politics of Palestinian Women in Israel."

[57] Greenberg, "'The King of the Streets,'" 244.

[58] Rayya El Zein, ed. *Shahadat: Exploring Popular Literature Series – Hip Hop*. (New York: ArteEast, January 2012). It should also be noted that there is by now a well-established genre of "Muslim rap" that explicitly infuses Muslim identity and piety into the music and lyrics, although this seems to be less prevalent among West Bank and '48 Palestinian rappers and more so in the Palestinian/Arab diaspora.

[59] Kahf, "Arabic Hip Hop," 359.

[60] Ibid., 381.

[61] Ibid., 360.

[62] Ibid., 372.

[63] Ibid., 381.

[64] Stein and Swedenburg, "Popular Culture, Relational History," 14-15.

[65] Ibid., 14.

[66] Shihade, "Not Just a Soccer Game"; Elia Zureik, "Arab Youth In Israel: Their Situation and Status Perceptions," *Journal of Palestine Studies* 3 no. 3 (1974): 97-108.

[67] See Maira and Shihade, "Hip Hop from '48 Palestine."

[68] Cited in Kahf, "Arabic Hip Hop," 376.

[69] For more on this, see Maira and Shihade, "Hip Hop from '48 Palestine."

Chapter 3

The Youth Movement

In spring 2011, a series of protests organized by youth in the West Bank erupted in the streets of Ramallah and in other sites across the West Bank, as well as in Gaza and inside Israel. This came to be dubbed the "youth movement," a label that referred to a range of political actions and campaigns by a loose coalition of young activists. The movement had a range of political orientations and organizing strategies, but the young activists generally shared a core political vision: an intense conviction that it was time for an alternative politics and a refusal of party-based factionalism, as discussed in the previous chapters. There was not often agreement among young activists on how that alternative could be achieved or what strategies should be used, and for some youth, no real clarity about what the alternative vision exactly was. Yet it was apparent that youth from this generation were moved to engage in protest politics, to publicly confront the PA and the framework of post-Oslo politics, and to mobilize outside of the established parties and factions in the West Bank, Gaza, and in Israel.

This movement of the jil Oslo was shaped by the post-Oslo political context, as mentioned in chapter one. Specifically, this context includes the historical events of the Arab revolutions in 2011, Mahmoud Abbas's bid for statehood in the United Nations in the fall of that year, and the dramatic hunger strikes by Palestinian prisoners that began in spring 2012, which some dubbed the "prisoners' intifada." Youth organized protests and erected camps in cities and towns such as Ramallah, Haifa, and Nazareth in solidarity with the Arab revolts and Palestinian prisoners, engaging in hunger strikes themselves and spearheading a protest movement that political parties eventually supported or tried to hijack. Young activists also mobilized publicly against rising prices and the PA's economic agreement with Israel. Additionally, many young activists had been involved in (ongoing) organizing against the Wall, settlements, the segregated Israeli transport system in the West Bank, and the Boycott, Divestment, and Sanctions movement. Within '48 Palestine, the youth movement has been mobilizing against police brutality and state violence, conscription into the Israeli national civil service, discrimination and repression in Israeli universities, land confiscation, housing restrictions, and other issues. One young woman activist from Nablus, Feryal, said, "The fact that there is this sort of youth movement is inspiring in itself. I'm not sure we can call it a 'movement,' because it's the same group of people who are involved everywhere, but to have that kind of commitment is very inspiring, given how depressing the situation is . . . there's so much that's disappointing so it gives us hope that we are doing something and not accepting the status quo." So while Feryal, like a few other people I spoke to, was hesitant to label this set of actions a "youth movement," she was also emphatic about the significance of these protests and political activities in the context of the post-Oslo political malaise in Palestine.

It was striking, furthermore, that nearly all of the hip hop artists I spoke to had been involved in this movement or these protests in one way or another. Every one of them spoke of the ways in which this political consciousness provided the context for their music and sense of political identity. Maisa said of political protests by youth in Haifa, "Everything we do involves the arts, it's huge here now." She added that while art had always been a part of the Palestinian national struggle in Palestine, what was different in her view was that "now young people make the arts . . . there's more space for people to do what they want." Many young artists were engaged in political graffiti and visual culture in support of the youth movement. Given graffiti's role in hip hop culture, this visual element is something that I will discuss in the context of the politics of youth culture and the youth movement's direct attempts to reshape public space. At the same time, I want to note that this movement does not represent all of youth politics or youth activism in the West Bank, Gaza, and '48 Palestine. There are clearly many young Palestinians who are not part of these protests (but who may agree to varying degrees with their political platforms) and others who may not share these political views or proceed from a very different starting point, or may be nationalist but within a different political framework.[1]

Spring in Palestine: "Still Colonized"

While there was a range of political arenas, campaigns, and strategies in the youth movement, what became known as the "March 15 movement" in the West Bank was sparked most immediately by the Tunisian and Egyptian revolutions in 2011. Public demonstrations by youth in Ramallah (and in Gaza City) in March 2011 were inspired by the youth protesters in North Africa who took over public space and Palestinian youth, too, decided to camp out in their cities as an act of political protest.

Stencil, "Tahrir (Liberation) is not a square," Jaffa.

'48 Palestinian youth also organized demonstrations in solidarity with the "Arab spring" and in support of a revived pan-Arab identity, with one rally in front of the Egyptian consulate in Tel Aviv including Palestinian youth holding the Egyptian flag and posters of Gamal Abdel Nasser.[2] I want to note here that the label, the "Arab Spring," is a contested one as critics have pointed out that it assumes a new or seasonal "awakening" of a population not generally engaged in democratic revolt, erasing the long history of Arab struggles against colonialism, capitalism, and oppression.[3] But what is important to grapple with is the impact of the radical political vision of these revolutionary movements and their attempt to forge a new paradigm for democratic politics, posing a "challenge to traditional political organizing" and traditional definitions of politics itself.[4] It should be noted that the Arab revolutions were also an expression of opposition to US and Israeli policies in the region, as evident in the protests in solidarity with Palestine.[5] Noura Erakat and Sherene Seikaly note in their writing on the Egyptian and Tunisian revolutions' reverberations in Palestine that historically "the figure of the Palestinian revolutionary has been an icon of the liberation struggle" in the region at large; in Palestine it was the Arab revolts that, in part, inspired a new generation of youth to take to the streets.[6]

The Youth Movement

The revolts by young people, workers, activists, and others that spread across the region sparked the flame of protest among youth across Palestine, yet these ripples exposed several contradictions. One of these was the repression of solidarity protests due to the fear that the uprisings would spark an internal revolt against the authoritarianism of the PA and Hamas, and in the West Bank, also due to the collusion between Fateh and the Mubarak regime in Egypt—an alliance based on shared opposition to the Hamas regime in Gaza which is tied to the Muslim Brotherhood. Young people in Ramallah took to the streets to show solidarity with the popular uprisings, but they found themselves attacked and, in some cases, arrested by PA security forces. According to Ahmed, a young activist in Ramallah, a young man who raised the Tunisian flag at a solidarity rally in the Manara, the central square in Ramallah, was "dragged to the police station," by PA security "and the flag was taken away." Ahmed recalled that when a group of youth rallied in front of the Egyptian Consulate in Ramallah, they were told that they were not allowed to protest; when they tried to demonstrate in the Manara on the night of the "camels' rally" in Tahrir Square (the violent assault on Egyptian protestors known as the Battle of the Camel on 2 February 2011), they were chased down the main street by PA security and Ahmed himself was physically assaulted. Another young man from Ramallah I spoke to, Hathem, was arrested for participating in an Egypt solidarity demonstration and pointed out to me that the crackdown was in the context of the PA being unwilling to "to take an official position on the Egyptian revolution," given Fateh's "backing from Mubarak" in the West Bank. But Ahmed also pointed out that the crackdown was less severe in Ramallah, where youth were mainly middle-class or from well-connected families, than at protests in other parts of the West Bank, so the repression of the protests was uneven. But the movement was an important site in which young activists attempted to develop new tactics and strategies, as well as a political analysis of the client regime's power and hegemony.

Camping out in the streets and being chased by the police also provided a context in which young activists met one another and created a social and political community. I found that some of these young people had become friends while participating in protests and had become part of a network of groups and campaigns that proliferated in subsequent months, such as Palestinians for Dignity (a coalition group), Youth Against the Settlements, Youth Against High Prices, People Against Corruption, Youth for Al-Quds, and Youth who Love the Homeland. Young left-leaning activists who organized a protest on 5 June 2011 memorializing the 1967 Arab-Israeli war, became part of what is called the June 5 movement and later merged with some from the March

15 movement to form the group *al-Harak al-Shababi al-Mustakil* (the independent youth movement). The "youth movement" thus became a shorthand term for this constellation of groups but also, as I use it in this book, an index of the emergence of a political current in a new generation of political actors.

It was also apparent that Arab hip hop played an important role in these youth protests across the region; in fact, the Arab uprisings brought a great deal of attention to Arab rap in the regional and international media. Global audiences began taking note of Arab rappers who had been taking courageous stances on questions of human rights, democracy, imperialism, and Zionism, and building pan-Arab alliances across borders that had previously gone unnoticed.[7] The Palestinian Street MCs said they had been inspired by Tunisian and Egyptian rappers, such as the famous El Général who defiantly critiqued the Ben Ali regime in Tunisia in his powerful song, "*Rayes Le Bled*" (Head of State) and who was arrested by Tunisian secret police.[8] In Egypt, songs such as Arabian Knightz's "Not your Prisoner" (with Palestinian British MC Shadia Mansour) and "#January25," a collaboration among Arab American/Canadian and Egyptian rappers, are examples of the ways in which hip hop was part of the soundtrack of the Arab revolutions. Palestinian rapper and producer Rami GB produced a song about Syria, "Najmat al-Sham," in collaboration with a Syrian rapper. In Haifa, Ministry of Dub-Key produced a song and online video, "*Al-Thowra al-Khadra*" ("The Green Revolution"), expressing Palestinian solidarity with the Tunisian revolution, and featuring rapper Mahmoud Jreri of DAM. According to Maisa, the song got hundreds of responses from Tunisia and was played at rallies in New York. The video for the song, which was shot in Haifa, shows the young musicians wearing kaffiyehs and singing in front of walls covered in Arabic graffiti proclaiming revolution and freedom.[9]

Rap was thus part of a political conversation, and a pan-Arab subculture, shared among Arab youth deeply engaged in questions about freedom, democracy, and solidarity, and using new generational idioms for cultural expression. 'Adi of We7, from Nazareth, said in a conversation during the Egyptian revolution in 2011 that many of the youth "revolting in the streets" of Cairo were identified with hip hop, and shared a subculture with Palestinian youth who participated in demonstrations "inside '48." Furthermore, Hisham of Palestinian Street astutely noted that the Egyptian street protests involving youth did not always include rap per se, but "many Egyptians were . . . chanting and they were improvising in the streets, for example, singing 'Go, go Hosni Mubarak.' So music was definitely part of the revolution." This broader notion of improvisational music underscores that rap was one element of the many forms of cultural production and creative performances which are part of revolutionary culture and the culture of protest. In addition to hip hop, other forms of music such as *sha'bi* (popular), or what could broadly be called "alternative," music also provided songs and performances reflecting a youthful culture of political critique of the status quo. The Egyptian punk band Brain Candy and electronic music groups that play new *mahraganat* (festival music) in Cairo are such examples.[10]

In the West Bank, there are alternative bands such as Dar al-Kandeel, a musical collective famous for their bold protest music. They used to have open jam sessions in the old city in Ramallah and, I was told, they have a following among Palestinian refugees in Lebanon who view their performances on YouTube. A broader understanding of music, poetry, and creative culture is certainly important to take note of when thinking about the Arab revolutions, youth protests, and political mobilization. While one must not exaggerate or fetishize the role of hip hop, and indeed of youth, in the Arab revolts, as some observers have tended to, it is still important to note the ways in which this generation understands youth culture and protest politics as closely intertwined in their struggle over what can be defined as appropriate, or necessary, "politics."[11]

Boikutt and Basel of Tashweesh also pointed to the ways in which the solidarity protests during the Arab Spring spilled over into artistic collaboration among hip hop artists from Palestine and the larger Arab region. As Basel pointed out, there was already a musical network spanning the region that included rappers from Palestine, Jordan, and Egypt, including Palestinian rappers in the Arab diaspora. Boikutt recalled that Tashweesh did a show in Cairo with rappers from Tunisia, Lebanon, Jordan, and Palestine in November 2011. The Egyptian Ministry of Interior attempted to shut down the concert because they were afraid that it would turn into a "protest, not just show," as it included families of the injured and martyred who had come to attend the event.[12] But the artists moved to another venue and managed to stage the event, called "Voices of the Street." Boikutt said incisively, "That's what it should be in Cairo now, not a show but a protest." He noted that the revolutions had galvanized a discourse among hip hop artists and youth of "Arabs speaking up and standing up"—this is what is perhaps a key element of the pan-Arab youth subculture identified with hip hop. In addition, Boikutt observed that hip hop MCs in the region had been among those who had been calling for revolutionary change even before the Arab Spring and had been "rapping about this before and were part of making it happen." Ruanne commented that the network of Arab hip hop artists across the region had been strengthened during the Arab revolutions leading to a reaffirming of pan-Arab identity and a "common history and struggle:" "When we did shows in Beirut, there was this talk of 'we are all one.'" Boikutt's song powerful rap song, "Ignite," says eloquently of the Arab revolts:

> Unbelievable
> How they made us obey
> At the funeral of the corpse of the [quintessential
> Arabic letter] Ddad
> Counter revolution: the revolution of wealth is in
> process
> Rise
> In the face of decades under an iron fist
> From here to a village without extension
> Without going too far
> Freezing of capital and nuclear war heads
> The interest of the primary beneficiary
> Melts with a flame from Sidibouzid
> Ignite … see how many dictators we'll uproot
> . . .
> The sound of revolution is everywhere, we make it
> heard
> From leaders to parliamentarians
> I do not exclude any of you/ But you don't care
> Until chants are directed at you and shake you
> Let me explain/ Tyranny leaves the street prepared.[13]

Boikutt's lyrics are full of the outrage and hope that was ignited by the courage of those who began the revolt against the repressive Tunisian president, Zine El Abedine El Ali, after the self-immolation of an unemployed young street vendor in Sidibouzid. The song also astutely observes that tyrannical regimes actually created the conditions of possibility of the uprisings in the street, despite decades of authoritarian rule. For Alain Badiou, the point is not just the Foucauldian maxim that where there is power, there is resistance, but also that resistance reveals the "the excessive power of the State;" "politics" is what interrupts "the measureless enslavement" of the state and the "resignation that characterizes a time without politics."[14] While the period before the revolutions cannot be described as "a time where politics was absent, it is this resignation that was shattered with the Tunisian revolution and in Tahrir Square, and later also in youth protests in Palestine. The youth movement, in this sense, was a site where various forms of knowledge of state power erupted into public view and in spaces of convergence between various movements. Therefore, it was not just a series of events but a site of knowledge production, both political and cultural.

But there was also a cautiousness, and in some cases ambivalence, among artists as well as among youth and activists, about what the Arab uprisings would mean for the region and for Palestine. One young activist who I spoke to in November 2011 pointed out that the United States and Western powers had been "catching up with these revolutions" and intervening in various ways, as in Libya, and that the "Arab Spring has been used as a tool for imperialism." In May 2013, Don Bassa worried about the outcome of the uprisings in Egypt, Syria, and Libya, which he described as a "military base for France and Britain." Mohammed, of Palestinian Street, commented astutely on the hypocrisy of the US stance on the Arab revolutions:

> I support the youth movement in Egypt but am
> against the idea of US politicians using the
> revolutions to support democracy when they are
> waging war in Afghanistan and Iraq and . . . support
> the biggest dictatorship in the Middle East which is
> called the state of Israel.

Others, such as a student at Birzeit, Mahmoud, linked the situation in Palestine to change in the Arab world, saying that Palestinian society had become "normalized" and complacent, and needed the inspiration of the Arab uprisings. He used the analogy of a frog who becomes accustomed to hot water if the temperature is gradually increased, but is shocked into action if suddenly thrown into hot water, suggesting that the frog is Palestine and the suddenly boiling water is the Arab world. Mohammed, the rapper from Dheisheh, noted that the Arab revolts rippled into Palestine in many locations: "The Arab Spring encouraged people to take local actions, for example, in al-Walajeh," a West Bank village where there have been protests against the Wall and settlements. The ripple effects of the Arab revolts thus led to a translation of the meaning of popular resistance into the specific Palestinian context of struggles for human rights and democracy.

Many youth were aware that the Arab revolts had very different implications for Palestine, and that a popular revolt would have different consequences for a population still living under occupation and colonization. As Boikutt observed, "No one relates to Fateh and Hamas anymore, their time is up. It's like with Hosni Mubarak. But it's a different situation because we're not in a postcolonial situation, we're still colonized." MC Dave said that he was drawn to rap as a teenager because it was a genre that encouraged confronting problems and in his opinion, one of the biggest problems facing Palestinian youth was the lack of challenge to authoritarianism. He said, "It's a problem that there is a fear of teachers in schools. Everything we did was because we were told to do so. We were not allowed to think." In fact, one of the popular graffiti motifs that sprouted on the walls of Ramallah was a simple stencil of the word *fakkir* (think). The political contradictions of internal repression, as well as external colonization, meant that the Palestinian youth movement had to grapple with the focus of their resistance on many levels. Along with artists, the youth had to create a framework and narrative that would address this unique predicament of revolting while "still colonized."

Stencils, wall near Beit Aneeseh.

The Statehood Bid: "What is this State?"

Following the Arab uprisings came President Abbas's bid for statehood at the United Nations in September 2011, and many celebratory events and advertising posters by Fateh sprang up to mobilize popular support for this in the West Bank.

But for many youth, including artists such as Basel, the campaign was viewed as "another propaganda bid" by the PA in the context of declining support for, and increasing criticism of, Fateh and Abbas. In fact, Ahmed noted that the youth mobilization which erupted in the streets in spring 2011 actually began in 2010. In response to plans for the UN statehood bid, young activists in the West Bank began discussing ways to call for "an end to negotiations" and reject the failed peace process, suggesting a "new juncture" in the search for alternative politics. The young activists' opposition to the statehood bid, however, was repressed by the PA in some instances that also targeted hip hop artists who were critical. For example, the Palestinian Street rappers said that the "UN bid agenda was not clear for Palestinians" and they wrote a song, "Who Put Abu Mazen in Place of Allah?" which they posted on YouTube; the song criticized Abbas's authority to go to the United Nations and the lack of democratic processes in the West Bank more generally. But the PA security, after sending warnings to the young rappers, sent the head of intelligence from Ramallah to visit them. They were forced to take down the video of the song which, ironically, addressed the theme of democracy. This cruel irony, of course, seemed to have been lost on the *mukhabarat* (intelligence) officer.

For some youth I spoke to, the problem with the UN bid was also the specific vision of the Palestinian state that it proposed, given that it remained within the Oslo framework of the two-state solution, confining a Palestinian state to only 22 percent of historic Palestine. One female student at Birzeit University (group 3) said, "It shouldn't have happened even though it may have created political awareness for us globally because it only asked for part of Palestine. It's a defeat for us." But some other youth in the same group vigorously disagreed with her sentiment, suggesting that it was "better than nothing" and that Palestinians were in too "weak" a position to ask for more. Marwan, a young activist from Ramallah, said that although he did not want a state that was just within the 1967 borders, he also wanted "some autonomy and self-determination" on some territory, and so was torn about the PA's vision of the state. Boikutt said emphatically, "I'm not for this vision of the state because Palestine is not just the West Bank and Gaza." He added that the bid was doomed to fail, commenting, "I don't think Palestinians are ready for another failure. Why did they do it? We don't need more failures, we've been failing for 63 years and even more!" This frustration, disappointment, and sense of betrayal by the national leadership was pervasive among the young artists and activists with whom I spoke and who rejected the dismembering of the Palestinian national body.

A young activist in Ramallah, Hafez, said that the Fateh leadership "wanted a state without 70 percent of the people," and astutely observed that "after Oslo, they wanted a state without looking at the core question of what formed us as Palestinians, which is the Nakba," and the struggles since 1948 (and earlier) that are key to Palestinian national identity. He went on to say,

> The Palestinians were meant to vanish, according to
> the Zionist plan. We didn't have a state ourselves
> before the Nakba. But we had a certain shape, we were
> a community. It doesn't matter what you call it, but it
> is fighting against this erasure that makes you a
> Palestinian, or fighting against oppression.

In this view, the issue is not just state-building or even nation-building. The issue is about being true to a vision of a collectivity that had the "shape" of a "community," and that was based on the core principle of resistance to injustice and to the settler-colonial project of annihilation. So the question for some youth was not just the borders of the state, but the national or collective vision that it represented, and whether that was consistent with the deeper vision of what Palestinians had struggled for in their resistance to colonial rule. What was apparent in many of the conversations I had with young artists and activists is that they had a more radical critique and were questioning the focus on the nation-state as the horizon for liberatory politics itself. They were also posing other questions that were about genuine emancipation from colonial oppression and neoliberal capitalism, critiques that were explicitly and publicly expressed in later protests by youth against the Oslo Accords.

Egtya7 Underground released a song on the same day that the UN statehood bid was launched, using the poetry of Tameem Barghouti, which rejected the PA's limited definition of the state and proclaimed: "We want Palestine, we want all of it! We want the refugees to come back, we want Haifa and Yaffa. The smell of Jericho won't substitute for it!" Basel Zayed, a young Palestinian musician from Jerusalem and founder of the progressive band, Turab (Soil), produced a popular Arabic song, "*Shu al-Dowleh?*" (What is This State?)"; the song critiqued the PA's vision of state-building and their regime of "thieves and police" and became popular among youth in this period. A performance of the song was shut down by the PA police at an event in Arafat Square in Ramallah on New Year's Eve in 2011.[15] But at a concert by youth groups from the West Bank and Nazareth in the Ramallah Cultural Palace on 18 September 2012, young musicians belted out the song to vigorous accompaniment from young people in the audience, who clearly knew the lyrics and began clapping and even dancing in enthusiastic support. The young MC at the event even called for a unified Palestinian state in his opening comments, to much applause from the crowd, echoing the view of rappers such as Boikutt, who said, "More and more, I think people want a one-state solution, and this government is not talking about that." Hip hop artists and youth activists were thus among those attempting to push the political debate about the future of the nation, the nature of the state, and challenge the boundaries of official political discourse.

The March 15 Protests

The challenge by jil Oslo to the PA's policies and the call for a different kind of national politics visibly erupted with the 15 March 2011 demonstration and hunger strike by young activists in Manara Square in the center of Ramallah, and the concurrent demonstration by youth in Gaza City. Yasmine, a young activist from al-Bireh, said, "On March 15, the Manara was established as a public space for anyone to come and express their grievances." This renewed politicization of public space, inspired in part by Tahrir Square, extended the mobilization that began earlier in 2011, in the West Bank, Gaza, and in '48 Palestine, with the solidarity protests during the Arab revolutions. Yasmine reflected that young activists also wanted to return to the collective resistance of the first intifada, the youthful revolution that epitomizes popular resistance in Palestine and also in the region. Some of the protesters also later became involved with the hunger strikes in solidarity with Palestinian prisoners in 2011. These strikes included young activists from '48 Palestine who set up a camp in the center of Haifa as part of a campaign eloquently titled "Hungry For Freedom," as youth in the West Bank set up a similar camp in Ramallah. The stenciled slogan, "Hungry 4 Freedom," reportedly created by '48 Palestinian youth, also appeared on walls around Ramallah as activists from both sides of the border were galvanized by this movement. According to Duaa, a young woman from Haifa who played a key role in organizing the hunger strike in the "Prisoners' Yard," a parking lot behind the chic restaurants in the center of Haifa, the protest involving twelve Palestinian youth was "very successful" because it continued for two weeks, much longer than most protests. She said that it sent a "powerful message to the Arab world," given that it involved young Palestinians from Israel collaborating with Palestinian youth inside the 1967 borders.

In the West Bank, the protests in the Manara revealed the political contestations and divisions among youth, and the attempts by the PA to undermine and hijack the movement. This dynamic is a clear example of the regime moving from coercion, which was apparently not always successful in suppressing young activists, to co-optation. The first, and most prominent, slogan raised by the young protesters was to "end the division" between Fateh and Hamas. Ahmed said that the protest was initially called for by a young activist on Facebook who was inspired by the Arab revolutions. There were many in the square who had different demands beyond unity between Hamas and Fateh and many who were critical of the framework of national politics itself. These other demands included the end of normalization with Israel and of dependency on foreign aid, elections for the Palestinian National Council, and the release of Palestinian political prisoners in Israeli jails.[16]

All the youth involved in the spring protests were acutely aware that the Manara was not Tahrir Square, and the West Bank and Gaza were not Egypt or Tunisia. Hathem, a young man from al-Bireh who was one of the hunger strikers in the Manara, said that although he and other youth were frustrated with the lack of democracy and the repressive polices of the regimes in both the West Bank and Gaza, "If we said, we don't want the *sulta* [the PA], we have [to deal with] the occupation." These young activists realized that they were caught between a rock and a hard place, between a colonial occupation and an authoritarian Palestinian regime. Hathem and other activists in the youth movement also observed that they were just a small group of protesters in the Manara, fifty to sixty youth at the time, and that many felt they needed a platform that would gain broad support. One young woman at Birzeit (group 3) said that she participated in the protests in Ramallah because "it was an important political expression." She reflected that although the protests "lacked organization and support," in her view it "was a good attempt, one among many."

Many of the youth in the protests that began on March 15 had previously been affiliated with various political factions, and had become disaffected or frustrated; some were independent and unaffiliated with any party, and some were affiliated but critical of the existing political framework and discourse. As Yasmine observed, the movement included people from Fateh as well as Hamas, leftists as well as liberals. Seif noted, in 2000, the widening of a "serious gap between the young generation and the leadership of the Palestinian political movements" which has "discouraged many young people, especially among the ranks of the leftist political organizations, from involvement in any political action."[17] As Hathem commented, "I'm an independent. For the March 15 protests, we said, 'Just hang the poster on your door, regardless of your affiliation.'" Marwan, who had been involved with the youth wing of a left-leaning political faction in college but had become increasingly disillusioned with the group, commented, "March 15th was the first time that young people took to the streets without orders from political factions," describing the protests as a "turning point" in youth politics.

Simultaneously, in March 2011, there was also a protest by youth in Gaza City who raised similar demands and who were in touch with youth from the West Bank as part of a network spanning the divided spaces of a politically and spatially fragmented Palestine. Hathem said he actually came to know a young activist who was on hunger strike in Gaza and who spoke to him on the phone while he was in the tents in the Manara. As Feryal observed, "What's inspiring about this group of youth is that they're from all over, not just from Ramallah, they're from all over the West Bank and from '48 [Palestine]. There's a connectivity... This 'bubble' of Ramallah didn't blur our vision of what's going on." So there was a deliberate and concerted attempt by youth to also forge unity on the ground, across borders and blockades that partition Palestine. The autonomous nature of the protests, and the inclusion of youth from different sites where there had previously been distinct political structures and frameworks, not to mention partisan loyalties, are significant aspects of what came to be known as the "March 15 movement."

Yet there was also deep disagreement among the youth, activists, and artists I spoke to about the March 15 movement, and particularly about the central call for "unity" between the ruling parties in the West Bank and Gaza that framed the demonstrations and hunger strike. For some, like Basel, the problem was that this was a call for "unity between two old, corrupt parties" and was hardly a radical demand, but in his view, an attempt to "imitate" mobilization by youth in Tahrir Square with a slogan that "even Obama" would support. Boikutt said,

> I support people coming out and asking for their
> rights, but I wasn't supportive of [the March 15
> protest].... it was calling for an end of division, but
> the Palestinian people are not divided... They should
> have called for a new Palestinian National Council.
> They shouldn't have come out on the streets for unity.
> And the PA co-opted them and it was over, *khalas*
> [finished]! The revolution was over.

Many of the youth I spoke to, including those from the March 15 movement, echoed this observation, that it was the minimalist nature of the protesters' most visible slogan that allowed it to be hijacked by the PA in Ramallah. Some, like

Boikutt, thought that there should have been a demand for elections to the Palestinian National Council (PNC), given that the Palestinian legislature has not had elections since 2007, after the split between Hamas and Fateh. The movement for democratic representation through the PNC calls for a larger body based on a restructured PLO which would include all Palestinians, not just those in the West Bank, East Jerusalem, and Gaza, but also in the diaspora and '48 Palestine.

As the March 15 protests persisted, however, the Fateh regime realized that it could not simply crack down on the demonstrators through violent confrontations, especially given the presence of international media in the Manara. So it tried to organize its own protest and actually brought falafel sandwiches to the youth camping in the square. (The irony of feeding falafel to activists on hunger strike seemed to have been lost on the authorities here). Yasmine, smiling wryly, described this moment as a political "comedy," acknowledging that it was an attempt by Abbas to appear like a "nice guy." But this was after some Fateh youth attacked the protesters and, according to Hathem, burnt the books that the young activists had put out on the street as part of a public library and almost set fire to their tents. Hathem recalled that some of the youth who were "beating the shit out of" the protesters were, in fact, Birzeit students affiliated with Fateh, suggesting the deep divisions among youth, with some clearly still loyal to the regime. The PA also tried to discredit the protesters by alleging that they were all working for NGOs. Ahmed said that "some Fateh guy burnt five one-hundred dollars bills to show that we were being paid by the United States," a theatrical insinuation that the protest was engineered by those receiving foreign aid as well as an "incitement" to demonstrators. Ahmed noted the paradox in this accusation from a regime dependent on international aid itself: "As if the PA's money is from their investments!" As he astutely observed, while Hamas physically attacked the Gaza protesters to crack down on the demonstration, in the West Bank, "The counter-revolution was organized by Fateh."

The theatrical nature of the protests and the responses it elicited were also critiqued by some young artists. Ruanne thought that the protests in the Manara turned into a "performance" that was easily appropriated. Initially, she observed, there was a demonstration that was more confrontational with the PA and that involved some young leftist activists, but they were violently attacked by security forces. For Basel, the media frenzy made the events into a "spectacle" rather than a successful action based on grassroots mobilization, which he felt was lacking in the March 15 movement. Yasmine, who was involved with the March 15 movement, acknowledged this critique and talked at length about the ways in which she and other young activists tried to make the movement a grassroots one, to go to "the streets" and beyond Ramallah, discussing how challenging it was to get people involved, even on very specific issues with a broad consensus. She recalled a street theater action in solidarity with Palestinian prisoners, "*mai w mileh*" (water and salt), in which youth dressed in prisoner uniforms offered people in the streets the two ingredients consumed by prisoners on hunger strike. However, she said, "people were not interested, and some were sipping coffee in cafes." These young people may have in some cases been disconnected from "the street," or the villages and camps, but it is also apparent that the street and the larger public it supposedly represents was also in some instances disconnected and de-politicized. It was apparent that the March 15 protests were indeed a dramatic moment of political theater in which various forces were colliding in the public square, literally, in a variously passionate, violent, and farcical struggle over political space and also political discourse, old and new. Even those who were critical of the protests' minimalist slogans were aware that the performative nature of politics was a dimension not to be taken lightly, and that winning, securing, or challenging the consent of the people to hegemonic rule is a political art, for all involved.[18]

Other youth, including hip hop artists, expressed somewhat different views about the March 15 protests that were more ambivalent. Mohammed of Palestinian Street said that one of the MCs in the group had participated in the protests in Bethlehem and performed rap at the tents in the Nativity Square. They had written a song critiquing the division between Fateh and Hamas that also challenged the notion of democracy under conditions where electoral representation has little meaning and are ultimately dictated by powerful external interests, critiquing "elections controlled by America." Not surprisingly, Mohammed noted, "People in the camp from Fateh and Hamas did not like it," but the children in the camps apparently still sing the song. Maqdsi, who had participated in the protests in the Manara, said, "As a first step, it was good to call for unity because we can't fight for occupation if we're divided. I did a song about that. . . . When it started, there were two groups of youth: one for and one against it." But Maqdsi, likeothers, was also skeptical about the outcome of the protests, given Fateh's attempts to ride the wave of protest in the West Bank and co-opt the slogans for unity, commenting: "The protests forced Abu Mazen to make a statement to offer to Gaza to make unity [with Hamas]. They [the protesters] felt they did the part, but shaking hands doesn't mean anything. It won't go that far." Mohammed said that he believed it was important for Palestinians to emphasize their shared struggle, beyond political affiliations, and was critical of party affiliations among youth which he thought were "about benefits." But he also wryly noted, "What I didn't like is that the people who were calling for an end to the division [from Fateh and Hamas] were those who helped to create the division!" In fact, the March 15 protests were followed by a meeting between Fateh and Hamas that was ostensibly focused on moving toward reconciliation. This and the subsequent rounds of "unity talks" between the two parties are described by Ramzy Baroud as a "unity charade," exhibiting the "miserable legacy of Palestinian factionalism," while Palestinian prisoners in Israeli jails engaged in a growing movement that—in contrast—had broad, popular support across factions, as he pointed out.[19]

So while some youth felt that the internal division that had led to violent clashes among Palestinians had to be addressed, and unity between the West Bank and Gaza regimes was a necessary first step to national liberation, others felt that the slogans and approaches of the youth protests did not go far enough in challenging the dominant political framework and building grassroots support. Duaa reflected in spring 2013 that while the hunger strike in Haifa went on for two weeks, such protests were still not part of an ongoing movement. In her view, there is "still a gap between political practice and slogans." Fajr pointed out that in addition to the contested issue of the movement's demands, many of the young activists did not have much organizing experience or had not worked with one another before, since they came from different factions or were independent, a factor which he and others thought had also allowed the movement to be hijacked in the West Bank. Hussein, a Birzeit student, commented that the youth did not have broad "support" nor a larger "structure for change," and that they did not "seem unified." One activist from Ramallah, who was critical of the youth protests because he felt they were not effective, also acknowledged that "young people feel lost, and they feel their whole life has been lost, so they're trying to do something."

Despite these limitations of the youth movement, not surprising for a political formation that was relatively new and outside of well-established political structures, the youth protests spawned many groups and political streams who found one another through organizing and in the streets. Fajr noted in September 2012 that his group had grown in numbers and that they had organized a demonstration against negotiations with Israelis directly in front of the President's office in Ramallah. It must be noted that many youth who did not themselves come out into the streets or participate in these activist groups and campaigns did share their political views. Hussein, for example, observed, "I'm against negotiations [with Israel] and this idea of only getting 22 percent of Palestine." Fajr was actively involved in organizing with a group that "decided that the call to unity was not enough and . . . wanted to unify all Palestinian people, not just Fateh and Hamas, and to include '48 Palestinians, the refugees and the diaspora." This group, Palestinians for Dignity, and others in the larger youth movement have foregrounded the unification of Palestinian nationhood beyond state borders and regional contexts as a core principle of a new political paradigm. This is a significant shift in jil Oslo and highlights the ways in which the youth movement has produced a public challenge to the Oslo paradigm of politics.

Some youth, including activists, criticized the movement as being largely male, while others said that it was mixed in gender—a point that obviously does not erase the reality of male dominance in Palestinian political leadership and movements in general as well as in the society at large. In Yasmine's view, it was individual personalities and proclivities to leadership, among males as well as females, that in part shaped who took the helm of organizing. In Haifa, Duaa commented that at demonstrations at the university, the person who "shouts slogans is usually male" and also straight, criticizing both the elision of women and also the heterosexism of the movement, though she acknowledged that heteronormativity was a complicated issue for young people to confront—as it is everywhere. Feryal even thought that youth groups in Ramallah who were sensitive to accusations of sexism publicized images of demonstrations that highlighted female leadership and participation, a complex question of representation and "inclusion" and one that I will explore in the following chapter. Issues of gender and sexuality were clearly on the minds of all the young activists I spoke to and it was apparent that they were grappling with this in their organizing as also in their daily lives.

The other critique I heard—much more commonly—of the March 15 movement and recent youth protests is that they allegedly involve primarily middle-class, Western-educated youth or young people affiliated with NGOs. Marwan commented wryly that one of the well-known young male activists who was involved in the March 15 hunger strike "drives a jeep, but the biggest thing that others drive is a vendor's cart." One artist described the protesters in Ramallah as "mostly middle-class kids with parents in NGOs or the PA." Al'aa, a young leftist activist from Birzeit University, thought that the movement was dominated by "liberal graduates from Western universities" who know how to speak to the (Western, English-medium) media and was critical of those who called themselves "anarchists," which he thought was a label not known to many local youth. Ahmed pointed out that young Palestinians who have studied abroad (as he had) sometimes become politicized in the context of activism elsewhere, and return to Palestine wanting to be engaged in local organizing. Undoubtedly, these youth bring vocabularies, experiences, and notions of political organizing from diverse contexts and are also influenced by histories of organizing within Palestine. Yet when I spoke to young people and students who had participated in the protests themselves, they described the protesters as coming from "mixed political, economic, and social backgrounds" and including "academics, students, and workers."

It did seem that the the hunger strike in the Manara, at least, largely involved middle-class youth, both male and female, and some of the activists were indeed involved with the youth NGO, Sharek, based in Ramallah. However, it was also apparent that youth from a range of class backgrounds who were not educated abroad and are not involved with any NGOs were, and are, involved in the larger youth movement that has continued to evolve. As Hathem pointed out, there is indeed sometimes a social schism between those from elite and middle- or lower-middle class backgrounds—the question of leadership by elite youth is a thorny one, as it is in all contexts. Some youth who became disillusioned with the "elite students" in the Manara protests formed a group, Free Palestinian Youth, that apparently consisted of middle-class youth who began going to protests in villages. Another group, called Intifada, emerged out of engagement in protests against the settlements and the Wall in Bil'in, Ni'lin, and Nabi Saleh with local, popular resistance committees. Independent, leftist youth (some formerly from PFLP and the People's Party), formed *al-Harak al-Shababi al-Mustaqil*.

For Feryal, while not all of the activists in the youth movement come from a "privileged class," a meaningful portion do and she also observed thoughtfully that by virtue of their participation, "those who are not privileged become part of a privileged group" through their association with the youth movement. Activism can bestow social recognition and give young people opportunities for leadership which they may have been previously denied or entry into a political space in which they had been—and may continue to be—marginalized. Ahmed acknowledged that activists in the youth movement were seen as "exclusive" and "elite" and that there was over time growing "fragmentation" among the groups in Ramallah. He commented that activists in the June 5 group came from "mixed class backgrounds" and also belonged to "clean organizations"—that is, not tied to problematic political agendas or funding sources—such as Addameer (the Prisoner Support and Human Rights Association in Ramallah) and the Popular Center for the Arts in al-Bireh.

There was also much discussion among youth of the larger question of what it meant to be an "activist" in the post-Oslo moment. Duaa commented, as did Hafez, that there is a youth subculture in places such as Haifa or Ramallah which for some involves going to a protest during the day and then going out to a bar at night for drinks, an activist culture both were uneasy with given its connotations of bourgeois decadence and also the compartmentalization of politics as its own "lifestyle." Furthermore, the politics of social life and youth culture is a complex issue, as I noted earlier in the discussion of Ramallah's public culture and bars, given the policing of social behavior of young women and men. Furthermore, the question of what it means to critically engage with consumption and—on a deeper level—pleasure and construct sociality in the midst of struggle is one that many activists, young and old, grapple with not just in Palestine, but the world over. There is also a regional and geographic dimension to the issue of activism as privilege, for as Duaa observed, in major urban areas such as Haifa or cities which are on the global media's map, "People get arrested and get out the next day, but people in al-Khalil [Hebron] get arrested and no one hears about it. We don't need to create events [that is, arrests] for the Western media, they are happening all the time." So, the uneven attention given to protest in the centers and peripheries of Palestine is an important one intertwined with the international context and mediascape in which the Palestinian struggle unfolds.

However, it is interesting to note another aspect of class privilege related to the youth movement which underscores how it has been produced in the post-Oslo context and in relation to the growth of a Palestinian elite. I think that, perhaps contrary to conventional understandings, this is a movement that has emerged not just because of youth unemployment and financial insecurity. There are, in fact, youth who have thrown themselves into political organizing who are doing so not because they are financially struggling or, proverbially, have nothing to lose, but because they are politically committed. Hathem thoughtfully observed that, in some cases, "other people can't related to the Ramallah bourgeoisie who are doing the same thing but with different motivations" for engagement in political protest. Fajr commented that the youth movement is also peopled with "many young, capable people who decided to stay here, maybe as side effects of this prosperity" of the Oslo era and belong to middle-class or affluent families, but are also "disaffected." Prosperity or financial stability, in other words, does not always have to be a disincentive for political protest but perhaps can in certain moments provide a secure base for taking political risks for youth who are acutely aware that they are "still colonized" in the virtual state, in Boikutt's words.

Clearly, there is a complex politics of gender, sexuality, class, colonialism, and capitalism that frames the issues of class location and gendered participation of young male and female activists—issues that are just the tip of the iceberg, in a sense, in a movement that is diverse, de-centralized, and constantly evolving. In some cases the protests involved youth who were not elite but middle-class or struggling with the impact of inflation and underemployment. Hathem and Marwan, who became friends after meeting at the March 15 protests and camping out together in the Manara, claimed that they helped spark the protest against the price hikes in Ramallah in September 2012, because they did not earn much income and were hard hit by the increase in the cost of cigarettes. As I sat with them at a coffee shop in downtown Ramallah—decorated with posters featuring political icons such as Ghassan Kanafani, Steve Biko, and Mahatma Gandhi—Marwan laughingly threw a pack of cigarettes on the table and commented that they had had to resort to buying the cheapest brand available. Marwan recalled, "So I posted something on Facebook and said, 'This sucks! I'm upset I can't even afford to buy my cigarettes. I'm going down to the Manara to protest the high prices.'" The call hit a nerve and to Marwan's own surprise, several youth responded to the spontaneous comment and appeared in the Manara.

One of the young protesters who was present at the rally in the Manara, a journalist who joined us at the café that day, was clearly not part of the English-speaking elite. He said that he brought a poster that declared, "When I go to the market, all I can do is hit 'Like'!" using a Facebook idiom to refer to his struggle to buy daily necessities. The protest, under the umbrella of Youth Against High Prices, spiraled into a series of larger demonstrations by youth that erupted across the West Bank in early fall 2012, some of them quite militant, where young people came out into the streets from Jenin to al-Khalil. According to Marwan, "In the recent protests, the youth who are burning tires in the streets are distancing themselves from the centralism of party politics." The protests clearly had taken on a life of their own and there were even calls for the resignation of the then Prime Minister, Salman Fayyad (leading some to believe that they were also linked to internal politics in the Fateh regime and a conflict between Abbas and Fayyad). But the demonstrations had also clearly struck a chord among those who were frustrated with the status quo and difficult economic situation and resentful of those who had benefited from the post-Oslo arrangement, culminating in a strike by taxi drivers against the increase in gas prices and also by teachers in the West Bank, with many stores and businesses closing in solidarity.

The rapper Rami GB wrote a song, *"Fesh Eshe"* ("There's Nothing"), that could be an anthem for these protests, even though it was written in 2009. The song, which layers male vocals over Arabic rap and melodic beats, speaks to the ongoing economic insecurities and challenges facing youth in the West Bank in the post-Oslo period.

> Our pockets are empty, there's nothing in them,
> Our stomachs are empty, there's nothing in them,
> Our heads are empty, there's nothing in them,
> Our eyes are empty, there's nothing in them.
>
> There's no money, no work, I'm sitting at home
> without work,
> My friend, my life is depressing, I'm paying taxes
> For something I don't own. I'm not Arab, I'm not
> Muslim,
> My situation is hard to explain. With tough times,
> We find ourselves with nothing . . . Pity us,
> They cheat us. We forget the past and
> we worship the present.

The song is a commentary on the economic struggles of youth, but also what Rami GB perceives as the intellectual and political bankruptcy in this new moment. It critiques the lack of a clear political vision in jil Oslo, alluding to the identity crisis among a new generation of Palestinian youth who have come of age in a globalized culture, disconnected from their past. It speaks to many of the issues which the youth movement has attempted to challenge and hip hop artists have highlighted through musical protest.

Opposing Oslo

The youth protests against high prices and economic insecurity, and against the divisive politics of dominant parties, grew into a larger critique of the very framework of politics in the post-Oslo moment and the current phase of colonization in Palestine. In February 2012, Yasmine recalls that young activists organized a demonstration against possible PA negotiations with Israel outside the presidential compound in Ramallah, raising slogans from early Fateh and PLO leaders such as, "Normalization is synonymous with treason." On 11 September 2012, a demonstration was organized in Ramallah by the youth coalition, Palestinians for Dignity, as frustration mounted with increasing unemployment and rising prices in the West Bank. The rally was called to protest recent price hikes and increases in taxation that were the result of the Paris Protocol of 1994, an annex to the Oslo Accords according to which Palestinian economic policies and the prices of goods are tied to the Israeli economy and Israel has control over Palestinian trade and customs revenues.[20] About two hundred people gathered in the center of Ramallah and began marching toward the Manara, chanting slogans such as, "Down with the Paris agreements! No more sitting with the Israelis!" and "You with the fat SUV's, where did you get the money to pay for it?"

The crowd consisted of a diverse group of people, young as well as older, including some families with children in strollers, but the vast majority were youth, both male and female. As the protesters marched through the downtown commercial area, they filled the street and swelled to about three hundred by the time they reached the Manara. A young man climbed astride the pillar in the center of the stone lions that guard the Manara and held aloft a Palestinian flag, while the demonstrators vigorously chanted, "We don't sit down to negotiate with criminals, we fight them!" and "It's not about gas prices, it's about dignity!" Some youth distributed photocopied fliers of a political statement and periodically threw them into the air, the sheets fluttering down above the crowd. The statement (in Arabic) read:

> We stand today for dignity, not just against hunger,
> but also against repression. You president, your
> politics is standing in the way of ending the
> occupation. It has become clear to everyone that these
> political, economic, and security agreements, from
> Paris to Oslo, are a burden on our people and are
> hindering our national liberation from Zionist
> occupation . . . How could our land be liberated if you
> make the people slaves?
> We say, stop the current course of politics and
> economics. . . . In plain Arabic, what connects us as a
> people is not the crumbs of your aid, but hope,
> dignity, and freedom.
> Down with the Paris economic protocols!
> Down with the Oslo strategy!
> Long live the just demands of the people!

Young men hoisted above the crowd, sitting on the shoulders of other protesters, yelled slogans through the megaphone such as, "You government of traitors! We want freedom, justice, and dignity!" PA security officers, including plain-clothes agents who were incongruously using old-fashioned and conspicuous walkie-talkies, lined the streets, as journalists photographed the rally. It became apparent that the protesters were actually going to make their way to the president's office, and not end at the Manara as most assumed. There was a slight ripple through the crowd, a mix of excitement and tension, as the protesters marched down Irsal Street toward the Muqata'a. Some of the young protesters yelled defiantly, "*Ya mukhabarat* [intelligence agents], *ya mukhabarat!* You are the dogs of the Shabak [Israeli intelligence]!" At the Muqata'a (the presidential compound), while security and intelligence agents watched the rally, a slew of journalists standing atop a wall on the side photographed and filmed the crowd.

Protest outside Muqata'a, 11 September 2012, Ramallah.

While the rally was devoid of violent clashes or a crackdown by security, it was apparent from the slogans that the young activists were opposing not just the price hikes and economic policies of Fayyad, but were challenging the very framework of Oslo and the repression of the PA. As Fajr observed, "The issue of high prices is a political issue wrapped in an economic cover." The protesters were calling for a radical reformulation of Palestinian national politics that would reject negotiations as a strategy for national liberation, not just the prime minister's neoliberal economic policies enforced at the behest of Israel and the International Monetary Fund. Ahmed later commented that "the recent protests against high prices and inflation would have looked different without the youth movement," underscoring the shift in analysis that had been staged that day that reflected this larger critique of Oslo politics—and signified by the fact that the protest was outside the symbol of the PA's authority, the Muqata'a, and not an Israeli office or prison. As Fajr pointed out, the youth protests that were directly opposing Fateh were also opposing repression in the name of "loyalty" to the party or regime, reflecting: "They use the language of family to shut you up, but now that talk of loyalty has evaporated." Censorship and self-censorship, in the name of loyalty to the nation, family, or party was thus being challenged, even if many young people as well as adults were still cautious. It was apparent that youth understood the political metaphors that had constrained them and were looking for new strategies and a new political language.

Later, after the 11 September rally, Fajr observed that many youth increasingly felt since the March 15 protests that the root of the problem was the "Oslo framework:" "We can't act in our own self-interest. The PA is a puppy dog of Israel. We're being blackmailed on everything from water to gas. We're fed up with negotiations, so we formed Palestinians with Dignity." Fajr alluded to Israeli control of basic resources such as water and gas and the power Israel wields over the PA, the West Bank, and Gaza; that is, Israel has the power to restrict or cut off essential services and supply routes if it wants to punish Palestinians. The concept of dignity (*karamah*) is key to this discourse of resistance to the Oslo paradigm of national politics, a politics associated with compromise, corruption, and the abandonment of collective resistance for a modicum of economic security, and for some, upward mobility and wealth. Baroud writes, "The perks of the Oslo culture have sprouted over the years, creating the Palestinian elite, whose interest and that of the Israeli occupation overlap beyond recognition of where the first starts and the other ends." This view of the complicity of the PA and the elites who have benefited from the material prosperity brought by Oslo was echoed by some activists and artists. For example, when I spoke to Hafez on Nakba Day (15 May) in 2013, as protesters marched in the streets of Ramallah and clashes with the Israeli military took place across the West Bank, he said, "The PA is frankly part of the occupation. It is ridiculous that they arrest people for confronting the occupation! In Bethlehem yesterday the PA military was at the Wall preventing protesters from getting there. They're even willing to shoot Palestinians. In Hebron, they do it all the time, and in Bethlehem, even Ramallah."

This violent repression by the PA, in coordination with the colonial regime, has met with resistance on the ground and from Palestinian hip hop artists armed with a radical critique. For example, Palestinian Street did a song with the rapper Stormtrap, of (the former group) Ramallah Underground, titled, "Get Out, the Oslo Authority," that was deeply critical of the PA.[21] The video, posted online in September 2012, featured images of president Abbas, contrasting him with earlier nationalist and revolutionary political leaders and artists such as Leila Khaled, PFLP leader George Habash, Edward Said, and Mahmoud Darwish. With a relatively simple rhythm and musical beats, the song is played over images dating from the exodus of Palestinian refugees during the Nakba and the first intifada to the signing of the Oslo agreement. The MCs rap:

> The corruption is not just by Abbas, they signed
> agreements to ruin our people
> We call on people to bring down the *sulta* (PA)!
> Keep thought free, and keep Palestine free from the
> water [Jordan River] to the [Mediterranean] sea.
> The problem is not just gas or electricity, the problem
> is corruption and treachery.
> See what traitors our leaders have become . . .
>
> You've changed us now to begging for food, and
> signing agreements
> that are corrupt.
> You play the role of security and intelligence
> gathering. . . .
> I don't want just cheap bread, I want dignity.
> Go down all of you! The game has become clear.
> Take your names and leave!
> We are hungry for freedom, not for bread!

Dignity, in this political critique by young artists and activists—as well as other Palestinians—is not just an individualized notion of self-respect but a recreation of the collective that insists on freedom, and rejects the material benefits of a colonial, neoliberal system understood as pacifying, containing, and suppressing resistance. The name of the youth group, Palestinians for Dignity, as Yasmine observed, stems from the vision that Palestinians "want dignity in our actions. It was inspired partly by [Palestinian prisoner] Khader Adnan because he was calling for dignity during his hunger strike. But it is also because a return to negotiations is not something dignified for Palestinians." Thus, the slogan "hungry for freedom" evokes not just solidarity with Palestinian prisoners on hunger strike, but also a deeper desire for liberation, not just "cheap bread," as the ultimate form of sustenance.

The fatigue with the limited paradigm for national politics provided by Oslo and enforced by the PA was very evident in my conversations with activists and also artists and youth. Boikutt incisively observed:

> People want resistance, whether it is violent or non-violent, that's what they really want. . . . They don't want someone who does security cooperation with Israel. How can this person represent them? They [the PA] are working more closely with Israelis than with Palestinians! Both these factions, Fateh and Hamas, are screwed up and have betrayed us, they're after more power and controlling this small piece of land that is already controlled. That's why Palestinians have given up, and corruption has become a normal thing, selling out has become a normal thing. Everyone's afraid of giving someone else something because they think it will hurt them.

The breakdown of collective support, an ethic that many recall characterized Palestinian life during the intifadas, is associated with an increasingly individualized ethos of upward mobility, pursuit of material goods, and flagrant consumption. This is particularly on display in Ramallah where gigantic billboards advertise consumer goods, fast food, and new housing enclaves while SUVs race past Mercedes Benz cars in the increasingly congested streets. For Hafez, who is a graphic artist, this flourishing capitalist ethos underlies a "neoliberal lifestyle imposed by government and economic policies" and a discourse valorizing individual freedom that permeates the increasingly institutionalized artistic culture as well. In the new arts scene involving Palestinian artists who are professionally trained or part of the global art circuit and market, according to Hafez, "art is about being free to say whatever you want even if no one understands it." Hisham attempts to challenge this socially detached and "neoliberal understanding of creativity" by making his political posters available online for anyone who wants to download them or use them at protests. He said that he refuses to "exhibit in a white cube" and that his exhibition space is the political demonstration. Hafez's critique underscores that there is an artistic as well as political practice that is needed to challenge the dramatic and unsettling recreation of Palestinian life and selfhood under Oslo. While these artists and activists do not necessarily have all the answers, they are clearly struggling with important questions and contradictions in cultural, economic, and political spheres.

The BDS Movement

One of the key features of the youth movement, and one that links the cultural and the political strands of its focus, is the commitment to Boycott, Divestment, and Sanctions (BDS), which was officially called for by Palestinian civil society in 2005 (www.bdsmovement.net). The BDS movement has provided an important framework for the politics of jil Oslo, and it has also integrated the arena of popular culture (though cultural boycott campaigns) with the economic (through consumer boycotts) and political (through sanctions and the core principle of opposition to Israeli occupation, apartheid, and colonization). Its three key principles—which represent a basic political consensus among Palestinians as well as rights enshrined in international law—include the right to return of refugees, equality for Palestinians living in Israel, and an end to occupation and colonization of Palestinian lands and to the apartheid wall.

For some youth of this generation, such as Fajr, it was the BDS movement that crystallized what a unifying and effective strategy of resistance should be in the post-Oslo movement—because it provided a framework to counter the normalization that marked this political phase and at the same time, called for engagement in grassroots politics beyond the structures of political parties and factions. Boikutt, whose own MC name highlights his commitment to this political strategy, said, "I think boycott is one of the best ways of resistance in this day and age." Commenting on economic boycotts, he added, "Economic power is what runs colonialism, it is the goal of colonialism and also the fuel. So if you can hit a percentage of its power, it's better than just sitting around." For Fajr, it was the BDS movement that "made a difference" and that offered a clear "direction" that would unify Palestinians in a fractured political landscape.

One young female activist, who is involved with the cultural and academic boycott campaign, commented, "The existing groups are fighting with one another . . . they're not doing any of the work. The organizing is by the youth, by the BDS movement, and by civil society." This young woman went on to discuss a campaign organized by students at an-Najah University in Nablus to boycott Tapuzina, an Israeli fruit juice very common in the West Bank. The young activists went to stores in Nablus and also to the university cafeteria and asked them to stop selling Israeli products. The campaign was successful, including at an-Najah, and I saw boycott fliers posted in other towns and at grocery stores in Ramallah throughout 2011, injecting politics into public space and otherwise mundane spaces of consumption. Feryal, who was involved with this campaign while she was at an-Najah recalled that it was an "uphill battle" as the university administration was opposed to removing the Israeli product, and commented, "The whole culture of boycott is very important. The concept of economic boycott has been there since the first intifada; people on the street know what *muqata'ah* (boycott) is, and people have a consensus that this is something we should do." For her, the larger issue was "reviving the culture of boycott and of resistance through boycott," so while BDS is not a substitute for a national movement, as some argue, it is indeed a means to revive the culture of collective mobilization.

Other youth also spoke about their involvement in cultural boycott campaigns and actions to resist normalization with Israel in the cultural arena, which has been a key premise of the Oslo political paradigm. There has been a proliferation of Israeli-Palestinian arts projects that focus on dialogue, peace, and reconciliation but that generally evacuate a political critique of the structural contexts of occupation and colonization.[22] Hisham, of Palestinian Street, said that since Oslo, "There were projects to show that we are friends, that we get along. There were so many dialogue workshops." Mohammed added that the group has been asked to perform for music projects that told them not to "do anything political." Feryal said that academic and cultural boycott campaigns that oppose collaboration with and funding and sponsorship by Israeli institutions were more complicated and difficult to undertake, even in Palestine. She observed thoughtfully that while the "notion of normalization (*tatbee*) exists in the media and public discussions," she felt that there was a lack of clarity about "why we need this or how to make it happen." I found that some Palestinian (visual and literary) artists I spoke to from Ramallah were themselves ambivalent about the cultural boycott—some because they still believed in "dialogue" even if it involved Israeli institutional support and others because they were concerned about being restricted in their access to funding and exhibition venues in an already restricted context—making it a contested issue on the ground; however, the rappers I spoke to seemed to be less equivocal. Clearly, Palestinian hip hop artists are generally underground rappers who have relatively little access to institutional support, at least compared to visual artists or writers, but the framework of normalization is one that frames cultural production in Palestine on multiple levels. In fact, Mohammed's only concern about doing an interview for this research was that I not publish an article in a book that also included a chapter about Israeli rap, in order to present "both sides" of the issue based on the fallacy of neutrality established through depoliticized cultural normalization projects. My conversation with Mohammed brought home to me how deeply aware these rappers were of how they might be used in activities that contradict their own politics and how explicit some were about resisting co-optation. This cautionary request illustrates the self-reflexivity of Palestinian rappers about the politics of representation through popular culture and what is at stake in the global interest in Palestinian hip hop, including in academic research.

This awareness of the risks of normalization in the post-Oslo era was very apparent among other youth as well and there has been increasing public resistance by youth to the project of cultural normalization in the West Bank. Marwan talked about a campaign organized in Ramallah in response to a New Year's Eve event in 2011 that featured Israeli artists and a Druze singer who performs for the IDF, Sharif Durzi, and that was hosted at a local venue charging a hefty price for tickets. In response, a group of youth decided to host an anti-normalization "open space" party in the streets of Ramallah. The event,which was free, was organized by a new youth group consisting of many journalists, Youth who Love the Homeland, and featured the song by Basel Zayed that was shut down by the PA, as mentioned earlier. The young activists also called on the venue to cancel the New Year's Eve event, and their boycott campaign eventually succeeded.[23] Furthermore, '48 Palestinian hip hop artists, such as DAM, have been strong advocates for BDS and for the cultural boycott, even though their own location within Israel means that they are inevitably speaking from a complicated and risky position in relation to boycotting the state—and one which has been deemed illegal for organizations by Israel.[24] In fact, because of the "boycott law" in Israel these campaigns by '48 Palestinians sometimes do not explicitly use the "word 'boycott.'" Despite this, young Palestinian activists from Israel, such as Duaa, have been involved in academic boycott campaigns with other Palestinian students at Haifa University calling for a boycott of collaboration with Israeli universities—a campaign that not many students initially wanted to join, she acknowledged.

Within the last two years, Duaa noted, there has also been a growing call from Palestinians asking Arab artists from other regions not to visit Israel (on

Israeli visas), even if to perform for Palestinian communities, as part of a rejection of normalization, campaigns which elicit a range of views among '48 Palestinians. For Duaa, the central issue was not just the issue of boycott or normalization, but what, in essence, the role of Arab (or other) artists could be if they are in solidarity with Palestinians facing occupation, apartheid, or invisibilization and how Palestinians themselves could engage in political solidarity with other struggles. She said eloquently that cultural "exchange" should not be for the sake of inter-cultural or cross-regional "connection" per se, but must be part of a "revolutionary music culture." Like Feryal, she was interested in the larger "culture of boycott" as a platform for cultural and political resistance through youth culture, a deeper political shift that these campaigns and strategic discourses could animate.

It is in this context, with all its possibilities and risks, that DAM and other rappers have used their global popularity to call for BDS at their performances and support Palestine solidarity campaigns across the world. They also continually participate in BDS campaigns across Palestine; for example, in late September 2012, DAM and other artists performed as part of a Freedom Bus Tour across the West Bank, sponsored by the Freedom Theater in Jenin, in support of cultural resistance and BDS. The tour featured solidarity events with protests against the Wall in different villages and teach-in's at universities as well as virtual dialogues with youth in Gaza (in March 2013, both DAM and Ministry of Dub-Key performed at a concert in a village near Jericho with the Freedom Bus Tour, in solidarity with Palestinian farmers and Bedouins in Area C who have been resisting expulsion by Israel). BDS has thus provided an important cultural tool and popular culture, including hip hop, is a space in which the politics of BDS is increasingly articulated, debated, and enacted in solidarity projects that connect different communities. This new youth culture of boycott that spans '48 Palestine, the West Bank, Gaza, and Jerusalem is interesting because it has highlighted the ways in which it is opening up space for cultural and academic freedom—rather than closing it down, as opponents of BDS often argue—for those whose freedoms are the most at risk due to occupation, siege, enclosure, and apartheid.

BDS is also supported and advocated by many as a tool for non-violent resistance that can be used by international civil society, as it was during the era of South African apartheid, to challenge state violations of international human rights. Artists, such as DAM, publicly support non-violent resistance but it is important to note that they are also critical of the liberal discourse of violence and "co-existence" programs, Jewish-Arab youth dialogues, and "peace" talks that evade political and structural inequalities. One of DAM's songs, "*Inqilab*" ("Revolution") from their album *Dedication*, incisively critiques the depoliticized discourse of "love" and nonviolent resistance as panacea: "This situation reminds me of apartheid and Nelson Mandela/Didn't he say Gandhi flowers [sic] don't always work/So to all the people of love and peace/How can we have co-existence when we don't even exist?/It takes a revolution to find a solution." Saz offers a similar critique of liberal notions of "co-existence" in the film *Saz*, which shows him in an argument about military service with Jewish Israeli youth at a Jewish-Arab youth program in Israel. '48 Palestinian MCs implicitly and explicitly challenge the use of Palestinian youth culture to evade the difficult realities of apartheid-style discrimination and undermine revolutionary movements, suggesting a self-reflexive critique of the politics of culture that is encoded within their music itself. The cultural terrain is thus an important site of both normalization and containment of political discourse, as well as of resistance and subversion.

The NGOization of Culture and Politics

Young artists and activists I spoke to were acutely aware of the ways the cultural arena is a battleground for constructing, repressing, and regulating national identity and the thorny issue of the role of institutions, such as local and international non-governmental organizations (NGOs), as well as foreign donors, in shaping the cultural sphere as well as political arena. The role of foreign NGOs and international donors, especially, is the central issue in an ongoing debate about the expansion of the NGO industry in Palestine in the post-Oslo moment. Adila Laidi-Hanieh, the first director of the Sakakini Cultural Center in Ramallah, traces the emergence in Palestine, and in the arts arena, of what she describes as the "aid machine" which "reified aid recipients according to donors' political priorities, often informed by neo-Orientalist concepts." These transplanted "Western models of cultural management" and donor-driven cultural agendas, she observes, generally avoided "controversial" issues.[25]

Many NGOs in the West Bank are focused on issues of participatory democracy, citizenship, self-empowerment, and governance, all in the context of a "colonized outpost in the postcolonial world" in which these concepts are paradoxical, at best, and, at worst, suspect for those who consider this a form of evasion or containment of resistance struggles.[26] Sari Hanafi and Linda Tabar argue that the transformation of Palestinian NGOs since the early 1990s and their articulation with the international "aid industry" led to a "disembedding of local organizations from linkages within society and their footing in popular movements."[27] The depoliticization of artistic and political movements and "weakening of the collective resistance movement" since Oslo is part of a larger neoliberal rationality that is focused on individual self-empowerment and entrepreneurship, according to Sibille Merz; this produces a "displacement of a political mode of action, in the form of mobilization, by a civic mode of action, promoting new subjectivities," as Hanafi and Tabar observe.[28]

Sakakini Cultural Center, Ramallah ("Free ? Palestine" on the left).

Rema Hammami and others have argued that NGOs have been part of the "retrenchment from a popular constituency that predated Oslo" and of the "ongoing political crisis in Palestinian society," thus playing a key role in the transformation of (what some would call) civil society and, most certainly, the public sphere.[29] While Palestinian NGOs, such as popular committees, have historically played a major role in political life in the absence of a Palestinian state, they have become increasingly professionalized and imbricated with the agendas of the international aid regime—one of which is to "minimize resistance to the peace process" and to the spatial and political fragmentation it has engendered, as Merz suggests.[30] Thus NGOization is viewed as contributing to rather than resisting the de-democratization and fragmentation of Palestinian society, as Penny Johnson and Eileen Kuttab observe.[31] Al'aa said, "Our whole civil society is set up with foreign funding, restricted and unrestricted, direct and indirect," referring to a situation in which some Palestinian programs and even political parties receive foreign funding that comes with restrictions, especially in the post-9/11 era, such as those related to US counterterrorism policies.

After the second intifada, many Palestinians from leftist parties ended up working in the NGO sector, which increasingly focuses on civic education, human rights, and training workshops, and targets "youth" and "women."[32] In Hafez's view, "NGOs that work for youth have destroyed the idea of the collective," in many cases, and promoted a shift to "volunteerism," within a framework of individualism and privatization of social services. Foreign-funded NGOs have thus played a growing role in the political arena, as grassroots groups have been sidelined, but it also means that foreign funding has become a lightning rod in debates about NGOization in Palestine and can be used to tar organizations and campaigns, as was the case during the March 15 youth protests.

Furthermore, as Taraki observes, NGOs have institutionalized cultural programs that "articulate not only new conceptions of 'culture,' but new ideas of the place of art in 'resistance.'"[33] For Hafez, the arts culture in the West Bank, and particularly in Ramallah, is shaped by neoliberal models of individualism that have detached artists from the collective spaces of cultural production through which they were historically linked to broader, popular struggles. Hafez said that such collective artistic spaces still exist, such as Funoun, the dance troupe of the leftist Popular Center for the Arts in al-Bireh, with which he is involved and which performs in villages and towns across the West Bank. However, Hafez was critical of arts institutions in Ramallah that he viewed as shaped by "Fayyadism," the neoliberal policies of institution-building and governance associated with the former prime minister (who previously worked at the World Bank). These policies, focused on individual freedom, consumption, and choice in the context of increasing "economic and political dependence on Israel,"[34] Hafez said succinctly, are "messing up the mess we are in." He argued that many arts programs and schools in Ramallah have produced a generation of contemporary artists who are increasingly connected to the global art market and funding structures and participate in international exhibitions but feel disconnected from the local community, even as they think "that their art represents Palestine." Individualized recognition becomes a conduit to these international circuits of arts production through particular aesthetic approaches or (specific) representations of the nation, that are generally legible mainly for a global audience.

Hip hop has been, in general, less funded and sponsored by institutions than the broad array of arts and cultural programs that have sprung up for Palestinian youth in towns, villages, and camps in the West Bank, as some of the youth I spoke to observed. Hafez noted that the Palestinian rappers he knows are "very critical" in their politics and there have been instances when they have "not been allowed to perform in some venues" in the West Bank. However, as awareness of this cultural movement has grown within and beyond Palestine, a host of entities have turned their attention, and their funds, to sponsoring hip hop groups and workshops—including even a global project of the US State Department—realizing its appeal for youth.[35] The Palestinian Street rappers recalled that after two years of working underground, almost in secret, they tried to get support and one organization, Seeds of Peace, offered to give them funding. However, they refused this sponsorship because the organization's political agenda, largely based on a liberal model of Israeli-Palestinian reconciliation and dialogue, contradicted their own politics. Eventually, the Ibdaa Cultural Center in the Dheisheh Refugee Camp itself supported the group, and they began using its space to practice and make music. Other rappers were also very careful about avoiding what they perceived as co-optation by sponsors whose cultural and political agendas that did not align with their own politics. Maqdsi, for example, said that in his view, "There is a lot of funding [for hip hop] from USAID and NGOs that are fishy, Israeli sources, so we decided to be independent."

There have also been independent hip hop projects initiated by Palestinian artists themselves. For example, the Palestinian music group Sabreen did a hip hop workshop for youth in the West Bank that was initiated by DAM. There have been several programs in refugee camps, such as a hip hop workshop at the Yafa Cultural Center in Balata camp, organized in 2011 with the help of artists from the Royal Court Theater in Denmark, in which Salim said youth wrote their own songs and skits. The Palestinian Street MC's have done workshops with '48 Palestinian MCs, such as DAM and Saz, in Dheisheh camp. The MCs from Dheisheh cannot travel to Jerusalem, due to Israeli restrictions, but they did a workshop for youth from Silwan, a neighborhood in East Jerusalem, who came to meet children in Dheisheh. These programs become a way of connecting youth across geographic borders and bantustans in Palestine, and also of providing spaces for cultural expression. On a deeper level, they also allow for expressions of "fantasy," according to Tina Sherwell, who organizes arts projects in Shu'afat camp. Sherwell remarked that "the young are yearning for that kind of space to be free outside of the home" in the context of restrictions on movement and expression, due to Israel's increasing colonization of physical space as well as increasing social conservatism in everyday life. These arts programs could also be considered, technically, "non-governmental organizations" or linked to NGOs, but it is apparent that they have different agendas and funding structures than those of the dominant "NGO industry."

For '48 Palestinian youth, the landscape is quite different as there are far fewer international NGOs that are interested in working with Palestinian communities in Israel. This is partly a result of the international community's general acceptance of the condition of '48 Palestinians as a "domestic" issue that absents them from political solidarity. This erasure is also partly due to the mythology of Israel discourse as the "only democracy" in the region and general ignorance about the systemic racism faced by Palestinian citizens of Israel. Compared to the West Bank, and Gaza, relatively less global attention is focused on the absence of an internal cultural infrastructure for '48 Palestinian youth who live in underfunded and neglected schools and communities, and in what could be described as internal "camps" or ghettoes in Israel. The Baladna study notes "the underdevelopment of the Arab localities, the lack of infrastructure, the unreadiness of Arab schools to organize after-school programs, the absence of clubs and public organizations and the tight budgets available in the Arab local authorities [municipalities]."[36] Thus, '48 Palestinian youth have little access to youth centers or cultural resources and, according to the Baladna report, spend most of their time on the Internet, as well as shopping, going to malls, and at home with family and relatives.[37] However, Duaa noted that the political sphere of youth activism in '48 Palestine is constricted by Israeli repression but also to some degree by NGOization, which even if relatively limited in the Palestinian community has created a context in which there is not often democratic leadership and "no healthy framework" for political activism. The workshops that DAM and other '48 Palestinian artists have conducted for youth are thus an important example of young people seizing cultural tools to create their own sphere of education and mobilization.

One of the implications, however, of the NGOization of the cultural sphere in Palestine is that imported models of "cultural management" attempt to define, and in some cases reshape, what is defined as "youth culture" and acceptable forms of cultural expression. Basel insightfully observed that there is a gap between independent Palestinian hip hop and the framework of cultural NGOs and institutions, such as "the British Council, the Franco-German Cultural Center, NGOs, the Ministry of Culture, radio stations, and corporations," and their basic definitions of "old versus young." Youth are considered objects of cultural projects focused primarily on absorption into the status quo ("mass culture") and the production of good citizens and subjects of the neoliberal order (proper national culture). But anything associated with hip hop, in this institutionalized framework, is inherently marketed to "young people," according to Basel. Beyond the issue of normalization and "proper" politics for Palestinian youth, there is also the issue of the core definition of what constitutes, and represents, "youth" itself in these contexts of cultural production and management.

Furthermore, there are progressive artists from the United States and Europe who come to Palestine in political solidarity but who are inevitably situated in a performance context in which potentially problematic notions of youth, and youth culture, are reinscribed or in which culturally alien models of performance are used. For instance, more than one person I spoke to cited the example of the progressive British Iraqi hip hop MC Lowkey, who had performed in the West Bank at a concert sponsored by the British Council, but who publicly said that he did not recognize the British flag. Al'aa said Lowkey used the concert as a platform to express a strong critique of US and British imperialism and was able to "use the system to see the situation here" in Palestine, but conjectured that he would probably not be invited again by the British Council. So in some cases, hip hop artists and musicians were able to subvert the framework generated by foreign institutions and NGOs for staging youth culture and acceptable political critique.

In other cases, however, there is a gap between local audiences and cultural programming due to what Taraki and Laidi-Hanieh both describe as a schism between imported and local cultural sensibilities and artistic practices.[38] For example, at a concert cosponsored by the British Council at the Cultural Palace in Ramallah in December 2011, Soweto Kinch, a black, British jazz-hip hop musician, performed songs about emancipation, capitalism, and the hollowness of celebrity culture for a packed audience. Yet, it was very evident that his music did not connect with the youth present, who were busy sending text messages on their cell phones, boisterously chatting with friends, and in one instance humorously yelling, "Allahu-akbar!" This disconnect seemed to be largely because Kinch was rapping in English, but in part it also seemed that the youth present did not relate to the musical idiom and also the format of the concert, which did not fit either with the cultural genres of Arabic pop or folkloric music. Basel, who participated in Kinch's music workshops for Palestinian youth sponsored by the British Council, was also frustrated with the ways in which the institutionalization of music and arts programming is regulated by those who do not understand what is an appropriate format or context in which to stage a performance of genres such as hip hop. In his view, hip hop is constantly relegated to the sphere of "mass culture" and of consumption by "kids," a genre not considered suitable for an adult audience. He pointed out that the music of Ramallah Underground, while it existed, did not fit with these existing cultural categories either and the collective only began getting more invitations to perform after they collaborated with the internationally renowned Kronos Quartet. Ramallah Underground also tried to perform in a range of venues, including community centers and outdoor spaces and even parking lots, to challenge the boundaries of performance and cultural consumption.[39]

On a deeper level, the question that the NGOization and regulation of the cultural sphere raises is that of the reshaping of cultural tastes and youth imaginaries in the context of the shifts in cultural consumption and production in Palestine since the 1990s. This is in the context of what Hanafi and Tabar describe as a "restructuring of knowledge and practice," including in popular and political culture, and "a new process of elite formation underway in the Palestinian NGO sector today" which has led to the emergence of a "globalized Palestinian elite."[40] Barghouthi points out that NGOs have provided a context for youth to work in new kinds of organizations, which operate with different cultural codes drawn from a Westernized global professional or activist culture. NGOs also provide Palestinian youth, who are confined and enclosed in the West Bank, opportunities to travel to international conferences and work with "internationals" (i.e. usually white Americans and Europeans).[41] As Taraki observes, the employment of many college graduates in the NGO sector, in concert with the exposure to "trans-Arab" urban culture, has led to a refashioning of cultural and also artistic sensibilities and to new "types of cultural and social capital."[42] Palestinian hip hop artists also increasingly tour the world and perform at concerts in diverse locations or with various cultural programs. Hip hop projects and performances are thus one site in a much larger cultural field that is continually produced, debated, and contested in relation to questions of globalization, nationalism, and neoliberalism.

Yet, it is interesting that for the most part, critiques of the corruption of "traditional" culture by youth did not address the role of NGOs in introducing new or Western cultural sensibilities. Perhaps this is because many of these young people have themselves either participated or worked in youth programs sponsored by NGOs, and so this has become just another facet of Palestinian life for the young. It could also be because they are all aware that the NGO sector is one of the few in which there are currently employment opportunities in the West Bank, and through an international NGO they may be able to get a well-paying, professional job, especially if they are fluent in English, even if they may be paid less than foreign employees. Seif observes critically that Palestinian youth who work in NGOs today have a "newly acquired affluence and social standing," and have acquired the accouterments and clothing styles of a global professional class, as well as opportunities for "frequent travels abroad to attend conferences and seminars."[43] It could also be that young people themselves desire the kind of cosmopolitan modernity that this cultural and economic sphere represents, even while they may be uneasy about the transformation that it has brought. In other words, there is an ambivalence among youth about the larger cultural and class transformation of cultural imaginaries, as well as material conditions, that cannot just be pinned onto a particular site, such as hip hop.

While more work probably needs to be done to directly investigate what young people think about the impact of foreign or local NGOs on their cultural identities and national imaginaries, existing literature has focused on young people's critiques of the ways in which NGOs are "isolated from the Palestinian street" and absent from grassroots or national movements.[44] It must also be noted that governmental organizations and entities also receive foreign funding, so the reshaping of the political and cultural sphere by donor agendas or international funding is not only through institutions that are, strictly speaking, classified as NGOs. However, while this debate is well established and ongoing in Palestine, it is apparent also that the Palestinian "NGO industrial-complex" is not a monolithic entity, but an assemblage of different kinds of organizations with a range of social actors working within them and sometimes against the grain of dominant agendas. Some of the young activists who participated in the March 15 movement, for example, were involved with Sharek Youth Forum (though they participated as individuals), an NGO based in Ramallah, which is largely staffed by young Palestinians, focused on youth development and political participation as well as advocacy for Palestinian youth. Sharek works with youth across the West Bank and its reports have documented the frustrations of Palestinian youth with the existing political structure and even criticized politicians, including some in the PA, for being indifferent to the political concerns of the younger generation.[45] At the same time, Sharek has been the target of protests by youth who are critical of the funding it receives from USAID, including by activists from al-Herak who protested at one of their youth conferences in Ramallah. Simultaneously, it has also been the target of criticism by Hamas for its mixed-gender programs and events in Gaza. In fact, the first manifesto of the youth collective from Gaza known as Gaza Youth Break Out (GYBO), which denounced the Hamas-Fateh conflict and repression by Hamas as well as the siege and violence inflicted by Israel, also criticized the shutting down of Sharek in Gaza by Hamas and the arrests of youth working with or supporting its programs.[46]

Youth NGOs occupy a complex and contradictory position in the larger cultural and political sphere in the post-Oslo moment and in the evolving youth movement in the West Bank. Wisam Shweiki, who coordinates Sharek's local youth council program in the West Bank to encourage young people's participation in local governance, acknowledged that such programs generate a contradiction in "speaking of democracy while under occupation." Yet he also pointed out that many youth in these local councils were challenging the domination of established parties and have often met with resistance in their villages and towns in trying to create "an independent space for politics," and, in some cases, have even been threatened by those defending the existing political order. Young people are thus acutely aware of the complexity of the political terrain they occupy, including youth who work in the NGO sector in the West Bank, and wrestle with its contradictions and tensions. This was perhaps most dramatically staged at an event hosted by Sharek in their center in al-Tireh on 25 September 2012, where then Prime Minister Salman Fayyad came to talk with a group of youth in a televised discussion, in the wake of the West Bank protests targeting his economic policies. He was confronted with passionate and sometimes angry criticism by the young men and women present, who asked questions such as, "How long will you use the excuse of the occupation to hide corruption?" and "How can we have a state if we have *wasta*?"

The vigorous discussion with youth even included the airing of a protest video featuring images of the recent youth protests in the West Bank against the price hikes and a satirical song critical of Fayyad. The young people present clapped and sang along in front of the squirming prime minister: "Ya Fayyad, watch out, ya Fayyad! We used to be a dignified people, now we are a people who beg." The eruption of youth into this *zajal*-style song vividly enacted a new sphere of confrontation of young people with their political leaders, in institutionalized as well as non-institutionalized spaces, which can be contradictory and complex. The event also illustrated the presence of various forms of music and performance in protest politics and in the struggle over what Palestinian national politics should look like, where youth culture and politics spill over into each other in often unexpected ways.

In the next chapter, I discuss the ways in which young Palestinian activists and artists have challenged repression and surveillance, using political tactics, forms of social media, rap music, and graffiti art. These cultural and political expressions are increasingly part of a public culture of protest against Palestinian as well as Israeli regimes of censorship and securitization.

---

[1] Obviously, there are many political movements in which youth are involved, Islamist politics being one of them, that were not part of the "youth movement" as commonly described and as discussed here, and that focused on various issues. For example, in September 2012, during the peak of protests by Muslims worldwide in response to the Islamophobic American film, "The Innocence of Muslims," stickers and posters were on display in some youth clothing stores in Ramallah, depicting a man unbuttoning a collared shirt to reveal a T-shirt with text in Arabic, and also below in English, saying: "I protest against disrespect our beloved prophet Muhammad" (sic). This Islamist politicization of youth culture was not, however, as visible in street protests in Ramallah and in the political mobilization by youth discussed here.

[2] Abed, "Youth and Students"; Rabi' Abed, "Youth and Students, Part 2: The Whole Story of the Youth Movement," *Zamnpress*, 30 April 2012. www.zamnpress.com, (accessed 30 May 2012).

[3] Steven Salaita, "Corporate American Media Coverage of Arab Revolutions: The Contradictory Messages of Modernity," *Interface: A Journal For and About Social Movements* 4 no. 1 (May 2012): 67-101; Magid Shihade, Cristina Fominaya, and Lawrence Cox, "The Season of Mobilization: The Arab Spring and European Mobilizations," *Interface: A Journal For and About Social Movements* 4 no. 1 (May 2012): 1-16.

[4] Aditya Nigam, "The Arab Upsurge and the "Viral" Revolutions of Our Times," *Interface: A Journal For and About Social Movements* 4 no. 1 (May 2012): 170.

[5] Reem Abou-El-Fadl, "The Road to Jerusalem through Tahrir Square: Anti-Zionism and Palestine in the 2011 Egyptian Revolution," *Journal of Palestine Studies* XLI no. 2 (Winter 2012): 6-26.

[6] Erekat and Seikaly, "Tahrir's Other Sky," 274.

[7] El Zein, Shahadat, 2012; Gana, "Rap and Revolt in the Arab World."

[8] "Hip hop and the Arab Uprisings," *Open Democracy*, 24 February 2012. http://www.opendemocracy.net/ulysses/hip-hop-and-arab-uprisings.

9 See: http://www.youtube.com/watch? feature=player_detailpage&v=w2RxmGriZlU.

10 Arian Fariborz, "Soundtrack of the Revolution: Pop Music as Rebellion and Social Protest," *Art and Thought* 96 no. 21 (2011): 4-7; Soraya Morayef, "We are the Eight Percent": Inside Egypt's Underground Shaabi Music Scene," *Jadaliyya*, 29 May 2012. http://www.jadaliyya.com/pages/index/5738/we-are-the-eight-percent_inside-egypts-underground.

11 See El Zein, Shahadat.

12 "Hip hop and the Arab Uprisings," *Open Democracy*.

13 From ArteEast album compiled by *Shahadat* (El Zein 2012).

14 Alain Badiou, *Metapolitics*, transl. Jason Barker (London: Verso, 2005), 145.

15 Jalal Abukhater, "Concert Interrupted by PA Police over Song Critical of UN Statehood Bid," *Electronic Intifada*, 1 January 2012. http://electronicintifada.net/blogs/jalal-abukhater/concert-interrupted-pa-police-over-song-critical-un-statehood-bid

16 Abed, "Youth and Students, Part 2."

17 Seif, "Youth in the Palestinian National Movement," 20.

18 Excerpts from Antonio Gramsci, *The Antonio Gramsci Reader: Selected Writings 1916-1935*, ed. David Forgacs (New York: New York University Press, 2000), 195-209.

19 Ramzy Baroud, "The Unity Charade and Prisoners' Intifada," *Ma'an News* 18 January 2013. http://maannews.net/eng/ViewDetails.aspx?ID=557063.

20 Similar protests against rising prices and increased taxes were held in end May, 2013 across the West Bank. "Nablus Demonstrators Protest High Cost of Living." *Ma'an News*, 1 June 2013. http://www.maannews.net/eng/ViewDetails.aspx?ID=601100.

21 See: http://postcolonialhubris.blogspot.com/2012/09/stormtrap-palestinian-rap-against-olso.html.

22 See Nasser Al-Taee, "Voices of Peace and the Legacy of Reconciliation: Popular Music, Nationalism and the Quest for Peace in the Middle East," *Popular Music* 21 no. 1 (2002): 41-61.

23 Abed, "Youth and Students, Part 2."

[24] On support for BDS from within Israel, see: http://boycottisrael.info/.

[25] Adila Laidi-Hanieh, "Arts, Identity, and Survival: Building Cultural Practices in Palestine," *Journal of Palestine Studies* 35 no. 4 (2006): 30, 39.

[26] Rema Hammami, "Palestinian NGOs Since Oslo: From NGO Politics to Social Movements." *Middle East Report* 214 (2000): 16-19, 27, 48; Laidi-Hanieh, Arts, Identity, and Survival," 34.

[27] Sari Hanafi and Linda Tabar, "The Intifada and the Aid Industry: The Impact of the New Liberal Agenda on the Palestinian NGOs," *Comparative Studies of South Asia, Africa, and the Middle East* 23 nos. 1-2 (2003): 207.

[28] Sibille Merz, "Reforming Resistance: Neoliberalism and the Co-optation of Civil Society Organizations in Palestine," in *Managing Democracy, Managing Dissent*, ed. Rebecca Fisher (London: Corporate Watch, 2013), 137; Sari Hanafi and Linda Tabar, *The Emergence of a Palestinian Globalized Elite* (Jerusalem: Institute for Jerusalem Studies/Muwatin, 2005), 30.

[29] Hammami, "Palestinian NGOs Since Oslo," 16.

[30] Merz, "Reforming Resistance," 140.

[31] Penny Johnson and Eileen Kuttab,"Where Have all the Women (and Men) Gone? Reflections on Gender and the Second Palestinian Intifada." *Feminist Review* 69 (2001): 40; see Hanafi and Tabar, "The Intifada and the Aid Industry."

[32] Merz, "Reforming Resistance," 140-1, 143; Seif, "Youth in the Palestinian National Movement."

[33] Taraki, "Urban Modernity on the Periphery," 77.

[34] Merz, "Reforming Resistance," 142.

[35] Hisham Aidi, "Leveraging Hip Hop in U.S. Foreign Policy." *Al Jazeera*, 7 November 2011. http://www.aljazeera.com/indepth/opinion/2011/10/2011103091018299924.html.

[36] Baladna, "Palestinian Youth Affairs in Israel," 47.

[37] Ibid., 49.

[38] Taraki, "Urban Modernity on the Periphery"; Laidi-Hanieh, "Arts, Identity, and Survival."

[39] Ray Smith, "Music as Resistance Inside the Ramallah Bubble," *Electronic Intifada*, 16 May 2011. http://electronicintifada.net/content/music-resistance-inside-ramallah-bubble/9967.

[40] Hanafi and Tabar, "The Intifada and the Aid Industry,", 209.

[41] Barghouthi, *Local to Global*, 24.

[42] Taraki, "Urban Modernity on the Periphery," 73, 74.

[43] Seif, "Youth in the Palestinian National Movement."

[44] For example, Barghouthi, *Local to Global*, 22-23

[45] For example: Sharek Youth Forum, *Palestinian Youth and Political Parties: From a Pioneering Engagement with Political Parties to Fear and Disappointment* (Al-Tireh: Sharek, 2010).

[46] See: http://gazaybo.wordpress.com/manifesto-0-1/.

Chapter 4

Surveillance, Counter-Surveillance, and Feminist Questions

Repression, Surveillance, and Counter-Surveillance

The youth protests in the West Bank that publicly challenged the national paradigm for politics, and economic, military, and political cooperation between the Palestinian Authority and Israel, came on the heels of demonstrations in Ramallah against the visit in early July 2012 of Shaul Mofaz, who was the Israeli defense minister during the Gaza war, to meet with President Mahmoud Abbas. This three-day protest was striking because it was a public expression of the battle being waged by youth to take their critique of the PA and the Oslo paradigm of politics to the streets, challenging both Israeli state violence and the violence and collusion of the local "authority." This demonstration was a key moment not just for public opposition by activists from jil Oslo to the PA's political paradigm and its military and security cooperation with Israel, but it was also a battle over internal political repression in the West Bank. Yasmine describes this protest as a "turning point" for the youth movement and public protests, a moment when activists did not simply go to the Manara, where protests are permitted by the PA police, "shout, and go home." This demonstration also highlighted core issues of repression and surveillance, internal and external, faced by young activists and addressed by artists, including through graffiti art in public space.

Young activists turned out in the streets of Ramallah on 30 June 2012 to protest Mofaz's visit and march to the "taboo area in front of the Muqata'a," as Fajr described it, where protests had generally not been allowed. The PA police physically assaulted the young protesters and arrested a few, yet two hundred protesters came out again in the streets the next day, and videos of the violent crackdown in the Manara were posted on YouTube.[1] The protesters waved Palestinian flags and carried signs stating, "No to negotiations with the murderer

Mofaz;" they called on Abbas not just to cancel the meeting but to also end all negotiations with Israel and its complicity with the occupying regime.[2] In fact, Yasmine recalls that the security forces attacked the protesters on the first day at the moment when they began chanting, "What happened? What happened? Mofaz has become one of us!" and "Down with the military regime!"

Although the protesters were prevented from reaching the Muqata'a, by the time of the third demonstration, according to Fajr, there were one thousand people in the streets. Only a handful of plainclothes security officers were deployed to monitor the rally, and the organizers declared: "With this march we emphasize that the people are the source of authority, and that we reject the use of violence against the Palestinian people by any and all hands."[3] Yasmine said that the last day of protests was "like Tahrir Square," with throngs of people coming out onto the street after they heard the news of the crackdown on the protesters, including assaults on females. "That was a shocking thing to everyone —how did we reach the point of Palestinians beating up other Palestinians, including raising the baton against women?" she says. The incident forced the PA to call for an independent investigation into the police brutality and the security forces were actually found guilty, which some activists thought was a notable step in exposing and challenging domestic repression. Abbas made a statement in support of "freedom of expression" and "the right to protest in a manner consistent with the law." Equally, if not more, significant, the meeting with Mofaz was cancelled, without any official explanation. Ahmed pointed out later that this "brutal" crackdown on the young protesters "destroyed the image of the PA police" that their public relations campaign had been trying to enhance, with large billboards in the city depicting smiling police helping schoolchildren and farmers.

Furthermore, as Fajr and Yasmine observed, one of the larger implications of the protests by youth in front of the Muqata'a and the mobilization since January 2012 was that they "managed to break the fear barrier" about public protests and direct popular challenge to the PA. In addition, Ahmed recalled that during the solidarity demonstrations with the Arab revolutions in 2011, young activists "managed to win the right to protest" by obtaining the support of the staff union at Birzeit University, for this alliance "shielded" them from the violent repression they had been experiencing at the hands of PA security forces in Ramallah. So the youth movement was pushing the boundaries of public protest and also building coalitions as part of a range of strategies and tactics to reclaim the public square, literally, at a moment when many young people—as well as adults —were skeptical, fatigued, hopeless, and fearful of public political engagement.

It is also likely that the strong media presence in Ramallah safeguarded the protesters to some extent, for as Fajr commented,

> We are privileged to be in Ramallah, which is the
> center. We're in a bubble, but we get the media
> attention. The PA has been doing horrible stuff in
> Jenin, in Khalil, they torture people, including torture
> to death, and there are no court trials. The
> demonstrations in Hebron and Nablus did not get any
> media coverage, and there are a lot of atrocities that
> have been going on at the hands of the PA for a long
> time in the West Bank. In Ramallah, we make things
> difficult for the PA by embarrassing them in the
> public sphere and they are getting nervous.

Fajr suggests that these young activists are using the fact that they are in a media bubble to engage in radical protests that, as they are well aware, are buffered from the more violent forms of repression experienced by protesters elsewhere (including arrests of Palestinian journalists who publish reports critical of the PA).[4] In effect, I would argue they are trying to turn the "bubble" against itself and strategically use the media to burst its pretensions to normalcy and normalization in the post-Oslo moment. Other young activists, such as those involved in the Freedom Riders campaign in fall 2011 who boarded segregated Israeli buses connecting the settlements in the West Bank in order to protest racial segregation and apartheid policies, and who were arrested by Israel, also used this protest strategy to galvanize global media attention. The Freedom Riders campaign deliberately used the language of the US civil rights movement and anti-racism to make an impact in the US media. While some young activists I spoke to criticized its focus on a Western audience, it is clear that the campaign successfully used the notion of desegregation and tactics of civil disobedience to make an impact on audience for whom this political framework would be legible.[5]

Activists in the youth movement also tried to be strategic in their organizing so as to counter local repression by the PA. Yasmine commented that the movement did not have designated leaders in order to be democratic and also because, "for security reasons, we didn't want one person to be singled out." After the PA investigation into the repression of the protests against Mofaz's visit, she said that some youth worried that the police might file a case against them, using allegations of drug use or immoral behavior to arrest them, an example of the ways in which the regulation of social behavior and youth culture becomes, literally, a form of discipline and punishment. But young activists also tried to directly confront and expose policing and surveillance of political protest. A tactic used to challenge surveillance and domestic repression by youth at protests, where there are undercover security agents, is to shout slogans such as, "Don't think he's a photographer, he's a *mukhabarat*! We know him."[6] This tactic of "outing" security agents posing as journalists directly confronts the embodied, personal, and intimate intrusions of surveillance in the streets.

Some young activists, such as Ahmed, pointed to the class aspects of the crackdown on protests and thought that middle-class or elite youth were generally shielded from the most brutal repression, not just those in Ramallah. Others commented on the gendered politics of the confrontations with the Palestinian and also Israeli security apparatus. For example, one young man affiliated with a left faction who had been imprisoned by Israel, commented that male members of PFLP have a very high rate of arrest, and are subjected to multiple arrests by Israel so they are often in and out of prison. Many young men from the PFLP were violently attacked in the spring 2011 protests and also arrested by Israel, which apparently "crippled" their youth movement. This activist noted that since women were "less likely to be arrested, they are at the forefront" of public demonstrations, suggesting that traditional notions of gender can be deployed as a tactical shield from the police, a complex issue that I discuss in the following chapter. Yet, it is apparent that PA security forces have indeed physically and verbally assaulted women at protests. Among young women activists I spoke to, there is an insistence that they "can take care of themselves" and do not need male activists to "protect" the women, as Yasmine remarked. There are various ways that young activists try to deploy class, gender, or geographic location as strategic or tactical responses to counter repression. These experiments in political strategy are part of a struggle that is being waged not just against Israeli occupation and colonization but also now against those who are seen as having abandoned national resistance and colluding with the colonizing regime.

I want to emphasize that surveillance by the Israeli regime is a major issue in the everyday lives of Palestinian youth, activists or not, as they navigate checkpoints and borders. They are constantly aware of the state of permanent surveillance in which they live, in the West Bank, Jerusalem, and within Israel. Ilan Pappe describes Israel as a "*mukhabarat* (secret service) state" for the logics of surveillance and securitization are key to militarized states; as John Collins argues, the Israeli settler colonial regime views the indigenous population as a constant security threat to be surveilled and contained, if not eliminated.[7] There is already excellent work on the ways in which the Israeli "architecture of surveillance and colonial rule creates not only a sense of prison, of living in multiple unending traps, but also forges a necropolitical situation with an economy of life and death," as argued by Shalhoub-Kevorkian.[8] Her research in Jerusalem examines the experiences of Palestinian youth living "under the constant surveillance of Jewish settlers" and with "closed circuit television cameras" and "hidden and invisible devices used by the state's security guards."[9] But Shalhoub-Kevorkian also argues that the "panoptic framework of the occupier" co-exists with "counter-technologies of resistance," such as the use of Internet or mobile and smart phones by youth for sharing photos or videos of Israeli military violence or settler attacks; for sending alerts about roadblocks or curfews; and for connecting with friends, relatives, and larger publics in a situation of "spatial confinement."[10] Similarly, in Ramallah, students at Birzeit University created a website, On the Ground in Ramallah, to provide eyewitness accounts of life under Israeli military occupation as early as 1996, and the use of websites, blogs, Twitter, and Facebook as forms of cyber-resistance has expanded rapidly.[11] While this research does not overstate the possibilities of "e-resistance" in the face of Israel's sophisticated security and surveillance apparatus, it suggests that these technologies are re-ordering political and social life, including for Palestinian youth.[12] There are also, of course, a range of other media that are used by Palestinian youth for documentation, journalism, and subversion of their confinement, such as photography, radio, and film.[13] Youth are developing a repertoire of diverse strategies and tactics and experimenting with new languages and forms of politics in the face of domestic and Israeli repression—as young artists are doing in experimenting with new idioms in the cultural sphere.

Visual Culture and Surveillance

In some cases, youth in the West Bank have tried to assert their right to freedom of political expression and to a democratization of Palestinian politics by visually challenging repression and surveillance for example, by producing graffiti and public art. There has been an explosion of graffiti art by youth on the walls of Ramallah and other towns in the West Bank, in conjunction with the youth movement and also with the emergence of hip hop subculture, with slogans and art splashed across public space. Hamza Abu Ayash, for example, has done graffiti art in many public places in Ramallah and al-Tireh featuring a signature white figure in various poses, such as holding a giant key symbolizing the right of return of refugees (see figure 1). One large painting on a wall along the main street in the center of Ramallah depicts the white figure carrying the map of historic Palestine strapped to his back, with the words "The Land is Hungry." Abu Ayash has also done a series of graffiti paintings in Ramallah and al-Tireh challenging police brutality and repression by the PA (figure 5). In fact, the walls next to Beit Aneeseh and on the street between al-Tireh and Ramallah have become informal galleries for an ever shifting array of political graffiti and stencil art.

Figure 1: "Here I was born, my crime is being Palestinian," graffiti, al-Tireh.

There has also been a flourishing of graffiti art by youth in solidarity with the prisoners' hunger strike, including ubiquitous stenciled images of Palestinian prisoner Khader Adnan with a lock on his mouth at various places around Ramallah (figure 2), that was produced by Hafez Omar. Some young activists painted slogans such as "Hungry 4 Freedom," in solidarity with the Palestinian prisoners' hunger strike, and "#Un-Occupy" or "Occupy Wall Street, Not Palestine," that were ubiquitous during the spring of 2011. Another artist, Majd Abdel Habib, plastered large black and white posters with photography and text on the walls of Ramallah. One of them features a photograph of a *Time* magazine cover of Yasser Arafat, as a "fedayeen leader," with the title, "Arab Commandos: Defiant New Force in the Middle East," and the other is of an older woman in a traditional Palestinian dress with the pointed question: "What's happening to us?" with some letters resembling the shape of a key, symbolizing the right of return (see figure 3). These images on the streets are variously critical, cynical, and exhorting of collective solidarity and political action in the post-Oslo context of political fatigue and frustration.

Figure 2: Khader Adnan, Ramallah.

"Revolution" (*thawra*) is also a popular slogan, and stencils of the word have popped up next to stenciled images of the faces of young men who were killed by Israel, for example, along the road between Ramallah and Birzeit. Feminist graffiti and stencils have also cropped up around Ramallah. Feryal revealed to me during our conversation that it was she who did the stencils of Handala (figure 4), holding the female symbol with a clenched fist inside, in the center of Ramallah and near Beit Aneeseh with the credo, "Freedom is a daily practice," inspired by a stencil from Beirut that a friend shared with her. There are various political movements and issues that are reflected on Palestinian walls, and that are engaged in conversations between political and youth movements spanning the region and the globe, from Wall Street to Beirut. Murid, a film producer from Ramallah who was involved in a documentary film about Palestinian graffiti in

161

the West Bank, said that graffiti is "an effective way to tell a story, especially when people have things to say and they are not always heard."

Figure 3: Poster, al-Tireh.

Graffiti has, of course, been a pervasive form of collective memory and public expression since the first intifada.[14] But Murid noted that there has been an "explosion of political graffiti," beginning in 2011 during the youth movement and prisoners' strike. He also observed that there has been an evolution from graffiti that was a display of political slogans or announcement of strikes to a more visually interesting form of public art, that involves painting, and that is also part of hip hop's visual idiom. Hafez recalled that as a young boy, he did graffiti during the night so that he would not be caught by Israeli soldiers, and commented that during the first and second intifadas, graffiti was mainly used for political communiqués and "walls were our mass communication" medium. He observed that those announcements in the street were not signed by individuals, but by parties or groups, and that graffiti art has also taken an individualized turn as it has become an "artistic practice in the street." So the nature of graffiti art today reflects larger shifts in politics and cultural production in the post-Oslo moment. Yet there seems to be some continuity between these different phases of street art as well, for as Murid commented, earlier communiqués on walls were also used to "connect the people," and while contemporary graffiti art by youth is generally not associated with political parties, it is often in support of political campaigns or aimed at creating public awareness about specific issues. In fact, much as political communiqués were criminalized by Israel and had to be anonymously splashed on walls before the era of Palestinian mass media, issues that are difficult to raise or are not discussed on Palestinian TV are now being painted or stenciled on the walls of Ramallah and other towns.

Figure 4: "Freedom is a daily practice/We are the revolution."

Murid pointed out that many of the youth who are producing graffiti are visual artists who want to display their work for the public—and are using walls and public spaces that are free and accessible—and in some cases also work with young activists or are part of the youth movement themselves. In addition, some graffiti artists work anonymously—apparently there are young women as well as men who do graffiti, such as an underground group of women I heard about who do political stencils around Jerusalem where they are under direct Israeli surveillance. It appears that street art provides an outlet for those who otherwise may be somewhat hesitant about public political activity, due to real political risk. It also provides a canvas to anonymously engage in political debate, as in the wry question ("where?") scrawled in the image of the wall, above, in response to the artist's statement, "The intifada is continuous" (figure 5). In many cases, the form and medium of graffiti art is determined by access to materials, for spray cans and professional art materials are expensive and so stenciling and posters are cheaper for many youth. There have also been graffiti workshops and collaborative projects between Palestinian youth and foreign artists. For example, a Danish graffiti artist has collaborated with local youth from Ramallah, Hebron, and Bethlehem, who had not met one another before, to develop new work together that is visible in the streets of Ramallah.

Figure 5: "No to repression" (on right) and "The intifada is continuous" (on left, under map of historic Palestine, with comment added underneath: "Where?!!").

A debate that cropped up in my conversations about graffiti art was about painting on the Wall, which is generally by foreigners. Some Palestinian graffiti artists and youth I spoke to argued that this was a form of normalization of an apartheid structure, and that doing graffiti protesting Israel on the side of the Wall visible to Palestinians was counter-productive. In addition, the well-known graffiti on the Wall encircling Bethlehem by internationally renowned artist Banksy, whose work is now distributed on postcards and T-shirts and even sold in a Banksy café in Bethlehem, was viewed by young artists from the Bethlehem area as yet another form of commodifying resistance. One of them had done graffiti on the walls of Dheisheh camp, where he lives, but was critical of the way the Wall was being absorbed into the Palestinian landscape by Palestinians themselves. The Wall is now used as a billboard for commercial advertisements or, as I noticed in Abu Dis near Al Quds University, for proclamations of love of the form: "Ahmed [heart] Leila."

Graffiti art is heterogeneous in form and motivation and persists as a successful technology of resistance and of politicization of the public sphere, especially by those who are marginalized or repressed by institutionalized politics. It is thus increasingly popular among those in jil Oslo who are attempting to use streets and walls for intervening in political discourse, but this visual resistance also elicits its own repression. While there has not been much crackdown on graffiti art in Ramallah, where Murid said "there's more freedom, as there are more foreigners and more eyes watching," in other locations in the West Bank, this was not always the case. Abu Ayash apparently obtained an official permit to do street art in Tulkarem, and yet the work was immediately painted over by Palestinian authorities (as often happens in US cities where graffiti is considered vandalism). Graffiti, it must be noted, is not illegal in the West Bank unless it is on private property, but apparently in most cases there has been little conflict even with property owners who have allowed their walls to become public canvases.

Marwan, who was involved in an experimental film that featured graffiti art projects in villages in which he himself participated, said that he has also tried to use Internet tools such as Facebook to counter surveillance. For example, he posted an article on Facebook about the repression of protests in the West Bank and uploaded a photo in which he circled police officers hitting demonstrators, asking "Do you know this person?" He said that people responded and identified the officers or provided other information and Marwan then used this to submit reports to the Palestinian Independent Commission on Human Rights. Visual culture, including new media and graffiti, is a tool to defend those whose own visibility makes them vulnerable to technologies of surveillance from policing, incarceration, and violence. Surveillance by the surveilled can be a form of sousveillance, or surveillance from below.

Other tactics involving digital media, such as hacktivism, have been used by Palestinians to target Israel since the second intifada.[15] In April 2013, a coalition of hacktivist groups, including Gaza Hackers Team as well as Algerian, Syrian, and Moroccan hackers, shut down the websites of the Israeli Defense Ministry and several other state agencies, as part of a second massive cyber-attack waged by the group Anonymous, dubbed #OpIsrael (v. 2.0).[16] This cyber-campaign, which began during Israel's assault on Gaza in November 2012, was quickly celebrated with T-shirts, emblazoned with the iconic Anonymous logo superimposed on a map of historic Palestine, that appeared at hip hop concerts and on the streets of Ramallah. Facebook has also been used by young activists in important campaigns such as during the prisoners' hunger strike. Yasmine recalled a faceless Facebook profile of a Palestinian prisoner, created by Hafez in solidarity with Khader Adnan, that was apparently very successful and adopted by thousands of people from all over the world.

Several young activists, however, approached social media with caution because they were aware it was also a tool of surveillance used against them, internally as well as externally. Ahmed said pointedly that with the reliance of activists on electronic media, "Facebook became like a Kalashnikov" because "anything on Facebook was monitored." As I mentioned earlier, the rappers from Dheisheh who posted a song critical of the statehood bid on social media were censored by the PA, which is evidently monitoring YouTube and Facebook as is the Israeli security apparatus. Al'aa said, "Here, if you organize a revolution on Facebook, they can find you." Furthermore, Dalia Othman, who is a young scholar of new media from Ramallah, said that while many Palestinian activists use social media, such as Facebook or Twitter, in her view they are not using it as effectively as they could or really understanding who their target audience is. For example, she thought that when "Palestinians used Twitter to trend on Palestinian prisoners, it worked well for the Western and mainstream media," publicizing Khader Adnan's hunger strike, but she thought that "it wasn't putting pressure on Israel."

However, Dalia thought that Facebook could be used more effectively by activists in organizing grassroots campaigns, given that there is a large population that uses Facebook in Palestine. It is apparent that Palestinian youth in the West Bank are indeed avid users of social media. One survey of youth cultural practices in 2012 found that almost 30 percent of young people between fifteen and twenty-nine years of age use the Internet for over three hours a day, and 40.8 percent said that they use the Internet for Facebook more than anything else.[17] However, there was also an awareness among young activists that there is a large segment of youth that is not always on Facebook or is perhaps wary about overly relying on social media. Facebook is also used to tar youth activists with the brush of suspicion, and in some cases it has become a code word for armchair or laptop activists and for a certain class profile, perhaps. Maqdsi said of the March 15 protests by youth: "After the protest started, people didn't think it was real because it was called for on Facebook." Hathem pointed out that estimates of attendance at events publicized on Facebook are sometimes exaggerated, given people click "join" but then do not show up (or "click-tivism," as Dalia noted). Al'aa felt strongly that electronic media was not a substitute for an organizing structure or a clear or revolutionary ideological framework, commenting succinctly, "Facebook is not Lenin!" In Hathem's view, face-to-face conversations and word of mouth publicity is sometimes better for political organizing, including the age-old practice of going to the coffee shop, where young men in particular regularly hang out, and talking to people in person. Echoing this critique, Yasmine said she realized during the youth movement, "The Arab Spring lexicon of 'youth,' and Twitter and Facebook is all bullshit! Going on the street was important to talk to people face to face; that's what happened in the first intifada."

At the same time, many youth and artists pointed out that electronic media allowed them to connect with other Palestinian youth who they otherwise may not be able to meet, especially across the colonial borders that have fragmented and divided Palestine, and also to connect with audiences beyond Palestine. The MCs from Palestinian Street commented that they engage with fans with Myspace and also with Palestinian youth in Israel via Facebook. Given that underground rap, as in Palestine, is largely disseminated via the Internet, it is a crucial space for auditory and social exchange and for building a youth subculture. Maqdsi said he takes seriously the "public space" of the Internet for interacting with fans and for discussion with various publics. Ramallah Underground, in fact, was first created as a website that provided the name of the collective that later became Tashweesh. Basel noted that the group had been "active online" since its inception, and before blogs and Twitter became pervasive digital tools for popular culture and activism.

Young activists and artists in Gaza also face political repression and censorship, which I do not discuss here since I did not do research in Gaza. But it is worth noting the ways in which youth face repression under the Hamas regime, as in the example from the March 15 protests in Gaza City cited earlier and also in the experiences of hip hop artists, who face both social and political repression. For example, Khaled, a rapper who is part of a Gazan collective called Palestinian Unit, wrote a song in 2011 that a local music studio refused to record "because it was directly against the government," and he was forced to "put in more metaphors . . . get out of the corner of Hamas to be more general."[18] Khaled said he preferred the direct, confrontational style of underground rap, but due to censorship he uses a more subtle approach: "A lot of times, we let the music speak, not only words." Palestinian Unit went on to produce a song, in collaboration with rappers from Denmark, that began with a defiant verse which could speak to both internal as well as Israeli repression, the corruption of Palestinian leaders as well as colonial theft: "We are not scared /We don't feel fear /We know what is going on /We know you steal /Hip hop is our way to deal."[19] So, political repression also intervenes in the music itself and reshapes aesthetic and lyrical styles but rap has also provided a lyrical form of sonic resistance.

Palestinian youth are using a variety of media and technologies, from the visual to the electronic, to challenge surveillance and repression, to engage in counter surveillance or sousveillance, and to "break the fear barrier" that has dampened public protest. This generation is also drawing on various elements of youth culture and hip hop, not just music, and a range of political strategies to offer a more radical critique of "normal" politics in the post-Oslo moment.

'48 Palestinian Campus Movements

Surveillance and repression are key issues for Palestinian youth in Israel, and for Palestinian students in Israeli universities, issues which are worth addressing separately because they are specific to the political culture in which '48 Palestinian youth are engaged in activism. Resisting surveillance and repression are also crucial fronts of the youth movement and political mobilization by young Palestinians in Israel, as evident in campaigns such as Academic Watch, a project of the Arab Culture Association's Ar-Rased Project that works with youth in "monitoring discrimination, racism and political oppression exercised against Palestinian Arab university students in colleges." What is important to note about the work of this youth activist project is that it links the surveillance and repression of Palestinian students and Palestinian protests on Israeli campuses to the militarization of Israeli educational institutions, revealing the deep links between "Israeli academia and the state's security and occupation systems."[20] Palestinian students from Israeli campuses are given legal training by the Ar-Rased Project and monitor incidents on their campuses, producing reports and publicizing this information on Facebook. The political framework of this network of '48 Palestinian youth activists is somewhat distinct from youth mobilization against repression in the West Bank because it is focused specifically on confronting Israeli state power and challenging racism and militarization in their lives as Palestinians in Israel. These terms—racism and militarization—are specific to the '48 Palestinian context and link this activism more directly to similar student movements in the United States that oppose the complicity of the US academy with the military-prison-industrial complex—in addition to the collusion between the US and its key ally, Israel, in global regimes of surveillance and warfare. In this sense, the logics of militarization, securitization, and racism link these different sites of imperial power and settler-colonial pasts and presents.[21]

Surveillance on Israeli campuses is used by both Zionist student groups and by university security to target Palestinian students and activists. Just by way of a few examples, at Tel Aviv University, the security unit has asked lecturers to "spy on their students who participate in protests and demonstrations," that is, in campus demonstrations critical of the Israeli state.[22] At Hebrew University in Jerusalem, the Zionist youth group, Im Tirtzu, published photos on Facebook of Palestinian students who participate in protests, such as a demonstration in solidarity with the Palestinian prisoners' hunger strike, with racist slurs and inciting comments such as, "Death to Arabs," "They should be burnt," and "This is the Hebrew University, not the Arab University."[23] After Palestinian students at Haifa University held silent vigils in solidarity with Gaza during the Israeli attack in November 2012, posts on social media called for penalization of the students and targeted a female student activist, asking Jewish students to report personal information about her and "to deal with her in a way that is commonly used with Arabs."[24] These racist attacks were in the context of the Haifa University administration and Students' Union calling the Palestinian protest of Israel's war on Gaza a "provocation" and the banning of all public campus activities—except for those in support of the Israeli military. These instances of campus repression of Palestinian student activism are just a few among many prohibiting Palestinian cultural festivals, documentary film screenings, and talks by Palestinian political leaders on Israeli campuses about issues such as Palestinian prisoners, anti-racism, and feminism.

Surveillance and repression of Palestinian students' political as well as cultural activities are linked to the larger project of Israel's erasure of Palestinian national identity and histories as well as to the militarization of the security state which views Palestinians as internal security threats and suspect citizens.[25] Israeli universities collaborate with the police and state security to censor, discipline, and expel Palestinian students so the campus is a battleground for Palestinian youth, and one where the stakes are high.[26] Right-wing groups have impunity in targeting and physically assaulting student protesters, for example, during campus activities commemorating the Nakba where Zionist activists have called the Nakba a "lie," destroyed signs, and assaulted Palestinian students who have then been arrested by the police.[27] In Safed Academic College, Palestinian youth —who constitute the majority of the student population—have been brutally attacked by religious Jews who have stoned student dormitories and called on landlords not to rent to Palestinian students, yet the college administration and police have not been able to protect them. The Safed Student Union even declared that students who were not discharged soldiers could not run for the presidency, and given that nearly all Palestinians do not serve in the Israeli military, this "bureaucratic" racism excludes Palestinians. It also highlights the centrality of service in, and loyalty to, the Israeli military and how that works to exclude Palestinians from campus politics.

For Duaa, who was a student at Haifa University and later at Hebrew University, militarization is a core issue for Palestinians in Israel and yet, she observed, it is not as well documented as discrimination against Palestinian students in entry to dormitories or admission to particular departments. This is why the Academic Watch project, in which Duaa is involved, is significant as it directly addresses the ways the militarized state and racial violence affects Palestinians within, not just those under direct occupation. While Duaa observed that it was important for student activism to be "based on our daily experience" and "not repeat the same slogans," in her view the problem was that there was not as much information about the militarization of campuses even though "there is a soldier in the middle of campus." This is a reference to Israeli campuses such as Haifa University which has a contract with the Israeli army and provides special programs for military intelligence, and where soldiers walk around campus in uniform, "brandishing their weapons."[28] Less visible in public, perhaps, are the military and Shin Bet (security) personnel who serve on the administrative boards of Israeli universities.[29]

The militarization of Israeli academia, and society, is embedded in racist regimes of violence and exclusion and it is apparent that Israeli universities are nationalizing institutions who are deeply tied to the Zionist state project on a number of levels, from curriculum to student activities. Duaa said astutely, "The aim of Israeli universities is to make Israelis better Israelis. If you do military service, if you talk better Hebrew, if you don't go to protests or don't challenge Zionism, you get more points, and you are a better student." The violence and surveillance of the Israeli military occupation in the territories conquered in 1967 are thus the other face of the violence and surveillance targeting Palestinians within the 1948 borders. For Duaa, in this context, there is a need for a clearer "Palestinian discourse" that gets to the "root of the issue" of the experiences of '48 Palestinians. She argued that protests that focus solely on discrimination and equality remain confined to the framework provided by the university and do not oppose the university as itself a "colonial institution," that uses the same claims to liberal democratic inclusion as the Israeli state. While Duaa made an argument for the strategic use of Israeli law, and the role of legal advocacy groups that challenge university policies, in her view, the problem was not with these strategies per se but a situation in which the "student movement is not leading" the wider challenge. But it is also apparent that the struggle to define resistance "from within" is an ongoing struggle for Palestinians in Israel that has persisted across generations. As Ahmad Sa'adi notes, the "considerable political involvement of Palestinian students" in Israel has not made them a "significant political force," partly due to state suppression and limits on their political freedom and means of resistance, given that '48 Palestinians are not internationally recognized as a colonized or occupied population with the right to resistance and self-determination. Sa'adi observes, as have others, that these "Palestinians are denied the two main options of radical change: the ballot box and the armed struggle," given the "Jewish nature of the state" which privileges Jewish citizens and political bodies and the elision of Palestinians in Israel from the Oslo framework.[30]

It is in this context, as well, that cultural resistance has always been a significant arena for '48 Palestinians, and that the collaboration and organizing linking artists and activists across Israeli borders is an important political act. As Maisa observed, "Now, there's way more resistance in the arts," citing the example of the hunger strike in Haifa in solidarity with Palestinian prisoners which included performances by young artists, such as Wala Esbeit from Ministry of Dub-Key. As I was concluding this research in 2013, young Palestinian (internal) refugees whose families had been expelled from the village of Ikrit in 1948 were occupying the remaining buildings in the village, where they had been camping for several months since summer 2012. They were hosting visits by young musicians, including Esbeit whose family is from Ikrit and Ramzi Suleiman whose family is from al-Bireh, as well as visits by activists and diplomatic delegations. This is part of a larger political project of symbolic "return" of '48 Palestinian youth to ancestral or destroyed villages, involving educational programs and visits by youth from other parts of Palestine as well. This movement focuses on the "core issue" of the Nakba and not just on the question of inclusion or representation within the state. While the Ikrit camp did not (for the first several months) receive as much as attention as the hunger strike in the Manara, it is a significant act of political protest by youth that foregrounds the framework of settler colonial dispossession and the ways in which the Oslo generation of Palestinians in Israel is exposing and challenging the core, settler and racial, logics of the Israeli state.

Feminist and Queer Politics

Surveillance and repression in various sites in Palestine, by Palestinian as well as Israeli regimes, are processes that are intimately bound up with a politics of gender and sexuality. As mentioned in chapter two, there are ongoing struggles over the politicization and gendering of public space that include contestations over youth culture and hip hop and the surveillance of gendered bodies and behavior. So questions of feminism are threaded throughout the discussions of youth movement and youth culture in this book, but I want to highlight here the important and complex ways that a feminist politics is part of movements and campaigns by youth, including those focused on surveillance and counter-surveillance. It was interesting to note the areas in which questions of gender and feminism surfaced among young Palestinian activists and the ways they are, or are not, articulated in discussions of political protests. On one level, there was the issue of the representation by, and participation of, women in political organizing and demonstrations. On another level, there was the deeper question of whether young activists were addressing issues of gender or sexuality as sites for political activism or critique and articulating this with national politics.

In discussions of protest culture with young activists, it was apparent that the representation and "inclusion" of women was a concern, for young women as well as men. For example, Duaa mentioned that although in recent protests in Haifa, such as during the prisoners' strike, "many Palestinian females are taking the lead," in other events, she observed that women are not at the forefront and the person "who shouts slogans is usually male" and also straight. She noted that this was also the case in the larger, Palestinian national movement in Israel, where women facilitate panels or talks or sing songs at events, but "they're not in the front;" with the exception, of course, of nationally and internationally renowned female political leaders such as Haneen Zoabi. In 2012, Duaa and a group of students from Hebrew University formed a Palestinian feminist group, Thoori (the female imperative, "revolt"), whose full name is "Revolution Against All Authorities." One of their events was with the queer activist, Haneen Maikey, from the Palestinian queer group, Al Qaws, and was titled "Queer in Arabic." Duaa said that the event was attended by many students, who were asked to define what "queer" meant to them, and that although some who attended said that queer issues were not a part of Palestinian culture, the event was not shut down. She also pointed out that gay Palestinian youth are becoming somewhat more visible at protests, acknowledging that inclusion of queers and queer issues is a difficult topic: "We are eighteen or twenty years old, so these issues are not clear." This is, of course, the case in youth activism in general, not just in Palestine.

Indeed, it is apparent that as in most contexts, questions of sexuality are complex and charged for young activists and doubly so in a colonial context where the Zionist narrative views the indigenous population as inherently culturally regressive, and essentially patriarchal and homophobic, inscribing a historical Orientalist narrative about Arab and Muslim societies. Israel's deliberate production of a (homonationalist) narrative of Israeli society as essentially liberal and tolerant in contrast to Palestinian homophobia evades the racism and violence of the settler colonial regime—what has been called "pinkwashing" and critiqued by scholars such as Jasbir Puar.[31] However, in recent years, Israeli homonationalism has been challenged by the emergence of young queer Palestinian activists from the West Bank and Jerusalem who founded groups such as Al Qaws and Palestinian Queers for Boycott, Divestment, and Sanctions (PQBDS).[32] In addition to their commitment to Palestinian national liberation and BDS, framing queer struggles as indivisible from anti-colonial and anti-racist politics, these queer Palestinian activists are also engaging in a cultural politics that creates spaces for a discussion for queer Palestinian sexualities and for queer youth across Palestine. For example, in May 2013 Al Qaws launched a youth music project, "*Ghanni A'an Taa'rif*" ("Singing Sexuality"), which included a website and concert in Haifa, as well as graffiti in Jaffa, Haifa, and other cities.[33] Youth culture is thus an important arena where the boundaries of feminist and queer politics are being challenged and pushed.

As Feryal observed, what is so striking about groups such as PQBDS is that they focus on homophobia and patriarchy as well as colonialism, occupation, and apartheid: "PQBDS sees the intersectionality of sexual, gender, and national rights." For her, politics meant challenging the "concept of authority" on many levels—the authority of the PA, the occupation, patriarchy, and also heterosexism —echoing the name of the young feminist group Thoori. While Feryal thought that "radical feminists" in Palestine see the "intersectionality of struggles," in her view, "the women's movement" was not open to addressing sexuality so it was important to have spaces such as PQBDS or Al Qaws where there can be "discussions of sexuality and sexism out loud."

The young women I spoke to seemed to concur, in fact, that they did not think there was an effective Palestinian "women's movement" or a truly feminist movement in the West Bank. Feryal said bluntly, "The women's movement of the past has died, it does not exist." Dalia, echoing this bleak view, said that there was "nothing inspiring right now" in terms of feminist activism or organizing, but added, "most women activists are feminists and their action is a form of feminism, trying to break taboos." This view suggested a rethinking of what feminist activism might mean, beyond "women's issues," for as Feryal astutely observed, "It's more about being out there. We are being the women's movement." Feryal went on to point that the NGOization of political movements, including the "women's movement," has made many in her generation—the Oslo generation—deeply skeptical of that form of politics. As Johnson and Kuttab observe, the "mass activism that marked the women's movement experience in the intifada has largely been replaced by an NGO model of lobbying, advocacy" and workshops, and political fragmentation in the wake of Oslo has also debilitated the women's movement—as it has the Palestinian left in general.[34] In addition, there is the complexity of having to struggle for women's rights in a context of a basic "lack of national and citizens' rights" for Palestinians in general.[35] Feryal pointed out that this has not precluded young Palestinian women from being "active" and rethinking their own political participation, even if this is not the "majority" of young women but still a "meaningful portion."

Yasmine, who was part of the March 15 movement and later Palestinians for Dignity, said that young women were "definitely involved in organizing and also leading" protests and that the latter group was sensitive to issues of gender, including in the writing of their political statements. This was part of a larger self-awareness that she described about gender and also class in the discourse and public face of the movement—who spoke for the group and in what language (colloquial or formal Arabic) statements were written—and what she saw as an attentiveness to democratizing political involvement. One of the interesting questions about women's political "participation" that surfaced in my conversations with these young activists I noticed was how to define political participation, from a feminist perspective. For Feryal, the question could not be reduced to one of simply "inclusion," and she was critical of what she saw as a shift to a tokenization of young women in demonstrations and images of protests. In many rallies that I attended in Ramallah organized by young activists that while the women who were present were generally fewer in number than men, they were often the ones vigorously waving flags or chanting slogans with a bullhorn. In Feryal's view, young women were sometimes "pushed to the front" of protests or photos were circulated on Facebook of "women climbing onto a tank" because some of these groups were "apologetic about sexism." The issue, for her, was not necessarily that women would have otherwise not climbed onto the Israeli tank, but that there was a desire to manufacture an "image of what resistance should look like." The implication of her astute critique was that there needed to be a genuine engagement of these groups with feminist politics, not simply the production of images for a global public and representation of female bodies enacting public or heroic resistance. This was not just restricted to the youth movement, in her view, but also to representations of the first and second intifadas and romanticized images of Palestinian women "fighting soldiers" that are circulated and consumed as a placeholder, in a sense, for feminism.

"Freedom is a daily practice," Ramallah.

It is important to read the production of these images of protest in the context of the ongoing manipulation of the gender question and pinkwashing by Israel, and the Western mainstream media, so the "romanticized" image of young women activists is used to "send a larger message in a politically and culturally charged space," according to Feryal. But she went on to contrast this with what she felt was an "inspiring" shift among young women who are currently in college, including some from an-Najah University in Nablus, and who are not only going to demonstrations and fighting with Israeli soldiers but also having conversations "about political participation, the PA, Oslo" and are "comfortable with their sexuality in a different way." It in this context that it is interesting to ponder the stenciled figure of the (ambiguously) female face, above, wearing a hijab with the slogan, "Freedom is a Daily Practice," which is on the Wall next to Beit Aneeseh in Ramallah—alluding to a more radical notion of emancipation.

Feryal recalled her own struggles while in college of "'coming out' as a woman who objects to the status quo," which for her included the "heteronormative structure, the Fateh-dominated university, and Obama being the 'hero' of the world!" Many young female activists are not affiliated with political parties, but they are deeply engaged with politics, according to Feryal: "These young women's participation is not just about 'politics,' but about the politics of being a woman in Palestine. There is a deep link between the participation of women in public space and the politics of being a woman in Palestine; no line can be drawn between where one begins and the other ends." This notion of thinking of the concept of public space as indivisibly feminist suggests that it is not just an issue of inserting women into the public sphere. In Feryal's conceptualization, public space is always already constituted as an issue of "being a woman in Palestine." So, "politics" resides not in the sphere of a formally politicized public sphere cordoned off from the "private" but in the everyday experiences of being a feminist and thinking about gender and sexuality in relation to the politics of the occupation or Oslo—a deeply feminist approach.

This critique emerges from a daily reality in which public space is indeed a fraught issue for young women in the West Bank, as is the participation of female activists in public protests. I had countless conversations with women (of various ages) about the growing problem of men on the street verbally harassing and in some cases physically molesting women in Ramallah, particularly those who did not wear hijab or looked "foreign." Some attributed this to the daily influx of men from villages and more conservative areas to Ramallah and also to the anonymity of public space in the city, not to mention the rapid shift in public culture. Dalia also observed that women in protests sometimes encounter verbal harassment from men on the street or even from police, and that the police would sometimes accuse women of being "the Beit Aneeseh type." A young male activist who was involved in the youth movement said that the hunger strikers in the Manara had been called "drug takers" and "prostitutes" by some who maligned them from Fateh. Yasmine also pointed out that harassment in the streets was less of a problem for female activists in Ramallah than in more conservative areas such as al-Khalil (Hebron), where young women who had participated in protests against the settlements have reportedly been sexually harassed. All of these issues co-exist with the ongoing experience of sexual harassment of Palestinian women by Israeli soldiers at checkpoints and sexual abuse and rape of Palestinian women in Israeli jails, so that young women (and men) are navigating a difficult territory between multiple forms of gendered/sexual policing and violence.

Dalia, who was involved with the 2011 protests in Ramallah, was actually involved in founding a project focused on sexual harassment, called Street Watch, in October 2011. The project was founded after a large group showed up in response to a Facebook posting for a meeting in Ramallah to address sexual harassment. A hotline was set up to report incidents of sexual harassment and Dalia created an online map where incidents could be reported via Facebook or mobile phones, but apparently, the Ramallah police refused to let the project continue. In a paradoxical response that illuminates the deeper tensions about the regulation of female behavior and national authenticity, the police officers were reportedly concerned that documentation of sexual harassment might damage the "reputation of Ramallah" as a place of loose and improper behavior or a "whorehouse," according to Dalia. So, in effect, the same logic that underlies acts of sexual harassment targeting presumably "loose" women was used to shut down organized opposition to sexual harassment that would, paradoxically, create the image of a "loose" city. As discussed in chapter two, it is not just the nation that must be guarded as authentic by defending the sexual and thus cultural purity of women, but also the city—and in this case, a city that represents the contested modernity of the nation and the emergent state.

The moral policing of social behavior and the PA's policing and crackdown on youth protests converge in contradictory moments where resistance is viewed as outside the bounds of "proper" national politics or proper cultural norms. The label of the "Beit Aneeseh" type is wielded as a social baton against youth and activists not just to besmirch reputations but to repress youth cultures that have been politicized in new and sometimes unexpected ways. The feminist politics emerging in these sites goes beyond a focus on sexual harassment, narrowly defined, to contestations over the right to public space, the right to the city, and the right to protest. "Being the women's movement" or feminist movement, as Feryal and others suggested, and being attentive to the production and policing of gender and sexuality on multiple levels, illuminates the radical concept of revolting against all forms of authority, as invoked by the group Thoori. This politics of "freedom as a daily practice" arises at the intersections of struggles against PA repression and normalization, occupation and surveillance, patriarchy and heterosexism, sexual harassment and gendered tokenism, and US imperialism and Obama's foreign policies.

---

[1] See: http://www.youtube.com/watch?v=Tvg76s1ShgM&feature=youtu.be.

[2] "Palestinians Stage Protests in the West Bank.," *Al Jazeera*, 3 July 2012. http://www.aljazeera.com/news/middleeast/2012/07/201273214025301804.html.

[3] Ibid.

[4] For a recent example, see: "Rights Group Blast PA Journalist Arrest," *Ma'an News*, 4 June 2013. http://www.maannews.net/eng/ViewDetails.aspx?ID=601909

[5] Jillian Kestler D'Amours, "Israel Arrests Freedom Riders Challenging Apartheid Road System," *Electronic Intifada*, 15 November 2011. http://electronicintifada.net/content/israel-arrests-freedom-riders-challenging-apartheid-road-system/10595

[6] Abed, "Youth and Students, Part 2."

[7] Ilan Pappe, *The Forgotten Palestinians: A History of the Palestinians in Israel* (Yale University Press, 2011); John Collins, *Global Palestine* (London: Hurst and Company, 2011).

[8] Shalhoub-Kevorkian, "Trapped," 12.

[9] Ibid., 12, 13.

[10] Shalhoub-Kevorkian, "E-Resistance," 56, 57.

[11] Makram Khoury-Machool, "Cyber Resistance: Palestinian Youth and Emerging Internet Culture," in *Being Young and Muslim: New Cultural Politics in the Global South and North*, ed. Linda Herrera and Asef Bayat (New York: Oxford University Press, 2010), 114-115.

[12] Shalhoub-Kevorkian, "E-Resistance," 56.

[13] See Julie M. Norman, "Creative Activism: Youth Media in Palestine," *Middle East Journal of Culture and Communication* 2 (2009): 251-274.

[14] Julie Peteet, "The Graffiti of the Intifada," *The Muslim World*, LXXXIV, no 1-2 (1994): 155-167.

[15] Khoury-Machool, "Cyber Resistance," 118.

[16] "Anonymous Launches Massive Cyber Assault Against Israel." *Russian Times*, 6 April 2013. http://rt.com/news/opisrael-anonymous-final-warning-448/.

[17] Yahya Hijazi, *Cultural Practices of the Palestinian Youth* (Bethlehem: Diyar Consortium, 2012), 44-45.

[18] "Wrapping the Rap in Gaza," *Rapolitics*, 30 March 2013. http://www.rapolitics.org/wrapping-the-rap-in-gaza/.

[19] "Politics, Raptivism, and Palestinian Unit," *Rapolitics*, 10 May 2013. http://www.rapolitics.org/politics-raptivism-palestinian-unit/.

[20] Academic Watch, "Annual Summary Report 2011-2012" (Nazareth: Arab Culture Assocation: Ar-Rased Project and the Youth Empowerment Project, November 2012).

[21] Collins, *Global Palestine*.

[22] Academic Watch, "Annual Summary Report 2011-2012," 25.

[23] Ibid., 17-18.

[24] Academic Watch, "Oppression in the Shadow of War" (Nazareth: Arab Culture Assocation: Ar-Rased Project and the Youth Empowerment Project, 2013), 8.

[25] Ahmad H. Sa'adi, "Minority Resistance to State Control: Toward a Re-Analysis of Palestinian Political Activity in Israel," *Social Identities* 2 no. 3 (October 1996): 395-413 (e-version); Shihade, Not Just a Soccer Game.

[26] Academic Watch, "Annual Summary Report 2011-2012," 19-20.

[27] Allison Deger, "Im Tirtzu Protests 'Nakba Bullshit' at Tel Aviv University," *Mondoweiss*, 14 May 2013. http://mondoweiss.net/2013/05/protests-bullshit-university.html; 27 Academic Watch, "Annual Summary Report 2011-2012," 28.

[28] Academic Watch, "Annual Summary Report 2011-2012," 5.

[29] Ibid., 5.

[30] Sa'adi, "Minority Resistance to State Control"; see also Shihade, *Not Just a Soccer Game*.

[31] Jasbir Puar, *Terrorist Assemblages: Homonationalism in Queer Times* (Durham, NC: Duke University Press, 2007); Ibid., "Israel's Gay Propaganda War." *The Guardian*, 1 July 2010 http://www.guardian.co.uk/commentisfree/2010/jul/01/israels-gay-propaganda-war (accessed 30 June 2011).

[32] See: www.pqbds.com.

[33] See: www.ghanni.net.

[34] Johnson and Kuttab, "Where Have all the Women (and Men) Gone?" 25.

[35] Ibid., 28.

Chapter 5

Conclusion

"No-bama"

On 21 March 2013, President Barack Obama arrived in Ramallah to meet with President Mahmoud Abbas after his visit to Israel. Disillusionment and anger were evident in the streets in the days leading up to the US president's visit, and red and blue graffiti sprang up on Ramallah's walls proclaiming "No-bama." Various political parties and groups of all stripes organized demonstrations in the Manara, with slogans and placards protesting Obama's support for Israel and the bargaining over Palestinian territory through negotiations between the PA and Israel, proclaiming "Palestine is not for sale." On 21 March, the day that Obama was scheduled to meet with Abbas at the Muqata'a, I returned to Ramallah in the afternoon to find that the street leading to the presidential compound had been closed off. Unaware that there was a protest just around the corner, I walked through the deserted Irsal Street to find that there was a row of police officers in riot gear blocking the street closer to the shops near the Manara, and then another row of police after that. Assuming the demeanor of a knowing journalist, or oblivious foreigner, I proceeded to walk through two rows of riot police to find that there was a group of about two hundred protesters who had been enclosed behind police lines and prevented from reaching the Muqata'a. Armed security officers were patrolling the entire area from the Muqata'a to the Irsal Street and adjoining neighborhoods, which were under lockdown. The irony that they were trained and armed by Europe and the United States was in full public view.

The protesters, who were mixed in age but predominantly young, were chanting vigorously, "Hey Obama! Out, out!" and holding signs in Arabic and English, such as "Obama is not a fair sponsor for any peace process in the Middle East."[1] As I approached the crowd that had been corralled behind the police, in front of the large Kentucky Fried Chicken outlet on Irsal street, the police tried to push the protesters back and a scuffle broke out. I found myself suddenly behind the line of police, who began shoving me and the protesters as they pushed back. I managed to slip out from the melee but a few other women were also being shoved by the police and were yelling at the PA security. One young man was arrested and hauled off to the side by police as a few journalists watched. I noticed that there were six or seven women police officers who were standing in the innermost line of police facing off against the protesters—as if somehow having female police cracking down on Palestinian women protesters would make this more appropriate. Perhaps "gender sensitive" policing had arrived in the West Bank? It was striking that the PA had earlier been willing to allow

"NO-Bama," Ramallah.

demonstrators to march to the Muqata'a to protest against Abbas's policies, but not to protest against the US president's support for Israel and the occupation.

... But Then, What Else?

I want to conclude here with some reflections by activists and artists who were part of the youth movement and whom I spoke to a year and a half to two years after the protests by youth erupted in the streets, from Ramallah to Haifa. Some of them commented on the ways "the youth movement" had evolved over the course of two or three years and touched on the issues and strategies with which they were now engaged but also the challenges and disappointments they faced. Ahmed said to me, in the fall of 2012, that the "work done since the last two years has shown that they [young activists] have matured," and observed, "Last year, we were concerned that there wasn't a framework to mobilize the masses. Since then we've been marching in the streets and found political approaches to connect to the street, we've been doing teach-ins." Fajr observed that while the youth groups had varying goals and strategies, "We're creating a new discourse, including a rights-based discourse. And we're going back to resistance," observing that the BDS movement has helped build a new framework for this resistance that "connects the internal to the international." A few reiterated that this youth movement had also broken, or at least begun to chip away, at the "fear barrier" that had kept young people from taking to the streets with slogans that would directly challenge the prevailing Palestinian regime. Young protesters, as well as rappers and graffiti artists, have been directly confronting issues of repression and increasingly bringing their critiques of the Oslo paradigm of politics into the public sphere through cultural production and protest cultures. Hip hop and youth culture is a significant new site where this political critique is being expressed, recreated, and contested, in conversation with the youth movement and youth activism. As Bayat and Herrera observe, countercultural music produces a "kind of solidarity building among the youth of the Middle East that conventional politics is unable to accomplish."[2] This is evident in the ways that Palestinian hip hop has emerged and expanded as a subculture and site of political conversation binding together Palestinian and Arab youth across the region and from the diaspora.

Several Palestinian youth who were engaged in these political and cultural movements were self-critical and concerned about the ways in which new cultural and political expressions produced by youth were developing, offering a nuanced critique that neither valorized nor dismissed the potential of youth protest and insurgent cultural expression. Duaa, for example, was particularly concerned that both youth activism and hip hop or "alternative music" should be original in approach, not derivative or standardized, and genuinely rather than superficially oppositional. She thought that "*wataniya*" (patriotic political) music was "not always good artistically" and that while Palestinian hip hop had "good and powerful lyrics," it also had to be musically sophisticated and interesting, remarking about nationalist songs in general: "We want to imagine this is a kind of Palestinian music, but using the same structure for all songs doesn't make it

Palestinian or Arab music. It's not just about the lyrics, but the sounds must be challenging."

Duaa's comments echo the debates about the politics of authenticity and the aesthetic quality of rap music that several artists discussed, as elaborated on in chapter two. She also highlighted an important notion, that political music and progressive artistic production should offer a genuine "challenge" to the status quo and to formulaic notions of political song. She reflected thoughtfully, "It's the same problem in the field of student activism. We use the same frame, and fill it with different content." One of the "frames" of student protests that she was critical of was the recurrent protests that led to arrests of Palestinian student activists in Israel followed by media reports, which she felt was a limited repertoire of political action and not "proactive" enough. Similarly, Fajr commented that young activists in Ramallah were cautious about raising familiar political slogans because "Palestinian politics for the last twenty years has just been slogans."

All these youth seemed to be grappling with how to rethink political resistance "in a deeper way," including in music and cultural production. Duaa was eager to see new, experimental forms of Arabic music that would represent a truly "alternative music" and politics. For her, "revolutionary art" had to be based in a democratic as well as anti-capitalist politics, and have a "connection to the local community." It was this "dialectical analysis" of the relationship between individual artists or groups and larger collectives, as well as between struggles—based on gender, sexuality, class, or nationalism—that she thought needed to be developed and deepened. In fact, Duaa seemed to be concerned that "alternative music" was becoming the basis of a new youth subculture in Haifa, with "alternative evenings" or "alternative parties," because for her this was ultimately based on the "idea of having a 'cool' nationalism or a 'cool' struggle." This touches on an interesting tension, and one which exists in many locations around the world: at what point does popular protest become too "popular," or even trendy, and not sufficiently subversive? Does popularizing political struggle mean that it inevitably becomes commodified? And how can youth walk this line between the popular and the radical when "youthfulness" itself is often seen as inherently embodying "cool?" These are complex questions and the young activists and artists I spoke to seemed very aware of them. It is important here to note that the overt expression of Palestinian national identity through even symbolic registers or items, such as bracelets with the colors of the Palestinian flag or Handala pendants, may not have been possible for '48 Palestinians to flaunt just a decade or so ago—let alone Palestinian flags at protests in the middle of Israeli campuses or cities. However, the point being made by some young activists is that these symbolic expressions are not sufficient for a radical critique of Israeli racism or Zionist colonialism and there needs to be a constant reflection on what is legible, challenging, or transformative.

In Ramallah, on a warm summer afternoon in May 2013 when I met Yasmine, at a café popular with the journalist and NGO crowd, she said thoughtfully about the protests she had been engaged in since 2011: "Demonstrating is good, but then, what else?" Yasmine discussed the "challenge" of trying to understand "what would draw people in [to the youth movement]" and focusing on "more concrete" issues, such as the call for elections to the Palestinian National Council, while not remaining too narrowly focused on single issues. She reflected at length about the ways in which activists in the youth movement struggled with internal issues of "cohesion" as well as "ideological issues," including differences between those who "wanted to reform the PA while others wanted to dissolve the PA." Tensions between reformist and radical critiques are present in every movement; for Yasmine, there was the added question of the "timing" of protests on certain issues, as young activists debated when the larger public would be willing to support a radical critique if they took it to the streets and whether the PA would arrest protesters in ever larger numbers or crack down more violently. She recalled, "We wanted to push the line more, we wanted to defy Oslo itself. But we realized that our numbers were small, and we were nobody." According to Yasmine, the fear of arrests and targeting by the PA security, not to mention by the Israeli military and intelligence, grew for some young activists after the crackdown on the youth movement, and this may have been a factor in the decreasing numbers willing to come out on the streets. She remarked that at the demonstration against Obama's visit, police used the "Egypt tactic" of "sending a random guy to harass women" protesters, provoking a fight among the demonstrators while the police stood "on the sidelines, watching." This was a very troubling moment for many young activists, in her view, for the use of provocateurs seemed to signal that the regime's tactics of repression were reaching a new "limit."

Yasmine spoke about these issues of repression and police violence matter-of-factly while sipping coffee, and it struck me that although the youth movement had been dismissed by many in Ramallah as the naïve actions of "Facebook activists," many of these youth had been thinking deeply about their role in a larger political field mired in skepticism and political paralysis and caught between authoritarian repression and colonial oppression. In the summer of 2012, these young activists organized a demonstration in front of the Muqata'a against political arrests by the PA in the West Bank and Hamas in Gaza, making sure that they did not only challenge Fateh but also political repression by both Palestinian regimes, and draw the public's attention to those arrested for political reasons in Palestinian, not just Israeli, jails. This is a complex and difficult issue, given the large numbers of Palestinians (including children and youth) still imprisoned in Israeli jails, often under conditions of "administrative detention" without due process, and given that Palestinian society at large is, in effect, imprisoned by Israel and so it is the disciplinary technologies of the carceral state that, understandably, receive the greatest attention within Palestine.[3] In fact, when I spoke to Yasmine, a young activist from Ramallah, Hassan Karajah, was still in prison, having been arrested a few months previously by the Israelis at his house, partly for his organizing with the youth movement.

Incarceration is a technology of repression and confinement that governs the lives of not just those Palestinians who are in Israeli prisons. Scholars such as Collins have addressed the ways in which Israeli colonialism "produces forms of material, psychological, and existential confinement that cut across the full spectrum of social life."[4] As Feryal said succinctly, "Israel wants to keep us in a zoo, they feed us in our cages and they want to move from one cage to the other" through the matrix of checkpoints, segregated roads, and the Wall which has expanded and been consolidated since Oslo. This is what Derek Gregory has called a "carceral archipelago," across which enclosed and incarcerated populations are moved around, directly or indirectly, by the settler colonial state through its policies and laws regulating residence, entry, marriage, work, and property ownership.[5] Young Palestinian activists have addressed the ways in which the biopolitics of colonial rule also regulate intimacy and romance, such as through the "Citizenship and Entry to Israel" law that prevents Palestinians from the West Bank and Gaza from living with spouses in Israel—a violation of international human rights law.[6] On 9 March 2013, a campaign involving many young activists, wittily titled "Love in the Time of Apartheid," staged a mock wedding near the Hizma checkpoint in the West Bank, with a bride from Nazareth in Israel and a groom from Abu Dis in the West Bank. The wedding parties that came from both sides of the border were disrupted while singing songs and waving Palestinian flags by the Israeli military; the groom and the bride in her wedding gown had to face stun grenades and tear gas.[7] Yasmine said, "This event highlights Israeli racist laws that forbid the two parts of Palestine to meet and fall in love and be together." The event also foregrounded the ways in which young activists from various parts of Palestine are connecting with one another through political protests, challenging the spatial and biopolitical confinement of the apartheid regime, and also using theatrical strategies to highlight the surreal nature of love and life under apartheid.

Yasmine also discussed the ways in which Israel's spatial regulations has led to a fragmentation that undermined the youth movement, in addition to growing social and class divisions in the West Bank. She acknowledged that the youth movement activists were "disconnected, but the reality is that we as a society are disconnected from one another, villages from the cities." Activists from Ramallah did not want to be "confined" to the city and had made concerted attempts to go to other towns and villages and work with activists on the ground elsewhere, attending weekly protests against the Wall and settlements in villages such as Bil'in and Ni'lin and attending protests against the negotiations in Nablus. Ahmed said that despite the splintering within the youth movement, "We had links to many places." These alliances and relationships s were also a means of providing support to other young activists in places where there was less media attention and impunity from Israeli or PA repression, as mentioned earlier, but Yasmine and others acknowledged that it was a "challenge" to build these networks of organizing with a small group of youth.

Yasmine pointed to another layer of contradiction that she and others struggled with in going to attend the weekly demonstrations against the Wall in places such as Nabi Saleh. She said, "At the end, for me it still remains a theater. You go to a protest, you demonstrate and then you return home." Protest as performance can be subversive and highlight in a single performative event the violence and racism of the state and its laws, as in the wedding staged at the checkpoint that was broken up by the Israeli military; however, if ritualized or even fetishized, it can slip ineffectively into something else. Yasmine pointed out that those fighting the enclosures of the Wall and confiscation of their lands and livelihood in places such as Nabi Saleh, one of many such places in the West Bank, have a "different stake" in these protests and have sacrificed with their lives, in some instances, during their struggles—as famously documented in films such as *Five Broken Cameras*.[8]

Collins argues that what is at stake in these popular struggles is what he calls a form of "habitational resistance" by Palestinians, that is, a "refusal to leave the land and disappear."[9] Protests by villagers in the West Bank, defending their right to live and farm their land and to tend to their animals in the hills, and the encampments by Palestinian youth from destroyed villages in Israel, who host music workshops in the remnants of a disappeared life, are all acts displaying that "existence is resistance," to use a well known credo in Palestine. When all else has failed—from armed struggle to peaceful civil disobedience, not to mention negotiations—to end ongoing processes of displacement, confinement, and annihilation, there is resistance through *sumood*, or ongoing resilience. While some Palestinians say that this notion of "staying on the land," if against all odds, is not enough, it is apparent that these forms of daily or habitational resistance reveal the "settler colonial nature of the situation" and bring to light the ways in which the aims of the Zionist project is to displace and erase Palestinians and Palestinianism itself.[10] This is what brings into sharp relief the indigenous nature of the struggle against the Israeli state and military and the Zionist project at large, linking it to the struggles of other indigenous populations who have used similar strategies of habitational resistance, from North America and Hawaii to Australia and Latin America.

This is why the vignette about Bab Al-Shams and the "resistance villages" with which I began this book is so compelling, as well as the youth camp in the depopulated village of Ikrit, because these dramatic actions highlight the imagination of what "habitation" on the land might look like, if a different kind of sovereignty were achieved in Palestine. Rather than focusing solely on the issue of the state and organizing based on traditional party affiliations, Palestinians from different locations created Bab Al-Shams, a new "village" named from a novel that told the story of Palestine as return, enacting resistance to the colonial present and ongoing Nakba. For Hafez, Bab al-Shams was a form of "peaceful" resistance which may have been staged for a global media, but it was still important because it was a "collective movement of people from different places" that went beyond the problems of a single village and included people who were not, conventionally speaking, "activists." It was also an exercise in democratic political life, for the dictum was that "whoever is part of the village can decide what happens in the village." Hafez, who participated in this protest, thought that it was "the first time in a long while" that Palestinians "initiated" and produced a political vision on the ground, something that was not purely reactive. Yasmine was somewhat more skeptical because she thought that the Bab Al-Shams experiment "didn't materialize something concrete on the ground," saying, "It was great, but what next?" But it was apparent that this question was embedded for her in a deeper frustration that the youth movement could not have accomplished more and a sense of hopelessness, a feeling that she said had increased as the youth protests waned. In fact, late spring 2013 was a "lull" in youth activism and these sentiments of disappointment were shared by some others, such as Dalia, who said, "There was a lot of hope after the March 15 protests and then it slowly burned out."

Clearly, the disappointment or fatigue expressed in these conversations arises out of a deeper despair and hopelessness among Palestinians in general and, simultaneously, in the context of ongoing Palestinian resistance. This political fatigue and disillusionment, as discussed earlier, is partly due to the lack of a unifying structure of collective liberation that people feel connected to and with which they can identify, the central dilemma in the post-Oslo moment for Palestinians. For Hafez, the "main challenge is to unite the people, to unite the generations," and like others, he argued that this unifying framework could be provided by the Palestinian Liberation Organization (PLO). Returning to the umbrella structure of the PLO, in his view, would be returning to a political "space" rather than an "ideological organization," for it "represents all of the Palestinian people," and is centrally focused on the Nakba, not only on the Israeli occupation of the West Bank, Gaza, and East Jerusalem. While this vision is reflected in the calls for elections to the PNC, mentioned in the previous chapter, it also seemed to represent for Hafez and others not just a programmatic shift but a deeper shift toward a different kind of collectivity, and a fundamentally different kind of politics of resistance. One of the many challenges to enacting this shift in the post-Oslo moment, for Hafez, is that "young people don't know their history," but the "PLO is the address of this past," suggesting that in a context in which Palestinian youth are increasingly unschooled in Palestinian history, even in Palestinian schools, there is a political and historical narrative of resistance that does not have to be invented completely anew. Furthermore, it is worth citing Feryal's observation that it is not "Palestinian society in general that is depoliticized, it is Ramallah that is depoliticized." Given that the majority of my interviews with activists were done in Ramallah, even if not all of these youth are actually from Ramallah, there was a palpable sense of political frustration and demoralization with the "five-star occupation." Yet as my conversations with activists, artists, and youth from other parts of the West Bank and from Israel, reveal, there is a healthy questioning and critical discussion of what an "alternative" politics and cultural expression really means that is ongoing across these borders, spanning cities, villages, and camps.

While the comments and conversations cited above and shared in the previous chapters may not necessarily offer a tangible or clear picture of what this truly alternative politics looks like—perhaps expressing more of the signposts on the way to get there and the clear points of departure to leave behind—I think they are important reminders that these discussions are not simply about a "return" to the political. Rancière critiques what he describes as a consensual call since the 1990s of a "return to a 'pure' form of politics," more clearly cordoned off from the "social," that "boils down to the assertion that there is a specific place for politics."[11] He argues that this return is generally to "the place of the state" and a "'proper' political order," governed by the logic of modern liberal democracy. The "return" to the political, in circumscribing what the proper spaces or subjects of politics are, thus is really an extinguishing of politics, according to Rancière. I think it is important to consider the youth movement in Palestine and the politics of jil Oslo not as an inscription of a return to politics, in this sense, nor as a purification of politics and a recuperation of something more authentic buried in a nostalgized past of "good" politics. While many of these young activists and artists hearkened back to the mass-based organizing of the first intifada, in particular, and deeply desired a revival of collective resistance, they understood that the post-Oslo, post-second intifada era was a different political and historical moment. They were critical of state-building, and particularly of the Oslo framework of the two-state solution, and they were also generally not focused on the state as the horizon of liberation or central paradigm of political resistance. Their struggles against repression, surveillance, and militarization did not resort to the discourse of liberal democracy, or even generally to civil rights, but rested on a language of freedom and dignity. Furthermore, narratives of proper politics or cultural purity, as I have demonstrated, are often laced in contradictory and repressive ways with gendered and sexualized tropes and moral policing. The young artists and activists I spoke to questioned the naturalness or inevitability of the political and social order in the post-Oslo era, but their political protests and imaginaries are neither conceived entirely anew nor simply echoes from the past.

In my conversation with Duaa, sitting in the garden of Beit Aneeseh on a spring evening in 2013, she said insightfully, "Our struggle should not become a tool, we need to understand where they're leading us, but it's very hard, especially in '48 Palestine." Duaa was concerned that Palestinian youth activism in Israel and protests by Palestinians in general should not remain on the terms or within the arena provided by Israel, where it is simply a struggle over reforming modern, liberal democracy but rather, should address the militarized and colonial nature of the state. Yet, as she acknowledged, this was a difficult struggle to wage by a colonized population within, who are subjected to daily repression but always already engaged in habitational resistance by remaining within Israel and maintaining a sense of Palestinian identity, in a variety of ways, including through cultural production. Duaa thought that it was important to be critical of the concept of "resistance through culture" so that this did not become a defanged resistance or form of containment; she mentioned a Tweet she received from a friend that quoted Slavoj Žižek, saying, "We have coffee without caffeine, and we have protests within an acceptable framework."

For Duaa, challenging the prescribed boundaries of proper politics—or acceptable artistic production—meant "always examining the gap in what we do." Constantly examining the contradictions or limits of "what we do" and what is considered possible or acceptable politically is in part what constitutes politics, and for Rancière, it is this "gap in the sensible itself" which is the basis of "dissensus," a shattering or disruption of political consensus or Gramscian "common sense."[12] The process of politics at its core entails the production of new political subjects that are not "natural," and new sites that are not pre-determined or viewed as outside of the bounds of conventional politics—an important intervention in a context where there is an evident exhaustion with existing political frameworks and the boundaries of political subjecthood. But this politics also means constantly and simultaneously exposing the contradictions generated by a colonial regime that claims to be a modern, liberal democracy, and by a Palestinian regime that is not actually sovereign but aspires to modern state-building based on the principles of neoliberal democracy. "To make the demand on freedom," Judith Butler observes, "is already to begin its exercise and then to ask for its legitimization is also to announce the gap between its exercise and its realization and to put both into public discourse in a way that the gap is seen, so that the gap can mobilize."[13] Activists in the youth movement and hip hop artists in Palestine are mobilizing this gap, or these paradoxes of democracy and sovereignty, in order to articulate and recreate new discourses and demands of freedom, trying relentlessly to make the contradictions of living under twenty-first century settler coloniality visible and audible.

Yasmine also suggested that there is another kind of gap, in the very discourse about the "youth movement" or youth revolts in the region, reflecting: "In a few years from now, we will no longer be 'youth.' We want to involve everyone, not just youth. Some of us are already older and this is part of the myth about the revolutions in Egypt and Tunis. You have to involve everyone to have a revolution." In this nuanced and self-reflexive critique, it is clearly not the generational category of youth per se that is central to the so-called youth movement, but revolutionary politics; this politics is one that is often conflated with those seen as inherently rebellious, unstable, and malleable—that is, the "young" or youthful. My conversations with these young activists and artists called into question the very production of the category of youth, as a site of radical, questionable, or suspect politics, and of liminal or corrupted desires. "Youth" is not simply a portent of the future or symbol of a (better) past, but one of many sites where the questions posed here, "but, what next?" or "then, what else" can continually be asked.

From the Farmers' Market to the French Institute

A series of events on 25 May 2013 brought home to me the ways in which hip hop has emerged as an element of Palestinian protest culture which is performed and showcased in predictable and also unexpected ways, and as a youth culture that has proliferated in various sites in Palestine as part of the production and transformation of public spaces and public cultures. There were actually three hip hop shows that day in Ramallah and Jerusalem, which seemed like a record number! It was also interesting to note the ways in which these shows connected artists from across Palestine and highlighted a range of political issues.

The first hip hop performance was actually at a farmer's market in Ramallah, organized by Sharaka, an organization founded and run by young volunteers focused on food sovereignty in Palestine and for supporting local Palestinian farmers (whose livelihood has been increasingly diminished as Israeli produce floods the Palestinian markets). This Saturday afternoon, the farmer's market, which was being held weekly outside the old Ottoman Court building in the old town, featured Stormtrap (Asifeh), the Palestinian MC who was a cofounder of Ramallah Underground. When I showed up, Stormtrap was setting up his equipment in a corner of the market with MC Gaza, a rapper from Gaza who had managed to travel to the West Bank. The crowd that afternoon was a mix of older and younger people, foreigners and Palestinians, some with children. It was a slightly awkward setting for a hip hop show as Stormtrap's laptop and speakers were set up next to a stall with farmers selling spices such as za'tar and sumac. However, MC Gaza, a slight young man in jeans and an orange T-shirt, was unfazed and began rapping with another young man, who had a long ponytail and was wearing baggy pants. Stormtrap, who was wearing a simple black T-shirt and black jeans, then did a song which was about the confinement of life under occupation, followed by a song critical of the PA and of Oslo. The beats played on the laptop were simple, not the complex mix of electronic music, Arab instrumentation, and sound recordings usually produced by Stormtrap, and it was unfortunately hard to hear him without a microphone.[14]

It also seemed that the setting was a slightly challenging one in which to burst into rap as the crowd was rather passive, and mostly busy shopping for olive oil and local cucumbers. Some people gathered around the rappers and a young Palestinian boy wearing a baseball cap and shorts intently filmed all the performances with his smartphone. There was also a film crew that recorded the performance, so all of the cameras were somewhat overwhelming in the small space. MC Gaza, however, had a strong voice and confident presence, managing with his energetic rap to create a "stage" in the middle of the market. On a bench to the side was a group of three Palestinian teenagers, in hip hop gear, who had clearly come to hear the rappers and not buy zucchini.

MC Gaza (left), Farmers' Market.

Stormtrap told me that he was actually scheduled to perform that night at the opening event of the annual Palestine Festival of Literature, at the Sakakini Cultural Center in Ramallah. It was striking to me that Palestinian rappers have become incorporated into major literary and cultural events in the West Bank and are being included in the repertoire of Palestinian music hosted by national cultural projects, such as the annual literature festival. MC Gaza, in fact, was performing at a Palestinian hip hop concert at the French Institute in East Jerusalem that same night, the third rap show in one day. I attended the concert in Jerusalem, which was held in the small garden outside the old building in which the French Institute is housed, next door to a popular bookstore/cafe and down the street from a couple of well-known Palestinian art galleries as well as the recently opened Yabous Cultural Centre. The stone terrace in the garden served as a stage where a table with a laptop and equipment were set up for the musicians. The audience gathered that evening was a diverse mix of foreigners and Palestinians, which seemed a likely crowd at the French Institute. There were several people with young children and a few Palestinian women of various ages wearing hijabs, as well as a group of young Palestinian men standing in a row at the front wearing baseball caps and baggy pants, one of whom was sporting huge red headphones.

The rapper, Maqdsi, came on stage first, in baggy jeans hanging below the waist and a white T-shirt, with a beaded necklace from which a map of Palestine dangled around his neck. He welcomed MC Gaza, to applause from the crowd, and reminded the audience jokingly that this was a hip hop concert so they should not sit demurely in the chairs at the back but come up to the front. Maqdsi launched into a set of political rap songs, with a younger rapper who was wearing a T-shirt emblazoned with a picture of Bob Marley. The MCs performed a song critical of NGOs in Palestine and about the failures of the peace process, while a third young man deejayed on the laptop. Maqdsi's signature style is low and brooding, and the beats were interesting and varied, with some samples of Arabic music and oud and a heavy dose of reggae sounds. The DJ, Khaled, then joined them and sang Arabic vocals while the two MCs rapped and moved around the stage. One of their songs, "*Ya Baladi*" ("Oh My Country"), referred to Jewish settlements in the West Bank, such as Gilo, declaring their refusal to leave Palestine to find another life and to stay on the land instead.[15] The young men at the front were throwing their hands up in the air and people in the audience were bopping under the trees, particularly the foreigners. Next up was a breakdancer, a young man dressed in a golf cap and vest. He was not just extremely agile in popping and locking but also very expressive, so it was a mesmerizing theatrical performance as he twisted in perfect synchronization with the music. There were at least three different people in the audience and around the stage filming the show, so once again, the small performance seemed to be almost overwhelmed by cameras and media.

One of the young men who was standing at the front of the audience jumped up on the stage and joined Maqdsi. MC Rayyan—who was not originally scheduled to perform—was much louder and seemed somewhat more at ease in performance than Maqdsi, leaning aggressively into the audience with the mike. He was wearing a baseball cap with the acronym "YMCMB" (Young Money Cash Money Billionaires), from the name of the hip hop crew that includes New Orleans-born rapper Lil' Wayne. This seemed, on the surface, to be somewhat of a contradiction as MC Rayyan's songs had nothing to do with billionaires or bling but were in fact politically progressive critiques of occupation and the political status quo. This incongruity could perhaps have been accidental, as Palestinian youth often sport clothing with English words without ostensibly identifying with their meaning (such as sweatshirts that say "FBI"), but it is also possible that the more hardcore sound of East Jerusalem rap is what was being indexed here. Next up was MC Gaza, to loud cheers from the audience, who began his song with a shout out, *"Min Gaza lil-'uds"* (From Gaza to Al Quds/Jerusalem)! His vigorous performance fired up the audience, as the evening darkened over Jerusalem. MC Gaza did one song which was about not having any fear, and another, along with all the other rappers, over samples of a Palestinian nationalist song, *"Samidoun"* ("Remaining Steadfast") with rousing beats. The young man from the audience with red headphones and baggy shorts also got up on the stage and did a rap song which declared that although Zionists had taken the land that belonged to Palestinians, the people would never give up and their spirit could not be taken. At this point, all the rappers were on stage together for the end of the show, the music pounding into the night on Salah ad-Din Street. The concert was inspiring, showcasing the variety as well as contradictions of hip hop culture in Palestine, staged in a neighborhood struggling to revive Palestinian arts and cultural life in the context of the strangulation of Jerusalem by Israeli settlements and restrictions on work, residence, and travel.

In 2012, El Far3i, the Palestinian rapper and percussionist from Jordan, recorded a jam session with a young musician whose family is from al-Bireh in the West Bank, Z the People (Ramzi Suleiman)."[16] In the Youtube video for the song, "Don't Want Your Life," Z plays the piano and belts out funk and soul in English as El Far3i raps in Arabic and plays the tabla. I end with an excerpt from this cross-border duet, distributed with the help of digital media, because its lyrics eloquently address settler colonialism and displacement, "peace" and superficial sympathy, the compulsion of securitization, and the need for revolutionary organizing and solidarity. The song is fundamentally a rejection of colonial laws and humanitarian aid and a call for a genuine political community and a life other than that imposed by imperial, capitalist modernity:

Z:

Don't want your life, I don't want your life.

. . .

I want mine! I want mine!

I don't want your laws . . . I don't want your peace.

I see through your heart, it's just pretending to know.

El Far3i:

The story is as follows: it's just an imperialist world.

A quick solution to a capitalist system?

You're delusional/Don't romanticize things

Focus your ideas, then take them in different
directions . . .

There is nothing called a "good moment to gather"

If you can't say good morning to your neighbor

How is the revolution supposed to shine?

So use that logic as a starting point, branch out to all
alleyways

Organizations, unions, universities, work places . . . .

Z:

I don't want your life, I don't want your life . . .

I want mine!

El Far3i:

. . . I can't just sit here quiet so refugees come out of
my mouth

When I spit East of the River rap, all borders melt
down

Colonialist eyes on this land so they send us
delegations

In the holy land of pain, we have sympathized with
the "settlers"

(little did we know) . . .

Aid coming sadly on top of ships . . . .

Z:

I don't want your control, what a burden on the soul

I wouldn't want your fear, it's kind of an addiction

I see through your eyes and they're missing the
picture
I don't want your life, I don't want your life.
[El Far3i rapping the same lines in Arabic]
I want mine!

---

[1] Alex Kane, "As Obama Visits Ramallah, Palestinians Vent Anger," *Mondoweiss*, 21 March 2013. http://mondoweiss.net/2013/03/palestinians-political-prisoners.html.

[2] Asef Bayat and Linda Herrera, "Introduction: Being Young and Muslim in Neoliberal Times," in *Being Young and Muslim: New Cultural Politics in the Global South and North*, ed. Linda Herrera and Asef Bayat (New York: Oxford University Press, 2010), 23.

[3] See publications and reports of Addameer: Prisoner Support and Human Rights Association at http://www.addameer.org/.

[4] Collins, *Global Palestine*, 86.

[5] Derek Gregory, *The Colonial Present: Afghanistan, Palestine, Iraq* (Malden: Blackwell, 2004), 125; Nadia Abu-Zahra and Adah Kay, *Unfree in Palestine: Registration, Documentation and Movement Restriction* (London: Pluto, 2013).

[6] Jessica Purkiss, "Love in the Time of Apartheid," *Palestine Monitor*, 11 March 2013. http://palestinemonitor.org/details.php?id=0n14spa3075yzmzibxc08; see also: http://www.loveinthetimeofapartheid.org.

[7] See: http://www.youtube.com/watch?v=3JYQMzl8nhs.

[8] *Five Broken Cameras* (dir. Emad Burnat and Guy Davidi, 2011).
The story of Nabi Saleh even reached the pages of the New York Times Magazine, in an unusually honest account of Palestinian popular resistance: Ben Ehrenreich, "Is This Where the Third Intifada Will Start," *The New York Times Magazine*, 15 March 2013. http://www.nytimes.com/2013/03/17/magazine/is-this-where-the-third-intifada-will-start.html?pagewanted=all&_r=0

[9] Collins, *Global Palestine*, 120-121.

[10] Ibid., 120.

Conclusion

[11] Jacques Rancière, *Dissensus: On Politics and Aesthetics*. ed. and transl. Steven Corcoran (London and New York: Continuum Publishing, 2010), electronic edition.

[12] Ibid.

[13] [From a dialogue between] Judith Butler and Gayatri C. Spivak, *Who Sings the Nation-State? Language, Politics, Belonging* (Calcultta: Seagull, 2007; 2010 ed.), 68-69.

[14] See track from Stormrap's recent album, *Iradeh* (Will): https://soundcloud.com/stormtrap/03-asifeh-iradeh?in=stormtrap/sets/iradeh-ep

[15] See: http://www.youtube.com/user/egtya7.

[16] See: http://www.youtube.com/watch?feature=player_detailpage&v=v9AcCUO4XPI.

www.ingramcontent.com/pod-product-compliance
Lightning Source LLC
Chambersburg PA
CBHW062055270326
41931CB00013B/3081